Performance
Assurance
for IT Systems

Performance Assurance for IT Systems

Brian King

CRC Press
Taylor & Francis Group
Boca Raton London New York

CRC Press is an imprint of the
Taylor & Francis Group, an **informa** business

AN AUERBACH BOOK

CRC Press
Taylor & Francis Group
6000 Broken Sound Parkway NW, Suite 300
Boca Raton, FL 33487-2742

First issued in paperback 2019

ISBN-13: 978-0-8493-2778-0 (hbk)
ISBN-13: 978-0-367-39401-1 (pbk)

Library of Congress Cataloging-in-Publication Data

King, Brian A.
    Performance assurance for IT systems / Brian A. King.
      p. cm.
    Includes bibliographical references and index.
    ISBN 0-8493-2778-4
     1. Information resources management. 2. Information technology--Evaluation. I. Title.

T58.64.K56 2004
004'.068'4--dc22

                                 2004047707

Library of Congress Card Number 2004047707

Visit the Taylor & Francis Web site at
http://www.taylorandfrancis.com

and the CRC Press Web site at
http://www.crcpress.com

CONTENTS

PART 2: TECHNICAL FOUNDATION

WHAT THIS BOOK IS ABOUT

The objective of this work is to promote the concept of Performance Assurance throughout the entire system lifecycle. It covers not only the technological aspects of performance, but also the relevant processes, plus company- and people-related topics. It provides sufficiently instructive material to allow the reader to understand the fundamental issues that surround performance and technology, and to apply the principles and experience that are expounded to formulate a coherent customized approach to performance assurance. The primary topics that are covered are hardware sizing, performance, and scalability for server-based systems, with the emphasis on those stages before systems go into production. Areas at the heart of the subject are discussed in some detail, including hardware and software technologies, vendors, technical infrastructures, application design, and observations on some of the softer issues. It is not a book about personal computers.

The book is heavily influenced by the increasing pressures to deliver systems or proposals in ever-shortening timescales. The watchwords throughout are "fit for purpose." Cost-effective, well-designed systems that perform satisfactorily can be produced without necessarily incurring great manpower cost.

The majority view tends to be that performance-related work kicks in close to the time when an application goes into production, possibly in time for any stress testing immediately prior to going live, but that it really gets into its stride thereafter. The views expressed in this book are that performance needs to be addressed from the very beginning, at the feasibility or bid stage, or even earlier where an organization is investigating suitable technologies for use in one or more proposed applications. Decisions that are made both before and during the design phase strongly dictate just how successful the system will be in meeting the performance and scalability requirements and, by inference, the costs of rectifying any problems. This book concentrates mainly, but not exclusively, on the pre-production stage, complementing the many publications that focus on tuning and other post-production issues.

When addressing performance before an application goes into production, for example, during a development project, it becomes clear that performance is ultimately just a byproduct of business requirements and volumes, the technical infrastructure, any software products that are used, perhaps the application development framework, the application design itself, and finally the code. This means that a solid understanding is required of these areas, particularly the technical elements. For those readers who are used to specialist roles such as performance analyst and technical architect, it may appear that I am straying into other people's territory. The book concentrates on the areas that need to be addressed, ignoring any problems of job demarcation. How an organization apportions the tasks to individuals will depend on local working practices and the skills of the people concerned.

Tasks that are addressed in the early stages of the system lifecycle are covered, including the evaluation of hardware and software products, the production of the nonfunctional aspects of Invitations To Tender (ITTs), and responses to ITTs by bidders. Two of the key areas, hardware sizing during the early stages when there is limited information and designing for performance, are covered in some detail.

It is important that technical architects and performance analysts take sufficient account of cost considerations when producing solutions, as cost is the ultimate driver in any IT system. Leaving all the financial aspects to the procurement or commercial departments until late in the procurement cycle can result in the need to rework the solution if it is considered to be too expensive. This requires some rudimentary financial awareness on the part of the technical team. Cost considerations are covered, particularly where procurement and product reviews are discussed.

Softer issues, particularly people-related matters, are as important as technology-related issues. Areas such as judgment, pragmatism, communication, and risk assessment are covered.

In summary, this book covers a range of topics, as shown in Figure 0.1, some of which the reader may not have thought had anything to do with performance *per se*.

CONTENTS

The book is split into two parts: individual areas of interest, roughly following the system lifecycle, and a technology foundation, a series of brief primers on various hardware and software technologies, written mainly from a performance perspective. Figure 0.2 shows the topics in Part I, and how they roughly map onto the phases of the development lifecycle.

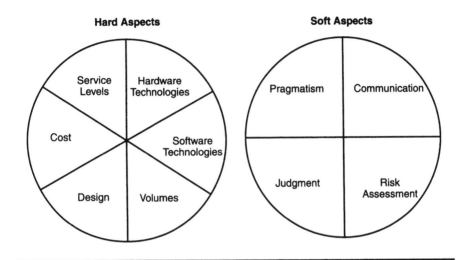

Figure 0.1 Hard and Soft Aspects of Performance

Subjects that tend to be covered sketchily in other publications, sometimes if at all, are discussed in detail. Subjects that are better understood, such as modeling and capacity management, where there is substantial published material, are summarized.

Chapter 1, Preparing for the Challenge, argues that performance- and technology-related issues should be addressed proactively throughout the system lifecycle: from initial investigations, through the bid or feasibility study, through development, to post-production. It introduces the skills that are required during the various pre-production stages, and it summarizes the concept of Performance Assurance, an approach for tackling performance proactively throughout the development lifecycle.

Chapter 2, Caveat Emptor (Let the Buyer Beware), looks at the issues that surround the review and selection of hardware and software products, including typical product lifecycles and the marketing approaches of vendors. It provides guidance on a focused approach to such reviews, particularly of software products.

Chapter 3, Lies, Damned Lies, and Benchmarks, discusses the problems that surround the use of benchmarks to aid the sizing of a system, in particular the methods that can be employed, knowingly or unknowingly, to produce highly optimistic, infeasible results. Typical "tricks of the trade" are outlined. It discusses how to approach in-house benchmarks, or benchmarks that are mandated by potential vendors, to ensure that they provide useful results.

Chapter 4, Nonfunctional Requirements and Solutions, looks at the effects of poorly written requirements. Although it applies to both in-house development and procurement, it is of particular interest to the

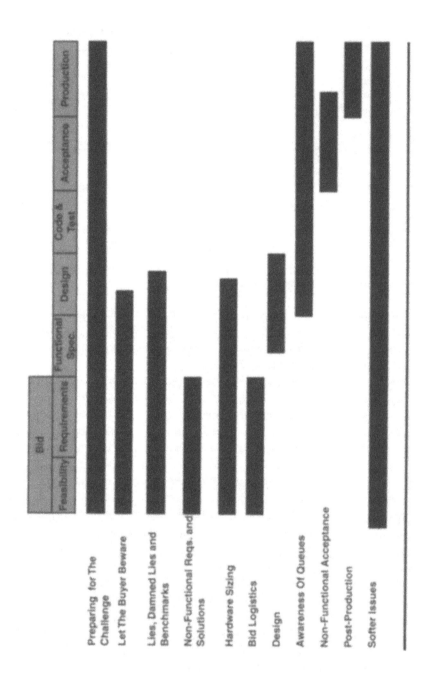

authors of ITTs, discussing the benefits of clear, unambiguous, and realistic requirements. In addition, it discusses general approaches to hardware sizing and deployment, plus the implications of high availability and business continuity requirements on the complexity and cost of a solution.

Chapter 5, Hardware Sizing: The Crystal Ball Gazing Act, focuses on the problems and potential approaches to this difficult subject when there is limited information to work with early in the system lifecycle. It is an area that many people seek to avoid because of the scarcity of information. A worked example is included, along with guidelines and useful rules of thumb.

Bids can be stressful, especially for individuals who are responsible for hardware sizing, as they are at the end of the solution chain, and consequently they have extremely limited time to complete their work. Chapter 6, Bid Logistics, contains advice for tackling bids in a coherent and pre-emptive manner, with the emphasis on catering for the shorter procurement cycles that are becoming more prevalent.

Chapter 7, Designing for Performance, Scalability, and Resilience commences with a review of some of the basic principles, including the need to avoid the extravagant use of hardware resources, the importance of partitioning techniques, the need for balanced configurations, and catering for resilience. Various design factors that can affect performance are discussed, along with suggestions for possible design approaches.

Chapter 8, Awareness of Queues, discusses the need to understand where they form, and their effects on performance, particularly the knock-on effects when there are networks or hierarchies of interrelated queues. It demonstrates that software queues and locks can easily prevent the full exploitation of the available hardware. It provides a brief introduction to performance modeling tools, highlighting their advantages and disadvantages.

Chapter 9, Nonfunctional Acceptance, focuses primarily on stress testing, covering the perceived need for such testing, the tools that can help, and general guidance on the preparation, set-up, and running of the tests. Soak testing and operational-readiness testing are also briefly covered.

Chapter 10, Post-Implementation, provides an overview of the classic capacity management processes that have been used for the last twenty-plus years. It goes on to discuss a minimalist approach appropriate for those organizations that have limited resources to cover the subject in any detail.

Chapter 11, Softer Issues, deals with nontechnical items. Personal skills are frequently as important as technical skills in producing effective solutions within ever more aggressive timescales. Many areas are touched on, including communication, the danger of overengineering, playing devil's advocate, awareness of cost and time constraints, team balance, mentoring, and client responsibilities.

Chapter 12, So What?, discusses some of the reasons why performance and scalability are not addressed adequately, typically on the grounds of cost or lack of time, and it covers the risks that are inherent in such an approach. It affirms the author's view that it is possible to tackle these subjects in a focused, cost-effective manner that will allow management to make informed decisions.

The foundation for sizing and performance work is a solid understanding of hardware and software technologies. Part 2 contains a selection of core technology tasters. All technologies have four to five key technical factors that heavily influence performance. These short primers attempt to distill the key points of a given technology in a succinct and, it is hoped, readable summary. They are in no way intended to replace a comprehensive understanding that can only be obtained by reading specific books, papers, and vendor material on a given subject matter. For example, at the time of this writing I have in excess of one hundred detailed papers on CPUs and server technology, in addition to several books that include sections that cover some of the same ground. The objectives of the tasters are simply to provide a useful initial understanding of a technology and its related performance issues with which the reader may not be sufficiently familiar.

THE TARGET AUDIENCE

The book is aimed at a general IT audience. To that end conscious efforts have been made to minimize the use of jargon.

Technical architects and performance analysts who have limited experience of addressing hardware sizing and performance issues before a system goes into production will find much useful information. There are so few people who are prepared to tackle hardware sizing early in the lifecycle that this topic on its own should be valuable to most people. Discussions on procurement issues will be helpful, particularly for those who are inexperienced in either writing or responding to an ITT, whereas the technology tasters will provide a slightly different perspective on those technologies that the reader may already be familiar with, plus a useful introduction to unfamiliar topics.

Application developers will gain a general appreciation of a variety of nonfunctional issues, helping them to appreciate the potential effects of decisions that they make during development, particularly in the areas of software product selection and application design.

Part 1 provides awareness of some of the nonfunctional issues that IT management is likely to encounter. Project managers, bid managers, IT middle management, and sales and marketing can all find useful information to aid in understanding the issues with which their technical colleagues are confronted. In addition, the technology tasters can provide an introduction to individual topics that they may be encountering for the first time, helping them to make informed decisions on technical risk.

THE TONE

This book may be described as critical. It is not a passive, teach-technology type book. It is based on my experiences, and although there may appear to be one too many "war stories," that is because I have encountered far more war stories than I have success stories. I classify myself as a realist, although the reader may consider me to be a cynic. I have been pleased to work in the IT industry, but it is far from being a perfect industry. As *The Standish Report* confirms, there are far too many unsuccessful projects, mostly based on misplaced optimism. My objective is to encourage the reader to think through the risks and implications of decision-making, rather than to attempt to provide the reader with any definitive views of my own on a given product or toolset.

ACKNOWLEDGMENTS

As with any book there is a cast of thousands, viz. all the people that I have dealt with directly or indirectly over the thirty-seven years that I have been in the IT industry. They have all contributed in some way or other to my make-up, even those individuals who have sometimes questioned my parentage, or attempted to debunk my recommendations when I have impertinently undermined their carefully constructed business cases.

While writing this book I enlisted the help of people in various areas of IT (technical, line of business management, project management, resource management, and development) to comment on the approach, content, and readability. I am extremely grateful for the time that they put in, and for their invaluable feedback. Any shortcomings are mine, and do not reflect in any way on their comments. My thanks go to Janet King (my wife), Adrian Brooks, Ken Burrows, Peter J. Clarke, Paul Coombs, John Morrissey, David Rowland, Brendan Ruck, and Mike Watts.

PART 1

INDIVIDUAL AREAS
OF INTEREST

1

PREPARING
FOR THE CHALLENGE

1.1 ABSTRACT

The performance aspects and related technology issues of new applications are frequently not addressed in any level of detail until just about the time that they are due to go into production. The reasons that are given for failure to tackle the subject include lack of information and lack of time. It is often assumed (or should that be hoped) that only a modest amount of tuning or a judicious hardware upgrade will be necessary to cure any problems. Unfortunately, neither tuning nor hardware upgrades are necessarily a panacea, particularly on larger systems. The original decisions that were made early in the system lifecycle on the choice of software products, hardware selection, technical infrastructure, and application design can all result in problems that are costly to resolve, and that can take significant time to implement. To overcome any fundamental problems, performance needs to be treated as an integral part of the entire lifecycle, from bid or feasibility study, through the project lifecycle, and on to post-implementation. Tackling performance issues before implementation requires a specific set of skills, including a thorough understanding of hardware and software technologies, an appreciation of vendors' financial status as well as their technical strategies and current product range, the experience to gauge the credibility of vendor claims, the confidence and ability to size the hardware when there is limited information to work with, and the capability to assess the effectiveness of proposed design techniques. In essence, the emphasis should be on pre-empting problems, rather than waiting for them to surface.

1.2   INTRODUCTION

Nowadays, views on the scope of performance work tend to be colored by the need to define specialist roles for individuals, with the attendant danger that some tasks can fall through the cracks and not be covered by anybody. A common view is that a performance analyst deals mainly with post-implementation issues, leaving technical architects to cover the subject up to that point. My belief is that performance is ultimately a byproduct of the functional and nonfunctional aspects of an application, and that therefore a sound knowledge is required of many areas, particularly hardware and software technologies and design techniques, in addition to the more accepted skills of performance monitoring, analysis, and tuning. The time to make best use of these skills is during the feasibility and early development stages when the key technical and financial decisions that may affect performance are taken. In this opening chapter, I discuss some of the background to the typical positioning of the performance analyst in the organization, a definition of performance, the skills that are required, and an outline approach to tackling performance during the project lifecycle.

1.3   IN THE BEGINNING...

When I began work in the industry back in the mid-1960s computing was arguably still in its infancy. IT departments were typically much smaller than they are today because the scope of applications was limited, whereas both hardware and software were somewhat rudimentary and immature when compared to what has subsequently evolved. Many companies used a single hardware IT vendor, and custom (bespoke) software was the norm.

The advantage of small departments was that everybody mucked in, and in the process they tended to acquire knowledge of many aspects of computing. In my first IT job I helped to operate the computer at busy times of the week, in addition to my normal job of programming, while I was also attempting to pick up sound design techniques. In retrospect, although our installation was extremely small (one analyst, one programmer, one operator, and myself) and the software was not particularly sophisticated, it proved to be an ideal training ground due to the variety of tasks, the environment (where I was working with sharp intelligent individuals), and the fact that I was working at a low level in an Assembler language that resulted in a broader understanding of the technology.

The growth of the IT industry, along with the advent of more sophisticated hardware and software, resulted in a tendency towards IT specialization from the mid-1970s, particularly in larger organizations. The role of performance analyst was one such area of specialization. Performance analysts were usually situated in the technical services area, sometimes as part of a dedicated capacity management team. This positioning tended to mean that they did not get involved in new applications until just before they went into production, and consequently any key decisions had already been made. The scope of their role was often limited to post-implementation tuning and capacity planning for production systems. This approach frequently meant that limited attention was paid to performance before the application went into production. At that time, this was usually not a great problem, as designers and developers had a good understanding of the available technology, a fact that tended to be reflected in the efficacy of their designs and implementation.

1.4 THE NEED TO ADDRESS NEW APPLICATIONS

However, the huge increase in the complexity of the software and of the hardware infrastructures has turned it into a potentially serious problem. Unfortunately, paying limited attention to performance during development is still quite widespread today. A commonly held belief is that a modest amount of post-implementation tuning will prove to be a panacea for any performance problems. This can be the case for small to medium-sized applications where the moderate volumes that usually have to be supported suggest that problems can be quickly resolved, or at least minimized, either by discrete tuning, or possibly by a judicious hardware upgrade. However, it is not necessarily a universal remedy. There can still be response time and scalability issues that are attributable to other factors, most noticeably to the technical infrastructure and application design.

Large-scale applications are more likely to suffer from performance problems that do not respond to the quick fix. Here it is important to address the issues during the early stages of the project inasmuch as it is usually significantly cheaper to design for performance, both in terms of the technical infrastructure and the application design, rather than to try to retrofit performance into the system afterwards.

One important caveat when mentioning "designing for performance" is that any design should be, first and foremost, fit for purpose. There is always a danger of overengineering the solution, for example, building a scalable multiserver solution where multiple servers are extremely unlikely to be required, or producing subsecond response times when two to three seconds would have been perfectly acceptable.

1.5 DEFINITION OF PERFORMANCE

Before discussing the skills that are required during the investigation and development stages, it is necessary to define what performance is. The

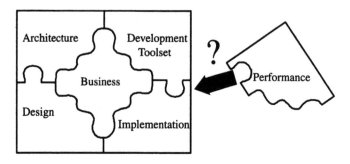

Figure 1.1 Where Does Performance Fit

obvious outward manifestation is system responsiveness, that is, online response times and batch job elapsed times. Taking one step backward, responsiveness can be viewed as a product of data volumes and transaction rates, plus hardware capacity and its use. These broad definitions can certainly fit in with the idea of a performance analyst who majors in post-production issues. However, performance is a much more all-embracing topic. As indicated in Figure 1.1, it is ultimately a byproduct of:

- Business requirements — functionality, volumes, peaks, and growth provisions
- Technical architecture — including resilience and scalability considerations
- Development technologies — frameworks, languages, middleware, and database management systems
- Application design — including provisions for responsiveness, resilience, and scalability
- Plus the physical implementation of the design — for example, the code and database

What I am saying is that many considerations have an impact on performance and that, particularly during development, it is not a subject in its own right, although it is frequently regarded as a discrete topic.

I have witnessed a number of development projects that started promisingly by appointing a performance analyst, but there was no clear understanding of the analyst's responsibilities. Unfortunately, these days of specialization tend to encourage a "Tick The Box" attitude. A Project Manager (PM) is convinced that a person is needed to tackle performance, somebody is appointed without defining the role, and the PM promptly relaxes, thinking that this particular angle is now covered. The appointed individual then attempts to carve out a role, trying carefully not to step on anybody else's perceived territory. I have seen performance analysts who spent a great deal of time in the early months setting up and running benchmarks in efforts to establish the feasibility of the proposed solution, occasionally making totally unfounded assumptions on the likely design. Similarly, I have seen individuals who spent the majority of their time preparing for stress tests that were to be run late in the project.

Benchmarking and stress testing are both essential tasks that have to be undertaken in a coherent manner. However, they are primarily validation processes. Somebody has to be involved in the key decision-making processes that surround the overall technical solution from a performance perspective. This may be a technical architect or a performance analyst, according to local taste and the capabilities of the individuals concerned, but it is important that it is a suitably knowledgeable person. The danger with a technical architect who has no knowledge of performance is that he may shop around for hardware and software products, concentrating on features and price, but not addressing performance implications. I should make it clear that the simple expedient of accepting a vendor's performance claims does not constitute addressing performance. The danger with a performance analyst who is used to looking after production systems is that she may have an insufficient understanding of the technologies and design techniques.

1.6 THE REQUIRED SKILLS

The ideal person is a hybrid of technical architect and performance analyst, although in my experience this type is scarce, not because individuals lack the ability necessarily, but merely because the typical project and support roles militate against the uncovering and subsequent flowering of people who have the necessary talents. Figure 1.2 shows a rough breakdown of the required skills and their relative importance.

The first comment to make is that the pie chart excludes two extremely important items, judgment and pragmatism. Suffice it for the moment to say that they suffuse all the items on the chart.

1.6.1 Understanding Hardware and Software Technologies

The initial prerequisite is a thorough understanding of hardware and software technologies. This includes the ability to translate the new jargon beloved by all vendors into a meaningful context. New jargon is particularly prevalent in the software arena where it is almost *de rigueur* to invent new terms. It is especially amusing, well, at least to my warped sense of humor, when not only the products, but also the jargon, get to be rebranded.

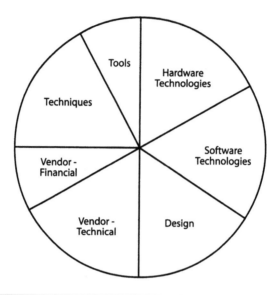

Figure 1.2   Skill Breakdown

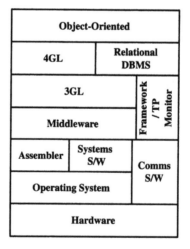

Figure 1.3   Layers Above the Coalface

Over time, IT developers have gradually but inexorably moved away from what I call the "coalface," that is, the lower layers where the hardware and low-level software reside. Figure 1.3 provides a sample illustration of how far away from the coalface various layers appear to be from the developer's perspective. It is not intended to be a definitive technical view: the precise placing of certain items is undoubtedly open to debate.

A performance analyst needs to be able to understand how functions and features in the upper layers are likely to be physically deployed lower down, including interfaces with the hardware, paying particular attention to any constraints, bottlenecks, or significant overheads that may be incurred as this mapping unfolds.

As the understanding of technologies is regarded as the cornerstone of performance work, Part 2 of this book contains basic information on a number of core technologies. They are called technology tasters because they each provide an introduction to a topic, deliberately limited to what I consider to be the key factors from a performance perspective. It is hoped that any detailed study of a specific technology will find useful fundamental information in a taster, but it should quickly move on to other literature that covers the subject matter in infinitely more detail.

1.6.2 Application Design

Sufficient understanding of application design techniques is required to assess that:

- The design can make full use of the available hardware capacity.
- It will meet the scalability requirements.
- Service level targets, for example, response times and availability, are achievable.

It is important that the effects of using any third-party products are assessed, as development frameworks, middleware, and database management systems can frequently influence, or even dictate, design decisions. On large-scale, high-volume systems, it is frequently necessary to design the application in such a way that the constraints that are found in almost all products are circumvented.

Arguably, the most important skill is the ability to break up a problem so that the system can be deployed as multiple partitions that can run concurrently, a process frequently termed "divide and conquer."

1.6.3 Vendors

Vendors take up a good portion of the pie chart in Figure 1.2. This subject is split into two areas, financial and technical. Before investigating a product in any level of detail, it is beneficial to have a rudimentary understanding of the vendor, including history and current financial status. Many people take the view that commercial matters are dealt with by their procurement or commercial departments. In my experience, any checking by these departments invariably happens quite late in the day after the technical investigations have been completed. It can obviously save time and effort if there is sufficient commercial understanding of the company before any technical investigations commence. I am not advocating duplicating the tasks of these departments or, perish the thought, attempting to do their job for them, merely that time spent getting acquainted with a company's fortunes can help to avoid unnecessary technical investigation.

I was involved in a bid where Compaq was offering Alpha servers at attractive prices, in comparison to the other major UNIX vendors. This happened to be shortly before it was announced that merger talks with HP were underway. A rudimentary assessment of Compaq's fortunes over the previous two years was sufficient to understand why the offers were attractive and what the risks might be. For example, the sale of the Alpha chip technology to Intel a couple of months previously, plus recent financial results, were obvious indications that all was not well. This is not to say that the choice of Alpha servers might have been inappropriate, merely that Compaq's situation came into the equation given that this particular bid involved running the developed system for 10 to 15 years. As it was a Greenfield site, the bid team decided on balance to go with another vendor despite the financial attractions and the undoubted technical pedigree of an Alpha solution.

Moving forward to a month or so after the merger finally took place, I was giving a talk to a group of developers and sundry technicians in a systems house. I was discussing the subject of vendors at some point in the presentation and I asked who was aware of the HP and Compaq merger. It was slightly disturbing to discover that only about 15 percent of the attendees were aware of this development. It was equally disturbing to find that current bids were favoring the use of HP's range of 32-bit Intel servers when the stated direction of the newly merged organization was to promote Compaq's Intel servers.

Although a technical architect may be investigating a particular vendor's products to meet a specific requirement, it is useful if he can keep abreast of vendor technical developments generally. For any given product, apart from its intrinsic technical merits and constraints, it is essential to understand where it fits in the vendor's strategy, its relative maturity, and life expectancy. In terms of the vendor's strategy, it is important to realize that few, if any, vendors offer a complete portfolio of products in any given hardware or software area. There are invariably gaps that the vendor may be forced by the competition to fill. The easy solution is frequently to buy a product from another company and rebadge it. The question then becomes one of whether it is merely a short-term solution to gain breathing space while the vendor develops his own solution, or if it is viewed as a longer-term solution that may take some time to be fully integrated into the existing range. The maturity of a product is always an important consideration. You will probably get bored hearing this as you go through the book, but V1.0 of anything invariably has reliability and performance issues, whether it is a hardware or software product, or a custom application. Life expectancy is the other side of the coin from maturity. Ideally, a mature product is preferred, but one whose life expectancy matches the projected lifespan of the system rather than one that is axed halfway through. Finally, on the vendor product front, it is useful to be able to differentiate between a new product and a rebranded product.

1.6.4 Tools and Techniques

Popular opinion has it that a good performance analyst has pockets full of tools and techniques. Tools are invariably software products such as performance monitors that can ideally produce sexy, real-time graphs, modeling aids to predict performance, homegrown spreadsheets, and stress testing tools. The skill is in the selection and use of effective tools. For example, there may not be much point in having a predictive modeling tool if there are unlikely to be sufficiently detailed performance metrics to plug into a model.

Tools have their place but they are far from the be-all and end-all of performance work. Although they can help to make a performance analyst more productive, they are no substitute for solid analysis, experience, and judgment. I am reminded of a concentrated one-day course on hardware sizing and performance that I delivered on a number of occasions for a large UK systems house for which I worked. The day was shaped around the experiences of a medium-sized project from bid through to post-implementation (I did say that it was concentrated!). The morning period covered bid qualification (to bid or not to bid), hardware sizing for the bid itself using very limited volumetrics, and design considerations. The afternoon session started with the assumption that some code and a database had been developed. It covered predictive modeling techniques using queueing theory (the company had developed a useful analytic modeling tool that was written in Visual Basic), implementation, and post-production issues. The course was liberally sprinkled with exercises, including a chance to use the aforesaid modeling tool. The feedback from the attendees, none of whom were experienced performance practitioners, typically went along the following lines (I paraphrase very slightly). "The most useful part of the day was playing with the modeling tool. The least useful part of the day was when the lecturer wittered about the role of judgment and experience in hardware sizing during the bid process when there is minimal information." A small number of attendees subsequently built models using the tool on their projects, with varying degrees of success. In general, the attendees ultimately realized that on many development projects the lack of detailed information made the use of a modeling tool problematic, and that perhaps less sexy techniques can be invaluable.

The major techniques in the performance analyst's kitbag are hardware sizing, performance analysis, and capacity/performance prediction.

- Hardware sizing is typically performed early in the lifecycle, quite often at the bid or feasibility stage. Invariably, there is minimal information to work with, a fact that frightens people from attempting it, as it can frequently be 90 percent judgment (based on experience) and 10 percent science.
- Performance monitoring and analysis is an ongoing task for production systems. Analysis is not necessarily as straightforward as it may appear. Except for simple problems, it is not just a case of looking at individual metrics such as CPU utilization or memory usage. Often, the trick is to use the various disparate metrics to build a picture of the interrelationships of the various hardware and software components to understand the reasons for unsatisfactory performance and to identify where any future problems are likely to surface.
- Looking ahead leads to prediction and capacity planning exercises where the objective is to take business projections for the next one to two years and to map them onto system usage. Predictions are then made as to how long the current configurations will support the workloads in terms of capacity and responsiveness, what upgrades will be necessary, and when they will be required. Predictive modeling tools can help although they seem to be less fashionable than they were in the late 1980s and early 1990s.

1.7 PERFORMANCE ASSURANCE WITHIN A PROJECT LIFECYCLE

This chapter concludes by looking briefly at the role of performance within the context of the development project lifecycle. Items that are tackled during feasibility and bid stages are covered in later chapters.

I have a penchant for using the term "performance assurance." It conveys the message that the emphasis is on being proactive throughout the project lifecycle, rather than being driven by events. What follows is a brief summary of the tasks that are undertaken at each stage. In keeping with my "fit for purpose" mantra, it is important to say that the precise scope of performance assurance will depend on the size and complexity of the application, the aggressiveness of the performance requirements, its relative importance to the business, and any cost constraints.

1.7.1 Requirements/Functional Specification Stage

The primary objective at this stage is to review, and where necessary refine, the initial technical solution that was produced during the bid or feasibility stage, in the light of a better understanding of the functional solution. This includes revisiting any hardware sizing. In particular, volumetric information is often virtually nonexistent before this stage is reached, and this can be the first opportunity to construct a coherent set of figures. Any changes or better understanding of business requirements that may have an impact on the original design ideas are assessed to ensure that they do not constrain the use of the available hardware capacity, and hence have an impact on performance. This can generally be a tricky time on two counts. It can frequently become clear to the project team that the original understanding of the functional requirements was substantially wide of the mark. Usually the problem is that the true size and complexity were not fully appreciated. This may result in the technical team being forced to revamp its solution, and it may have to commence this work in a vacuum while the functional team struggles to complete its understanding.

The second potential problem is invariably self-inflicted. It usually occurs when there is a lack of continuity of staff from the feasibility or bid phase to the project. It is an unfortunate fact of life that many IT people suffer from the not-invented-here syndrome. This means that anything that was done by others, especially when they are no longer around, is considered to be inherently inferior and unsuitable, and must be changed out of all recognition so that all remnants of the previous solution are completely obliterated. Okay, so I exaggerate, but only very slightly. I accept that there are occasions when the original solution is unsuitable, usually when the full scope of the business requirements were not appreciated, but more often the lack of continuity means that the project team is frequently unaware of the assumptions that were employed, or of any specific constraints that were in operation. It would be extremely useful if the feasibility or bid team actually documented the assumptions that they had to work with, particularly any cost constraints, for the benefit of those that follow.

1.7.2 Design Stage

This is potentially the point in the project when there is the greatest opportunity to ensure that performance will be satisfactory. There are a number of major pointers here.

- There should be a design! There is an increasing tendency to believe vendor hype with respect to the capabilities of development frameworks and to do away with the design stage. Although there are undoubtedly small systems where the risk may be justified, any reasonably sized system should have a design.

- The design must be able to exploit the proposed hardware and software platform. A very simple example from the dim and distant past was a system that was based on a TP monitor. The plot was to run a single system on a dedicated server with multiple CPUs. Unfortunately, at that time the TP monitor in question could not exploit multiple CPUs.
- The design should not be overambitious. It should be fit for purpose; that is, it should not be fully scalable if it does not need to be, as the costs are unnecessarily increased, and there is the increasing likelihood of reliability and maintenance problems.
- Last-minute pressure to use the latest and greatest technologies should be resisted unless there are solid reasons to do so.
- Some design methodologies promote discrete logical and physical design stages. Time constraints can have an impact on the quality of the physical design, frequently leading to its total omission, thus greatly increasing the risk of hitting significant performance and scalability problems by trying to implement the logical design.
- The design should make the best use of the development toolset. This means that wherever possible the design should "go with the flow," avoiding the temptation to battle with the toolset.
- The use of in-house benchmarks should be considered to investigate any area where there is a lack of confidence in the likely performance, for example, any questions that there may be over throughput or response times. Ideally, any fundamental areas of risk should have been identified earlier in the project, and the benchmarks performed at that stage.
- Finally, the design stage is the ideal opportunity to review all hardware sizing calculations and to refine them as necessary. Any detailed predictive modeling is likely to be commenced at this stage.

1.7.3 Code and Test

The main objective is to encourage developers to think consciously about performance as they are building the application. There are several strands that can be followed:

- Setting up guidelines for the developers to promote good practice, for example, good versus bad SQL, details of any perceived idiosyncrasies in the development tool set, and so on. Do not get too carried away. I have seen some fairly large documents that were somewhat daunting to the majority of developers who promptly tended to ignore them. A concise one- or two-pager is preferable. Alternatively, structure the document so that the really important items are highlighted at the front of the document and readers are referred to the rest of the guidelines later in the document.

- Ensuring that code reviews take account of performance aspects.
- Testing and monitoring the performance of the key functions as soon as code is available. Many systems have a relatively small number of functions (up to six) that handle 70 to 80 percent of the total transaction volume, and it pays to concentrate on them, certainly in the short term. The resultant metrics can be fed into a detailed performance model, where there is one. It is at this stage that the greatest benefits are likely to accrue from the use of predictive modeling techniques. Modeling results should be fed back into the design and build process. Ideally, subject to time and cost constraints, this should be an iterative process until performance is considered to be satisfactory.

1.7.4 Performance Acceptance Testing

There are two main areas, stress testing and soak testing. The main elements of stress testing work are to:

- Investigate how a representative stress test can be set up and run with the minimum of effort. The effort that may be required to set up databases and test scripts should not be underestimated. The use of stress testing tools should be considered (a) to minimize the amount of manual effort and (b) to allow tests to be repeatable.
- Ensure that the application is ready for a stress test. Items include the removal of development aids such as debugging and traces that will degrade performance, the sensible set-up of the database across the available disk capacity to minimize bottlenecks, optimum memory cache sizes for the DBMS or file system, and optimum use of multitasking where it is appropriate.
- Review the results of the performance test and identify any problem areas.
- Extrapolate the results to the full production volumes if the stress tests were run on a subset of volumes.

Stress tests are usually short in duration, typically running for no more than one hour, as the main objective is to ensure that system responsiveness is satisfactory under peak load. Subject to time constraints, they are usually followed by soak tests that assess system reliability over time; for example, they check for memory leaks whose effects may be slow to show. They can run for many hours, or indeed many days.

1.7.5 The All-Phases Stage

I have roughly followed the Waterfall model where project development is split into discrete stages. However, as anybody who has ever worked on a semi-frantic project will know, there is the All-Phases stage. This stage usually commences with the start of the coding and testing, but it is seldom to be found in project plans. It occurs when the functional requirements have still to be bottomed out, and not only has the design team had to take a flier to keep the project on track, but the coders and testers now have to take their lives in their hands by commencing work without completed specifications. This parallel development can continue right through to the end of the project. The religious fervor that surrounds the Rapid Application Development (RAD) versus Waterfall debate is quite amusing, as I have seen extremely rapid development occur under the guise of the Waterfall model. This stage is mentioned because if a project ends up in this position the benefits of using judgment earlier in the project (usually at the bid or feasibility stage) are likely to be realized, and hence the amount of any rework that may be required will be minimized. Judgment is discussed later in the chapter on hardware sizing, but in essence it is the ability to assess the credibility of the information that is available and the likelihood of the goalposts being moved, and to make decisions that seem appropriate, sometimes in spite of the generally accepted views at the time.

1.7.6 Post-Implementation

The application should be closely monitored during the early stages of production running. This can take longer than expected as any volume-related problems may take some time to surface; for example, it may take three to four months, possibly longer, for the database to get to a sufficient size for inefficient accessing problems to manifest themselves. At some point responsibility for the application will transfer from the project team to the support team, and performance tasks will pass to the capacity management team, or equivalent. This is usually around the three-month mark, particularly when the application has been provided by a third party, as warranty periods tend to be 90 days.

1.8 SUMMARY

In this chapter, the main messages have been:

- Performance analysts tend to get involved around the time that a new application is due to go into production but the major benefits, particularly on larger projects, are likely to accrue from involvement both before and during the development phase.
- Performance is ultimately a byproduct of business requirements, architecture, volumes, design, and implementation. All these subjects have to be assessed from a performance perspective in a timely manner. The person who is involved at each stage does not necessarily have to be the ubiquitous performance analyst. It may be a technical architect. The choice depends on the skills of the individuals concerned. Referring to the phrase "what goes around comes around," I consider that the nurturing of technical all-rounders who can cover performance issues is long overdue.
- There should be a person in every organization who has the knowledge, skills, and experience to make dispassionate judgments on the relative merits and constraints of individual IT technologies. Every project team needs ready access to this person.
- Performance issues need to be tackled in a proactive manner. A performance assurance plan provides a solid foundation that can underpin such an approach.

2

CAVEAT EMPTOR
(LET THE BUYER BEWARE)

2.1 ABSTRACT

Smaller projects may be afforded a degree of latitude in making errors of judgment when choosing hardware and software products. The scale of such projects invariably means that any significant problems that may arise can mostly be resolved, or at least minimized, without significant cost implications. In other words, they are better placed to have the luxury of making mistakes and learning from them. Larger projects have less room to maneuver in this regard. Poor decisions with respect to the technical infrastructure or the software solution can be difficult and costly to resolve. An understanding of software and hardware product lifecycles, an appreciation of marketing techniques, coupled with a coherent approach to product selection, will all help to improve the decision-making process.

2.2 SOFTWARE PRODUCT LIFECYCLE

Very few software products, or indeed applications, perform satisfactorily when they first go into production — the "V1.0 syndrome." This is not a recent phenomenon. Even when there was seemingly more time available for design and implementation in bygone days, there were usually performance problems.

Software product vendors typically have to take a long-term view, as they may not get into profit with a new product for two to three years after the initial release (see Figure 2.1). During the initial development, money is being burnt with no revenue coming in to offset the cost. Pressure will build inexorably to get V1.0 out on the streets to provide some necessary revenue. Companies with reasonably deep pockets will

19

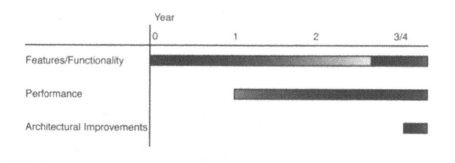

Figure 2.1   Software Evolution (darker: more detailed attention given)

also face pressures, although they are more likely to be competitive rather than financial pressures. It is quite usual for some of the functionality to be de-scoped in an effort to shorten the time to market. In addition, the comprehensiveness of testing may be affected, while performance will be lucky to get any sort of look-in.

Revenue from the initial customers of V1.0 will help to fund continued development. Although the performance may be poor, the overriding clamor from the customer base, and from potential customers, will tend to be for increased functional features. Therefore, the focus will remain on functionality to widen the customer base, although some rudimentary performance improvements may be included where they are simple and straightforward to implement.

There may be several functional releases before the preoccupation with features will start to abate and the performance problems begin to take center stage. A major release that concentrates on performance may be shipped in the third year. The scope of these performance improvements will depend on how sound the initial design principles were. Any shortcomings may have to wait for a fundamental re-architecting of the product. This may not occur until the fourth or fifth year, by which time there is, invariably, renewed customer focus on features.

2.3   HARDWARE PRODUCT LIFECYCLE

There is more pressure on hardware vendors to get performance right the first time, as it can be difficult, although not insuperable, to rectify problems. This is not to say that achieved performance will necessarily match the marketing hype that precedes the launch.

The size and complexity of a hardware product, plus the amount of bespoke design work that is required, will have a direct bearing on the costs of development, which in turn will affect its life expectancy. For example, a new generation of server technology has to last longer than a given disk technology, to claw back the original investment and to maximize profits. There are obviously ways to ensure that a server technology can achieve a satisfactory lifespan, for example, gradually increasing the clock speed of the processors, obtaining speed improvements through compiler changes, and implementing faster chipsets. Ultimately, the demise of a technology will be brought about either because the vendor considers that he has had full value from it, and he now perceives that he can obtain a competitive edge by replacing it with a new technology, or because the vendor is lagging behind the competition and he is forced to introduce a new technology, probably sooner than he would wish.

The actual life of a supported hardware product will vary according to the vendor and the type of product. For example, modern UNIX and W2K-based server technologies may last four to seven years, whereas a particular disk drive may only be actively shipped for two to three years.

2.4 MARKETING

In addressing a typical product lifecycle I have concentrated mainly on the view from the technical and overall commercial perspectives. Apart from the obvious financial pressures there are also pressures that are brought on by the competition. There is frequently a massive incentive to decrease the time to market out of a fear of missing the window of opportunity when it is possible to establish a place as a key player, or indeed to achieve some sort of competitive edge.

Although strenuous efforts are made to ship the product sooner rather than later, the product is usually pre-announced. This is partly to interest potential customers, but also a method of trying to prevent them from straying to the competition, particularly if the competition is likely to ship their offering earlier. It is this latter element that tends to dictate how far ahead a pre-announcement is made. Announcing too far ahead, particularly if development falls behind schedule, brings the attendant danger of a possible loss of credibility. Where any significant delay is encountered, the name of the proposed product will sometimes be changed, as well as the jargon that was used, in an attempt to make people think that the latest name relates to a totally different product. These rebranding ploys are more likely with hardware products, as they have longer development cycles and are therefore more prone to significant delays, although they also occur with software products.

These tactics can also be adopted when a product requires a makeover. In this case, an established product using older technologies is suddenly caught out by the appearance of newer products. An obvious example was the advent of object-oriented techniques. Products that never mentioned the use of such techniques were suddenly bristling with references to objects. In many cases, this was mostly talk with limited substance. Where software changes have occurred in an attempt to make up lost ground (e.g., with the advent of Web interfaces), it may be that the implementation is a rudimentary, possibly poorly performing, add-on rather than any fundamental, and hence potentially expensive, redesign.

Beware "David versus Goliath" confrontations. Here, Goliath decides that he should have been in a given product area some time ago and threatens to make up for lost time by using the full weight of his financial muscle. From a technical perspective, the effectiveness of this ploy is not the foregone conclusion that most people assume; it depends very much on the underlying complexity of the software. At one extreme, in the field of operating systems it can take many years to make any appreciable inroads into the head start that the leading players have, much less catch them up. It is a well-worn but valid observation that simply throwing bodies and money at a problem is no guarantee of providing a quick solution to a problem. However, from a marketing perspective the simple warning that the big guys are coming often seems to have the desired effect of causing potential customers to dither in their deliberations.

There are many ways to market a product but ultimately it is the written word that is important. Large organizations have their own publishing outlets and can afford to produce books on technologies or products, or they can encourage professional writers to write books by funding them, or by providing access to detailed material. Standard marketing material is frequently difficult to comprehend, especially for software products. Descriptions of the technical aspects can be vague, using invented jargon with little or no explanation of their meaning. Indeed, it can be difficult sometimes to fathom whether there is a real product, or whether they are just talking about a concept or architecture.

For established products it is usually necessary to convince customers that improvements will follow thick and fast. This can be achieved by publishing a roadmap. Do you know of any roadmap that turned out to be vaguely accurate? I cannot personally remember any. Where graphs are published with respect to past and future performance, they invariably follow the trend in Figure 2.2, showing that improvements have been modest, or even static, in the last couple of years but they are now going to accelerate out of all recognition.

2.5 TECHNICAL REVIEWS OF PRODUCTS

In the ideal world new technologies and products are investigated as part of an R&D process, not as part of a project. However, in my experience, project-driven investigations tend to be the norm. Management, which is

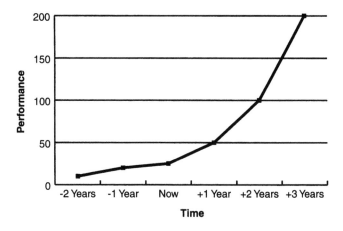

Figure 2.2 A Typical "Jam Tomorrow" Roadmap

usually reticent to sanction project-driven product reviews, quickly becomes impatient when it is perceived that they are dragging on. I have some sympathy, although not a great deal. IT people are inquisitive, and they usually want to uncover as much information as possible before they are prepared to commit themselves. Unfortunately, project investigations do not usually allow that luxury. Equally, there is the danger that investigations are too high-level, and that consequently they do not probe deeply enough. I have encountered some investigations that have a "tick the box" mentality; that is, they are simply looking for a product or a technology to plug a gap and therefore any probing is limited.

Assuming that time is limited, investigations have to be focused. The first task should be to doublecheck that somebody else in the organization has not been there before you. I remember one company where each division had performed its own review of document management systems. In fact, in one division at least three different projects/bids had carried out their own detailed investigations. The next task is to identify your key criteria, for example, price, key features, solid but flexible architecture, scalability, maturity, performance, resilience, and so on.

It is vitally important to see through any marketing-inspired obfuscation and to develop a pragmatic understanding of the product, its suitability and usability. This includes:

- An assessment of the likely risks
- The identification of any poorly performing or nonscalable aspects that should ideally be avoided
- An indication of any workarounds that may be necessary to compensate for unsatisfactory elements

■ Any impact on the preferred technical infrastructure (e.g., lots of small servers are required rather than a small number of large multiprocessor servers)

2.5.1 Preparation

There is no substitute for being up to speed on technologies in general, and on vendors and their individual product offerings. As mentioned previously, any reasonable-sized organization should have a person who keeps abreast of technologies and products. A full-time role is not being proposed, although larger organizations may consider it worthwhile. One approach is to split the responsibility and have a number of individuals who each keep their eye on a particular sector of the marketplace. An alternative approach is to subscribe to a company that specializes in R&D and makes its findings available. Care is required with this approach, as some outfits may be strong adherents of a particular technology, and therefore their advice may not be as impartial as it should be.

It is important to start with a rudimentary understanding of the financial status of the vendor. It is essential not to waste time going through a review process, recommending a particular product, only to discover that it may not have been a wise move from a commercial perspective. In general, basic financial information (e.g., accounts for the last year or two) can often be found on the vendors' Web sites. Rumors of profit warnings, takeovers, bankruptcy, and so on can be found in the financial or IT press. Online newspapers such as *The Inquirer* and *The Register* will invariably fasten on to this type of information, in addition to the more usual provision of technical information.

From a technical perspective, it is important to obtain an understanding of the current status of the technology: is it bleeding edge, moderately mature, or approaching the veteran stage? It is preferable to start with books or papers that at least pretend to be impartial, before graduating to vendor material. Beware of articles, seemingly impartial, that mostly just regurgitate material that the authors have been fed by vendors. Look for balanced assessments in books and articles and be wary of test results that seemingly substantiate an author's view. I read a book recently where results from very small, unrepresentative tests were used to justify an approach to the development of large-scale systems (wrongly in my view). Read material from as wide a range of vendors as possible on a given type of product, as the stance that is taken by different vendors, such as what each tends to emphasize, downplay, and even avoid, frequently provides clues as to the relative strengths and weaknesses of the individual products, and to the general issues that surround this type of product.

2.5.2   Reading Vendor Literature

It is possible to write a book on this subject. However, this is not the place to go into any particularly gory detail. Scanning techniques that are based on identifying key words or phrases, particularly in indexes, are extremely useful. This is the ability to home in quickly on the important parts of a document, that is, the parts where the really interesting information resides, as opposed to the general material. This is a skill that I have gradually acquired over the years. It is akin to speed-reading although it is not quite the same thing.

My first step when reading a document is to get a general feel. If I have difficulty understanding what they are talking about, to the extent that I am not sure if they are describing a concept or a product then there is the danger of my dismissing the product. Now it may be that the product deserves attention but that it is simply being let down by the marketing material. It could also be that the marketing material is just covering the cracks, and the product should indeed be dismissed. In fact, I will always go back to the vendor and give them another opportunity to provide some reasonable material. To illustrate the point of vague descriptions, a friend rang to ask me if I had heard of a particular product (that will remain nameless) as there were some questions on its suitability. I confessed that I had not heard of it but I promised to look into it. I looked at the material on the company's Web site and after 15 to 20 minutes I was just about confident that it was a product that was being described but I had absolutely no idea what it did. The material consisted solely of a mixture of marketing-speak and jargon. As I was pressed for time, I had to give up. In my experience, if a product has good, or even just promising, features the vendor can usually be relied upon to describe them *ad nauseam* in plain English.

With regard to architectural aspects, many vendors, particularly in the software arena, seem loath to provide a sound description. They appear to think that they will be giving away highly prized information that will aid the competition. I have to say to them that I have lost track of how many times I have signed nondisclosure agreements (NDAs), only to discover that there was either nothing that I did not know already, or that the information was of extremely limited value, and that it was unlikely to be worth anything to anybody! It is eminently possible to provide a sound view of the architecture without giving away the crown jewels. Reviewers are typically not looking for information on those really important algorithms that give the company an edge (although that might be worth signing away your life for!), merely a coherent view of the architecture, down to the protocol or process level, enough to understand the implications for performance, resilience, and scalability.

Make sure that all claims are read carefully. Marketing people can be extremely economical with the truth, but they tend not to lie, at least not in print. Here are a few tongue-in-cheek examples:

- "Will support" — not in this version then
- "Can support" — depends on your definition of "support"
- "Can integrate with" — only with some difficulty
- "Can coexist" — oh dear!
- "Scalable" — can support at least one more transaction
- "99.999 percent availability is obtainable" — math is not my strongpoint
- "Today, many of the top companies are using our product in systems that are designed to deliver 99.999 percent server uptime" — that little box over there in the corner is running our product that is responsible for 5 percent of the solution

Finally, the reviewer's solution to the marketing problem used to be simply to bypass that material and head straight for the white papers, those useful technical documents that provide the "nitty-gritty" information. Unfortunately, marketing has invaded this territory, and in recent years too many so-called white papers have degenerated into rather grey, insipid documents that are often little better than the straight marketing material. This should not be surprising as many of them betray the hand of a marketing censor. Perhaps we should be looking for black papers!

2.5.3 Vendor Meetings

Meetings with vendors have to be focused. I have sat in on too many meetings or presentations that were not productive, and a series of meetings was required to make any progress.

- Decide on the agenda and agree upon it with the vendor ahead of time. Too many meetings have either no agenda or a vague unfocused agenda. Agree upon any specific topics that must be covered.
- Ensure that the vendor will have the necessary technical expertise available. This usually means that they have to be booked well in advance. If the vendor is a reseller it is doubly important to ensure that they have suitable expertise available.
- The vendor's offices tend to be the preferable venue as they are more likely to be able to get hold of the necessary technical expertise.
- Ensure that any requirements to sign nondisclosure agreements (NDAs) do not cause unnecessary delays.

- Do not go with the expectation of being entertained.
- Do not attend without having done some homework on the technology/product. I remember one particularly turgid meeting where useful information had been provided ahead of time by the vendor (a rare occurrence) but it had not been read by one individual who promptly managed to get away with wasting several hours getting up to speed by asking questions that were largely answered by the reading material.
- Provide the vendor with a *précis* of your requirements beforehand. There is an unfortunate tendency for bid teams especially to refuse to provide sufficient information. If it is truly sensitive, and much is not, it is eminently possible to disguise the client, the market sector, and the system with some thought. It is totally counterproductive to refuse to give the vendor reasonable information with which to work.
- Do not forget that vendor sales material will usually tell you every last thing that the product is capable of doing. Concentrate on the areas that the glossies do not cover.
- Start off the first meeting by providing a succinct background to your requirement.
- If the meeting does not appear to be fruitful, call a time-out at some convenient point to discuss progress and, where necessary, shape the rest of the session. Do not be afraid to bring the meeting to a halt if reasonable progress is not being made.
- Arrange any necessary follow-up meetings. Try to ensure that the vendor passes on the background of your requirements to any technical specialist who is made available in future meetings, as you do not wish to waste time explaining them again.

2.5.4 Technical Review Checklist

This section focuses mainly on software product reviews, as they tend to be more frequent than hardware product reviews. It contains an outline checklist of items that should be covered in a technical review. By necessity, it occasionally dives down into fairly detailed criteria. Readers who require more background material or criteria for hardware reviews should read this section in conjunction with Chapter 7 and the relevant Technology Tasters in Part 2.

2.5.4.1 Architecture

Investigate the background of the product.

- Establish its maturity by looking back through its history.

- For what platform was it originally designed? For example, it may have been designed for a client/server, whereas you are interested in the Web-based version of the product.
- How many major releases have there been? Beware attempts to convince you that the product is more mature than it actually is, by quoting an unusually high version number. For example, version 5 in year three would sound a bit suspicious. A major release once a year is reasonable. Occasionally, versions are jumped; for example, version 2.2 is followed by version 4.0. There can be genuine reasons for such a jump. Version 3 may have been behind schedule and a decision was made to merge it with a later release. Whatever the reason, it is important to understand the rationale.

Check that the version that you are interested in is actually being shipped. If not, when will it be available? Is it delayed? How confident are you that the revised date will be hit?

Insist on a jargon-free detailed description of the architecture, where possible. Software architectures should be described at the process or main component level.

Investigate the deployment options, that is, how the individual elements can be mapped onto hardware components. Can all components coreside on a single server, or can they be implemented on separate servers?

Check what the prerequisites are, for example, platform, operating system, and other software products. It is particularly important to check the required versions of any prerequisites, particularly if you already have a version earlier (or later) than that supported by the product under investigation.

Request details of the proposed future releases for the product, including any plans for its eventual replacement.

2.5.4.2 Scalability

How does the software scale on a single hardware server (scaling up); does it use multiple processes or multithreading techniques?

What are the effects on throughput and response times as CPUs are added to the server? (Hardware and software overheads on multiprocessor servers may significantly constrain performance.)

What is the ultimate constraining factor on a single server?

Can the software scale by deploying multiple hardware servers (scaling out)? Are these scaling features inherently designed into the product or does it rely on underlying software from another vendor for example, cluster technology?

On a multitier solution, which elements can be scaled out, and which cannot? For example, the front-end and middle tiers such as the Web and application layers may be scaled out but the back-end database server may not be.

Investigate how scalability is achieved on each tier. Is a master–slave approach adopted, and if so, at what point does the master become a bottleneck? Find out if a user is assigned to one server (e.g., an applications server) for a complete session. If so, check what load-balancing techniques are used to decide which server a user is allotted, and how successful the load balancing is in terms of spreading the load evenly. If a user is not tied to a single server, again check what load-balancing techniques are used, and how the user's state information is maintained between transactions.

On back-end servers, can multiple hardware servers combine to act as a single data repository; or can they only act as discrete individual repositories that require some form of hard partitioning in the design?

If a single repository is supported across multiple servers check to see if there are any disk-writing restrictions, such as, only one hardware server can write to the repository at a time. Is some form of distributed lock mechanism employed to enforce integrity across hardware nodes? If so, investigate how it is implemented. Note that disk-based locks may perform poorly.

In a multi-server file system, is there a separate master process that controls a session between a client node and the repository for data access? What restrictions are there with this approach?

Where memory caches are kept on the individual client nodes of a multi-server file system to improve performance, check how the caches on other nodes are maintained when the data is changed by one node (cache coherency issues).

On high-volume systems query the proposed use of network file systems such as CIFS or NFS for shared repositories as they may limit performance.

2.5.4.3   Resilience

Check what resilience features are built into the hardware, for example, redundant power supplies and fans, network connections, battery backup for disk subsystems, and so on.

Check that the disk system is adequately resilient. If RAID 5 is employed ensure that there are no performance issues; that is, write-intensive systems are not usually suitable for RAID 5.

Check to see if the software has any inbuilt resilience features. For example, if a process fails or hangs, are there any features that may allow it to be restarted? In the same vein, can the number of retries for a failed process be controlled?

Are there any fail-over mechanisms whereby a service can be made resilient? A service is usually defined as a collection of hardware, software, and associated network addresses that typically comprise an application. In the case of a software failure, the service may simply be restarted, or in the case of a hardware failure it may be moved to another hardware server. How is the failure of a service detected? The normal mechanism is via a "check heartbeat" mechanism that continually pumps "are you alive requests" to the service. Failure to respond within an acceptable timeframe will result in the service being deemed to have failed. The question is, what if the service is still functioning and the problem actually lies somewhere on the network connection between the two servers (split brain syndrome)?

How many hardware nodes are supported in a cluster, and what limits the number?

Check what distance limitations there may be for the hardware nodes in a cluster. Is there a concept of a "super cluster" where a number of discrete, possibly geographically dispersed, clusters can be controlled, and where services can be moved between clusters, for example, from the production data center to a disaster recovery center?

Check what recovery is necessary when a service is moved ("failed over") to another hardware node. Is fail-over seamless? That is, there is no noticeable break in the service for a user whose transaction is affected. If it is noticeable, what factors affect the time taken to complete any necessary application recovery? On a middle tier server does a user lose state information? If not, how is state maintained and what are the associated overheads, for replicating state across servers or persisting state to shared disk?

Where data is replicated to another system either for resilience purposes, or as part of a distribution of data, check the overheads, as they can be quite onerous. Is the replication performed synchronously, in which case response times may be affected, or asynchronously? If both are supported, what are the advantages and disadvantages of each approach?

What are the dangers of data corruption if replication fails due to a hardware or network failure? Are there any distance issues where the servers are more than 10 to 15 km apart, particularly if the replication is performed synchronously?

2.5.4.4 Performance

Verify what performance, in terms of throughput and response times, can be expected for the proposed size of the system. Be wary of claims that are based on results that were achieved on smaller systems, as they may not be valid on larger systems.

Be very wary if the product has not supported a system as large as this, particularly if the vendor appears to have done no performance work, for example, never performed any stress testing, has no information on performance characteristics, and so on. Understand what factors have the greatest effects on performance. For example, what effects are there on response times for deploying a scalable, multitiered solution?

Do resilience features affect performance?

What tends to be the primary bottleneck — CPU, disk, network, software locks, and so on?

If benchmark figures are available insist on seeing a full disclosure report.

2.5.4.5 Other Elements

It is invariably useful to talk to existing clients about their experiences with the product. Be wary that the vendor will want to steer you towards satisfied rather than dissatisfied clients. Check which version and features of the product they are using.

Investigate the size/location of the vendor's development and support teams, particularly for software products. How many senior technicians are there who fully understand the product? Beware of moderately sized vendors who may only have one person who is based on the other side of the planet, who can never be got hold of, because otherwise she would never get any work done!

It is beyond the scope of this book to go into any detail on price implications and commercial negotiations. However, here are some general pointers.

- Question the rationale behind algorithms for pricing software products that will run on multiprocessor systems. The pricing of different sizes of system has been a thorny problem for a number of years. It is particularly galling if you consider that you need additional hardware due to the inadequacies of the vendor's software, only for him to charge additional license fees for the privilege.
- Similarly, question any additional cost implications for running the software on a standby node or on a DR system. Although only one instance of the production system may be running at any one time, some software vendors may try to charge you for each instance, whether it is running or not.
- Question any insistence by the vendor to apply a mandatory charge for installation or training where you do not consider them to be

appropriate. This frequently happens with respect to back-end clusters.

- Understand the rationale behind any apparently cheap prices. Is the vendor in financial trouble; is the product about to be axed or replaced?
- Obtain the costs of appropriate maintenance cover. For example, is hardware cover required from 9 to 5, Monday to Friday with a four-hour call-out time, or on-site 24/7, or 24-hour phone line support for software?
- Check when maintenance is payable (e.g., monthly or annually), and whether it is payable in advance.

2.5.5 Custom Software Versus Product

A custom approach may sometimes be considered where the products are too rich in features and (most important) too expensive, or where there are serious concerns with respect to performance and scalability.

I encountered an example of this recently. The project had a design requirement to store 30 documents per second at peak, and to subsequently retrieve them at the rate of 15 documents per second. The storage and retrieval requirements were lightweight in terms of functionality, being one part of a large complex case management system. Products were investigated but they were overrich in functionality for the needs of the project, and hence prohibitively expensive. There was also a question mark over performance and scalability, particularly for one of the products. It was decided, on balance, that a custom approach would be significantly cheaper; it would meet the current performance requirements, and it would produce a scalable solution.

Ideally, any custom element should be designed and implemented in such a way that it could be replaced with a suitable product in the future, as and when appropriate.

2.5.6 Drawing Conclusions

Arguably, the primary skill is the ability to remain dispassionate despite the numerous distractions. This includes:

- Countering your own innate biases towards particular products and vendors.
- Not being seduced by the latest technology that will look good on the CV.
- Remembering the "fit for purpose" mantra. Vastly superior products usually have a price tag to match. They may be extremely attractive

but they may not represent value for money if many of the features are likely to be unused.

■ Disregarding the near-religious zealotry of colleagues and vendors who consider that a particular technology is akin to the Holy Grail.

■ Ignoring the endless competition bashing in which vendors sometimes indulge.

■ Forgetting that really annoying salesman.

I find that a useful technique is to discuss and agree upon a set of selection criteria before the reviews commence, and to establish a relative weighting for each criterion. Items such as maturity, sound design principles, effective resilience and scalability features, and credible performance claims tend to rate highly with me. Where possible, I tend to perform a purely technical comparison in the first instance, taking commercial considerations into account separately. I do this so that if there are significant financial constraints that may ultimately affect the choice of product, any technical risks can clearly be seen.

All major risks and any requirement to develop workarounds must be identified and costed.

The comprehensiveness of any written findings will naturally depend on the time available. Where time is limited I usually find it possible to summarize the key points of a product in three to four pages in most cases. Major technologies may be two or three times this figure. For readers who are used to producing voluminous reports, remember that we are primarily interested in the big questions of maturity, architecture, performance, scalability, resilience, future enhancements, price, and risk; and there is usually little opportunity to write any weighty tomes. For readers who subscribe to the current fashion for not writing anything, I am sure that you can live with short summaries.

The outcome of any reviews should be a firm set of conclusions and recommendations. This may seem to be an obvious statement but many technicians have a propensity for sitting on the fence, a luxury that the speed of modern projects does not permit.

Finally, the findings should be made available across the company in an effort to ensure that other projects may benefit from the investigation, and that they do not have to reinvent the wheel unnecessarily.

3

LIES, DAMNED LIES, AND BENCHMARKS

3.1 ABSTRACT

Benchmarks seldom, if ever, reflect the complexities of the production systems that they purportedly seek to imitate. At best, they may constitute a credible subset of a proposed system whose usefulness is ultimately constrained by a lack of time to build a more lifelike representation; at worst, they can be unrepresentative systems that produce misleading results.

Three main categories of benchmarks are identified: industry, vendor, and custom in-house. Industry benchmarks can be useful if their functionality can be equated in some way to the functionality of the proposed system. The objective of many vendor benchmarks is simply to promote the vendor's product. The results are often used as marketing material to demonstrate that their product is superior to the competition. This means that there is always a temptation to produce impressive results by using techniques that are unlikely to be deployed in a typical production system. Such techniques are more likely to be used on immature products. There is less reason to employ them on mature products that have gained general market acceptance, not least because they have been around long enough to resolve serious performance issues. Custom-built and in-house benchmarks have the best opportunity to provide meaningful results, as it is possible to dictate the scope and rules of the benchmarking. However, they are frequently encumbered by time and cost constraints.

It is the conclusions that are drawn from benchmark results that are important, not the results themselves. No benchmark results should be taken at face value unless there is supreme confidence that the benchmark truly reflects the proposed system.

3.2 INTRODUCTION

Let me start by apologizing to Benjamin Disraeli for hijacking his quotation about statistics. However, it does seem to be a particularly apt description for many benchmarks. The objective of a benchmark should be to provide clear confirmation of the likely performance characteristics, throughput, and scalability capabilities of the product(s) or proposed custom system under investigation. For many reasons considered in this chapter, they seldom provide this confirmation. Let us commence by detailing the types of benchmark and highlighting various tricks of the trade that are knowingly or unknowingly employed, before discussing possible approaches to constructive benchmarking. Discussions center on benchmarks that produce results on throughput and responsiveness, as opposed to more hardware-oriented benchmarks that may provide figures on the relative speed or performance of a hardware component, although the latter are mentioned.

3.3 INDUSTRY BENCHMARKS

In any comparison of hardware/software products it is imperative that every effort is made to produce a level playing field. The major industry benchmarking organizations, Standard Performance Evaluation Corporation (SPEC: http://www.specbench.org/) and the Transaction Processing Performance Council (TPC: http://www.tpc.org/) try hard to ensure that their benchmarks are both representative and fair. Vendors run these benchmarks by adhering to the precise rules on the workloads (or by using the supplied source software in SPEC's case), test set-up, test running, and reporting. Over time, vendors invariably find loopholes that allow them to achieve highly optimistic results. It is therefore a perpetual task for these organizations to keep ahead of the game by producing new versions that will restore the level playing field.

Industry benchmarks provide a useful mechanism to compare products but they are not foolproof and therefore they should be used with care. One of the reasons that they are not foolproof is that they are based on defined workloads, but they are not your workloads. Although you may have a preference for hardware vendor A over vendor B from a performance perspective, an industry benchmark is not going to help you to work out how much hardware will be needed to meet a particular requirement. It follows that an estimate needs to be made of how closely the project requirement matches the benchmark. For example, how many database calls will the proposed application be doing, in comparison to the TPC-C workload?

Table 3.1 SPEC Benchmarks

Benchmark	Type of Performance
CPU2000	CPU and memory
SFS97_R1	File server
WEB99	Web server
WEB99_SSL	Web server using SSL
jAppServer2001	J2EE 1.2 Application server (based on ECperf 1.1)
JBB2000	Server-side Java
JVM98	Java Virtual Machine
MAIL2001	Mail server (SMTP and POP3)
HPC96	High-performance computing
OMP2001	OpenMP (high-performance parallel software)
Apc	Graphics performance
Viewperf	OpenGL

Table 3.2 TPC Benchmarks

Benchmark	Performance
TPC-C	OLTP
TPC-H	Decision support ad hoc queries
TPC-R	Decision support business reporting
TPC-W	Web e-commerce

SPEC is a nonprofit organization that was originally formed in 1988 by a number of workstation vendors. The aim of the original benchmark was to test CPU performance. It has gone through a number of iterations, the current version being CPU2000, and it is still arguably the most popular of SPEC's benchmarks. Over the years other benchmarks have been added, as summarized in Table 3.1.

TPC is also a nonprofit organization, and by coincidence it was also founded in 1988. Major hardware and software vendors are members. Its original benchmarks TPC-A and TPC-B related to OLTP performance and they were based on the TP1, alias the DebitCredit benchmark. These benchmarks were useful initially, but they were extremely rudimentary and hence flawed. TPC-C, a much more comprehensive OLTP benchmark, eventually replaced them. Table 3.2 shows the current range of TPC benchmarks.

3.4 VENDOR BENCHMARKS

Vendor benchmarks have become much more of a marketing tool over the last five years. The move to standard development environments and deployment software, such as Java and J2EE Application Servers or .NET, has undoubtedly increased the intensity of the competition between vendors. This recently led to an outbreak of what can only be described as puerile behavior with the Pet Store benchmark incident. Pet Store is a simple sample application that was made available by Sun to allow developers to understand Java and J2EE. It is in essence a training aid. It was not intended for benchmarking and it was not suitable for bench-marking, not least because there were no rules governing the set-up, running of tests, and reporting of results. Two battles ensued: various Java application server vendors, including Oracle, IBM, and BEA, claimed superiority in the Java arena; and arguably more vociferously, a J2EE versus .NET dogfight commenced after Microsoft implemented Pet Store in .NET. They were akin to boxing matches without the Marquis of Queensbury rules. Without going into the gory details, it is sufficient to say that an unseemly squabble ensued with outlandish claims, counter-claims, and general mud slinging by all concerned. If you are interested in the details, simply key "Pet Store benchmark" into a search engine. None of the participants come out of it well. It has simply been a lot of marketing hot air that contained no substance, certainly nothing that could be considered useful to customers. There have been comments that if this is the only benchmark available to compare J2EE and .NET then we have to use it. I could not disagree more; all Pet Store results belong in file 13 (the bin). On a more positive note, the introduction of the ECperf bench-mark (now called SPECjAppServer2001) promises a level playing field in the Java community. This does not help Microsoft, of course, and it is perhaps understandable that they might wish to continue with Pet Store.

Some vendors get carried away with the idea of quoting stratospheric numbers. I have seen one benchmark where to start with the claimed transaction rate per second was suspiciously high. This number was then mapped onto an extremely low usage profile assumption. The net result was a claim to be able to support one million users. Similarly, I have seen a message-based benchmark where many small messages were packed into a single physical message. By using lots of hardware, a claim was made to support many millions of messages per day. The results of such benchmarks should be placed gently in file 13.

It is probably an unfortunate fact of life that vendor benchmarks will continue to be more of a marketing tool, and less an effective means of providing useful information. Therefore, the message has to be *caveat emptor*.

3.5   INDEPENDENT BENCHMARKING

Vendors sometimes quote benchmarks that have been performed by independent, third-party organizations. Without wishing to malign the efforts of all independent benchmarking outfits, there is a danger that a company may have been hired by the vendor to perform the benchmark, according to a stated set of rules or criteria that have been defined or influenced by the vendor, in order that its product be shown in the best possible light. It may of course be eminently possible to change the rules/criteria and come out with a different set of results! Therefore, it pays to check the basis on which an independent benchmark has been performed.

3.6   IN-HOUSE BENCHMARKING

The final type of benchmark is the in-house variety where it is developed and run by the project team. The tricks of the trade apply equally here although it is more usual to find that they have been done subconsciously. The typical problem that faces the in-house project team is usually a lack of time. The following illustrations are indicative of the problems and their subsequent effects.

A project was faced with a requirement to accept and store a high volume of raw data, somewhere in the region of 3 MB/sec. Note that this was a number of years ago when it was a bigger problem than it might be today. The objective was to secure this data to disk, before analyzing it, and making the data and the analyses available to the users. As there was concern surrounding the ability to handle this volume of raw data a simple benchmark was developed to assess that part of the system. The confident conclusion was that it could be handled. Unfortunately, with the time constraints the team trivialized the problem. The actual system had to perform a reasonable amount of validation, mainly via the use of database lookups, before writing the data to disk. This validation was not included in the benchmark. The other major flaw was that in assessing the results the team had failed to factor in the other tasks that would be concurrently active, such as the analyses and the user activity, and hence would eat into the available resources. The overall result was that the system failed to perform, and a significant amount of remedial development work and hardware upgrades were ultimately required to rectify the situation.

A second project had software processes that would sit on separate machines and pass messages among them using sockets. A benchmark was set up. Due to a lack of hardware at the time, the test was run on a single server. Although the lack of a physical link was factored into the results, the team was unaware that when the sender and receiver are on the same server the operating software was clever enough to realize this and to send the messages from process to process via memory, thus avoiding any communications software overheads. The net result was very good benchmark performance that was not repeated on the production system.

Finally, a third project had to support high volumes, up to five million readings per day initially, with the strong likelihood that this would increase by four- or fivefold fairly quickly, in line with strong projected business growth. The client was very concerned and requested the vendor who was developing the custom software to demonstrate that the system would be able to cope. The client went about this in an interesting way. They wanted to see 20 times the required throughput in a benchmark, although the vendor was allowed to use all the tricks of the trade. The client's thinking was obviously that they would be confident about getting 1/20th of this throughput in the actual system. The software vendor did indeed use lots of go-faster techniques, the main ones being heavy database denormalization, semi-hard data partitioning, and an overspecified hardware configuration. Everybody was happy with the benchmark results, and the eventual system did indeed perform well with the initial volumetrics, and more important, it was successfully designed to be scalable. So what was the problem? Unfortunately, the software vendor was a large organization. Other project teams within the organization that were faced with high-volume requirements discovered, mostly by word of mouth and invariably at third hand, what amazing results had been achieved. It became something of a *cause célèbre*, but nobody ever bothered to check up on the details of the benchmark or what was ultimately achieved in the production system. They simply accepted the headlines and assumed (wrongly) that they would achieve similar results.

3.7 TRICKS OF THE TRADE

Benchmark performance can be influenced in many ways. The intention in this section is to highlight some of the main methods, although it is not meant to be an exhaustive list. Any of the methods mentioned can be considered perfectly valid if they will be used in the actual system. If they will not be used in the actual system they should, in most cases, not be used in the benchmark. These techniques are sometimes knowingly used, and occasionally subconsciously. They are divided up into a number of subheadings.

3.7.1 Simplifying the Problem

Arguably the most frequently used ploy is to simplify the processing. As a simple example, an application might perform comprehensive validation on input data before writing it to the database. In a typical benchmark there may be only rudimentary validation, and sometimes none at all.

Relational databases are the most commonly used type of database management system in current use. One of the advantages that they bring is flexibility in the way that data is stored and accessed. A favored technique is to "normalize" data. This means that data items are kept separate and that where possible they are not replicated. An extremely simple example may be a portfolio where you have products of different types, such as equities, bonds, savings accounts, and so on. In this case you might have a product table (one record for each product that you hold), a type of product table, plus separate tables for dealings and receipts. Although all this data is held separately, the powerful SQL join facility allows a developer to access data from multiple physical tables as if it were a single logical entity. The advantages of this normalized approach include better modularity, easier maintenance, as well as flexibility. The disadvantage can be performance degradation. For example, when reading the details of a deal it may be necessary to access the product, type of product, and the deal tables, that is, three table accesses to produce the required single logical deal access. Many implementations will adopt a fully normalized approach until performance becomes unacceptable and some degree of denormalization becomes necessary; that is, two or more tables are merged to reduce the number of table accesses that are required (e.g., the product and type of product entities might be merged in our example). In short, denormalization may be good for performance but it reduces flexibility. Actual systems need to take a pragmatic view of the relative merits of normalized and denormalized approaches. I have seen benchmarks that use high, and hence extremely unlikely, levels of denormalization to ensure good performance. Using our simple example again, I have seen cases where it would have been implemented as a single table in the benchmark.

3.7.2 Improving Disk Performance

A favorite technique is to hold all data (or as much as possible) in memory. Permanent data is ultimately stored on disk but accessing it from a disk is much slower, in relative terms, than accessing it from memory. It follows that if data can be kept in memory, better performance will ensue. Caching, as it is termed, is a common and legitimate technique that is used to improve performance. Whereas a real system will endeavor to use memory where possible, memory is a finite resource and therefore actual performance will consist of a mixture of accesses from memory and disk. Benchmarks can achieve better performance by configuring more physical memory than is likely in the actual system or by having a smaller database than is likely so that a greater percentage of it will fit into memory. On the same theme, the database may be full size but the benchmark only makes use of a small disproportionate subset of the data, and hence caching is likely to be more effective.

Where significant disk access is necessary, a high specification disk subsystem will give better performance. Examples include a disk controller memory cache to hold data and thus minimize the need to access the disk plus the configuration of many disks over which to spread the data to minimize delays caused by contention for access to a specific disk. High-specification disk subsystems are fine if they are deployed in the production systems. Unfortunately, this is sometimes not the case.

A final observation on disk performance is that database writes are much more expensive in terms of resource usage than database reads. Many benchmarks are therefore either read-only or they perform minimal writes. In a recent vendor benchmark, the transaction mix included only 1 percent database writes, whereas the system for which the product was being considered had 40 percent writes.

3.7.3 Unrepresentative Deployment

Another technique is the use of unrepresentative hardware. One approach is to use a larger and more powerful server configuration than is likely in the target environment. Alternatively, the benchmark may be deployed across more servers than is expected. For example, part of the software may not be able to provide satisfactorily scalable performance as CPUs are added to a single server. A solution may be to configure multiple single-processor systems rather than a single server with the requisite number of CPUs. Once again, this is fine if the client ultimately decides that such an approach is acceptable. However, although the approach may be acceptable at the level of 4 uniprocessor servers it may not necessarily be acceptable at 104 uniprocessors. Another example is the provision of what appears to be excessive LAN bandwidth in order that a network device can be fully exploited.

A potential problem with a multiple server benchmark can be that the overall system has been separated into a number of hard partitions; that is, there are multiple self-contained systems where data is not shared between the partitions. This is not acceptable if the requirement is actually for a system where data can be shared/accessed by any server in a multiple server configuration.

In modern software architectures the emphasis is on the implementation of multi-tier solutions. For example, a common approach is to have presentation, business, and database layers. There is usually a reasonable amount of flexibility in this type of solution as to where a given piece of processing resides. Business logic elements could theoretically reside in any of the layers. Therefore, if the middle tier that is supposed to house all of the business logic does not perform well enough for benchmarking purposes then parts of it may be moved to the database tier, as DBMSs are more mature and better-performing products. I have seen an example of this where the vendor concerned was, somewhat perversely, trying to sell middle-tier software!

3.7.4 Minimizing Overheads

If a benchmark contains a high volume of messages that have to be transmitted between components using communications protocols there is usually a significant software overhead involved in setting up connections and the sending/receiving of messages. The actual length of the message is much less significant in this respect. Superior throughput performance can usually be obtained by employing larger messages, for example, packing several application messages into a single protocol-level message, and thus minimizing the communication software overheads. Network devices typically show better throughput performance with larger messages. Once again, it is a question of whether the use of larger messages is feasible in the actual system.

The performance of individual hardware devices can vary depending on their usage. Disks provide a good example. The largest element of the time taken to access a disk is the seek time, that is, the time taken to move the read/write heads across the disk to the position where the required data resides. Latency is the next largest element; this is the time taken for the disk to rotate until the desired data is beneath the read/write heads. The time taken to transfer data to or from the disk is typically minute in comparison to seek and latency times. This type of disk access is usually called random access; that is, the data is somewhere on the disk and it has to be located and retrieved. Alternatively, where data is being accessed sequentially, track by track, only a small percentage of accesses may require a seek, and even then it may only need to move to the next track and thus incur only a minimum seek time. The addition of large data transfer sizes and readahead techniques can all add up to impressive sounding throughput rates for sequential access and they are the headline numbers that are often quoted. It is important to use figures for the type of access that is required in your situation.

Similarly, magnetic tape performance can be inflated. The secret with tapes is to keep them going at top speed to maximize the likelihood of driving them at somewhere close to the drive's maximum data transfer rate. In a backup benchmark this can be achieved by using very large files as small files will result in loss of speed while the backup process closes the file and finds/opens the next one. Note that there are valid software techniques that can be employed to minimize such delays, usually by having multiple concurrent threads.

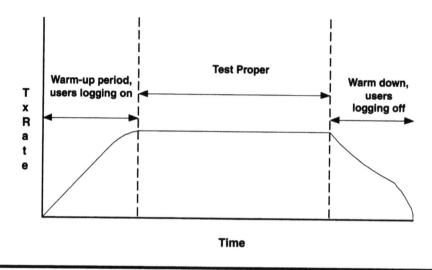

Figure 3.1 Benchmark Test Timeline

3.7.5 Reporting

Reporting benchmark results can provide further opportunities to overstate performance. A technique for ensuring that the product is seen in the best possible light is to simply not mention those aspects that exhibit unimpressive performance. RFC 2544 is a fairly comprehensive document that describes a benchmarking methodology for network interconnecting devices. It recommends various tests that should be performed and reported upon. They include throughput, latency, and frame loss rates. Using firewalls as an example, it is common to see vendors quoting figures for throughput and frame loss as they frequently tend to appear impressive, relatively speaking, whereas it is difficult to find latency figures being quoted, that is, the overall time taken to get through the firewall (processing time plus queueing time), particularly at varying throughput rates. Latency is a key metric, as it will have an impact on system responsiveness.

An individual test will typically consist of three elements, a warming-up period (e.g., while users log on), the test proper, and a warming-down period, as shown in Figure 3.1. A comprehensive report will show the entire test where each of these elements can be readily identified. Performance can be overstated by only mentioning the highest throughput obtained which may have occurred only once during the test, possibly just for a matter of seconds. Another approach that can be adopted where performance cannot be sustained for any reasonable length of time is to reduce the duration of the test. I have seen some tests with durations of less than one minute. The usefulness of such tests is highly questionable.

A common approach on vendor benchmarks is to compare the vendor's new, recently released product against the competition's old product that may in fact have been "end of lifed" (as they say).

The results from small to medium-sized tests are used to reach vague but enticing conclusions such as "the product scales."

Finally on the reporting theme, vendors routinely go through verbal gymnastics to paint their products in the best possible light; so it pays to read the wording carefully. Although they may indulge in being "economical with the truth," the majority tend to avoid outright lies. Be particularly wary of strained language, for example, the words "shows a capacity to support." What does that mean? It pays to be vigilant, as there may be some vendors who are tempted to resort to lies, usually when under severe pressure from the competition.

3.8 USING BENCHMARKS

It is time to discuss how to navigate this particular minefield.

3.8.1 Using Published Benchmarks

If a comparison is required of the relative performance characteristics of competing products it is absolutely imperative that there be a sufficiently level playing field to allow a reasoned judgment to be made. Industry benchmarks, where they are appropriate, may help, as they are generally more credible than vendor-specific benchmarks. Try to ensure that "apples versus apples" comparisons are made; for example, only currently shipped versions of products are compared, similar hardware configurations are used, and, where appropriate, similar costs. Read the full disclosure reports that vendors have to submit, along with their results. Industry benchmarks are useful but they are not infallible. For example, be on the lookout for forced (multiple hard partitions) as opposed to natural scalability.

It can be necessary to treat even valid vendor claims with care. I have come across substantiated transaction volumes that were being supported by existing customers but they were not using the same technologies that the proposed system required; often they were using more mature and leaner technologies.

Ignore any claims that a vendor may make comparing the performance of its product against the competition; it is seldom an apples versus apples comparison. Ignore all "world record" claims. If you read such claims carefully you will see that it is eminently possible to devise a category that has a population of one at a given time, for example, "the best ever performing hot tango colored server."

If a vendor provides a nonindustry benchmark, insist on seeing a complete report on the benchmark that will allow you to make a reasoned judgment. Such a report should include:

- Details of the benchmark environment
- Information on the software tools and hardware that that were used to drive the test
- Details of the workloads that comprise the benchmark, including their functional complexity, the number of concurrent users, and transaction rates
- Details of the database/file systems, including the number of occurrences of major entities and the overall size, plus information on how they are spread over the available disk capacity
- Details of all performance enhancements/tuning plus details of any components that are not available in the currently shipped release
- Logistics of the test(s), for example, warm-up period; duration of the test; any warming-down period
- Detailed test results (throughput, response times, and the utilization of major hardware components) over time, such as by minute
- Vendor's analysis of the results including an assessment of any actual or potential bottlenecks or choke points
- Scalability assessment in concrete terms, as opposed to vague "it is scalable" statements
- Scalability limits (all products have them, as no product is infinitely scalable)

Understand which performance factors are important. For example, the results of firewall benchmarks seem loath to mention latency, that is, the time taken for a packet to pass through the firewall. As this will affect response times it is a potentially important metric.

If the results of independent benchmarks are made available it is important that you understand who commissioned them, the vendor concerned or another, what rules/criteria were used, and whether the third party has performed similar benchmarks that have produced different results.

3.8.2 Requesting Benchmarks

Companies that have mandated the short-listed vendors in an ITT (Invitation to Tender) to run benchmarks as part of the procurement should clearly define the rules of engagement to ensure a level playing field so that a comparative review is possible. The rules must be tight and reflect the requirement. Be aware that meaningful benchmarks invariably take longer to prepare and run than expected. Therefore, it is important to set achievable targets, preferably after canvassing the views of the short-listed vendors on what is feasible in the timescales. The rules should typically cover:

- The scope of the benchmark ideally should concentrate on the top three to four key business processes or that part of the system where there is significant apprehension over performance or scalability
- Mandatory or acceptable hardware environments
- Database and file system sizes, including the number of occurrences for each major entity
- Constraints, for example, database denormalization may not be allowed, cache sizes may be limited, and so on
- Description of the workloads that comprise the benchmark and their associated numbers of concurrent users, and peak transaction or message rates
- The number of test iterations, for example, the transaction rate may be steadily increased or the database size increased to reflect different peaks or business growth
- Test rules, for example, when rebooting of the system or reloading of software components between tests is mandated or forbidden (mandating the reloading of software components may ensure that beneficial caching effects are not carried over from one test to another, and forbidding it may help to flush out memory leaks); the duration of tests including any need for warm-up and warm-down periods; any requirements to witness benchmark runs and to check that they are working correctly
- Format of reports (see the suggested format in the previous section)

When the mandatory benchmarking has been completed, if time permits, allow vendors the opportunity to modify the rules, as there is always the danger that by being too pedantic a vendor may be prevented from using beneficial features. The only caveat here is whether such features can be realistically deployed in the actual production system.

3.8.3 In-House Benchmarks

In-house benchmarks should broadly follow the rules for requested benchmarks although they may be less stringent in certain areas, for example, reporting. Time constraints are the primary limiting factor. Too many benchmarks run out of time and are left incomplete. Therefore, it is important to be brutally realistic as to what is achievable in the available time, perhaps concentrating on the area of greatest concern. To do this, it is necessary to plan the task in a fair degree of detail, particularly the amount of preparation that is required, and to assess whether the software is stable enough to be stressed; high-level planning only induces a glossy, ill-founded perspective on what is possible.

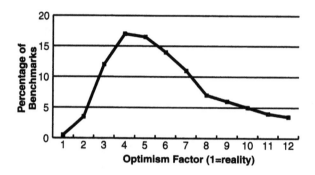

Figure 3.2 Benchmark Optimism

3.8.4 Drawing Conclusions from Benchmarks

As stated previously, the usefulness of any benchmark ultimately lies in the accuracy of the conclusions that may be drawn from the results. The first step is to decide if it tells you anything at all. I have come across some benchmarks that I have totally dismissed, as I had absolutely no confidence in them. Reasons include:

■ Lack of a disclosure report
■ Strained marketing words (do not flow naturally) that I suspect of being economical with the truth
■ Stratospheric throughput claims
■ Competition bashing

If the benchmark has not been dismissed the next step is to judge how it relates to the proposed system. Almost all benchmarks understate the complexity of real systems. The trick is to decide by how much. This has to be an individual judgment, based on the particular circumstances and the degree of faith in the vendors/in-house team. Figure 3.2 provides an indication of how benchmark results compare with reality in my general experience. Items to look for include:

■ Any heavy-duty use of tricks of the trade, such as heavy database denormalization
■ Excessive hardware used to obtain good results
■ Hard unnatural partitioning of data across multiple servers to obtain better throughput when the technique will not be used in the proposed system
■ Failure to fully exploit the hardware, for example, CPU utilization is only 25 percent
■ Lack of any coherent analysis of the results

The third step is to decide to what proportion of the overall system the benchmarking is applicable, and what to do about the remainder. For example, only 50 percent may be covered by the benchmark. The quick, potentially risky solution may be to estimate the remainder by analogy to the benchmarked element. The preferable solution is to size it separately.

Throughput has been mentioned above, but what about response times and scalability? It requires a great leap of faith to believe that response times in benchmarks will be reproduced in the actual system. Similarly, be extremely wary of believing scalability claims that are based on published benchmarks. If scalability is important it is preferable to ensure that it is directly addressed in a requested or in-house benchmark.

Although it may appear that I am quite negative about benchmarks, they can be very useful. My preference is for small, targeted in-house benchmarks that focus on particular areas of concern. Published benchmarks can provide useful information, as long as there is sufficient data to understand how they were run and just how representative they are.

4

NONFUNCTIONAL REQUIREMENTS AND SOLUTIONS

4.1 ABSTRACT

There are few examples of clear, coherent nonfunctional requirements that are realistic in both the technical and commercial senses. The main reason for this state of affairs is that the nonfunctional aspects receive insufficient attention. The same individuals who are responsible for the functional requirements frequently write them. These authors tend to have limited technical knowledge, as they usually come from a business analysis or application development background. The result is that the requirements are often vague, ambiguous, and lacking in basic sizing information, and the expectations are often technically unrealistic and financially unaffordable.

Where the requirements form part of an ITT that is sent to external organizations they invariably lead to a protracted tendering process when each bidder makes different assumptions, and adopts different approaches, thus making it difficult for the purchaser to compare solutions.

This situation is eminently avoidable. Modest attention to detail by suitable personnel can produce a coherent set of requirements that includes sufficient information for bidders, both internal and external, to which to respond. This can be achieved without sacrificing prized objectives such as value for money.

This chapter focuses more on Invitations to Tender that are responded to by external organizations as the issues are magnified. However, many of the observations on possible technical solutions are also applicable to in-house systems.

4.2 INTRODUCTION

I pondered for a considerable time before including any discussion on ITTs. The reason is that from my perspective there seems to have been a pronounced shift over the last three to four years whereby some procurements, particularly the larger variety, concentrate ever more on price and, relatively speaking, the pros and cons of the proposed technical solutions appear to assume less importance. The most impressive part of one particularly large ITT was the detailed complexity of the spreadsheets that were provided to bidders for their use in providing a highly detailed breakdown of their proposed prices. The quality of the remainder of the ITT suffered in comparison.

This observation is not meant to infer that the technical excellence of the solution should be more important than the price, or even as important, merely that there is a certain lack of balance in some ITTs. "Value for money" is becoming an ever-more quoted mantra. I have no problem with value for money; in fact I wholeheartedly endorse it. Unfortunately, I have yet to see or hear a coherent explanation on any procurement that I have been involved in, of what precisely constitutes value for money and how it is factored into the decision-making process. However, I eventually decided that despite my innate cynicism a discussion on the nonfunctional aspects of procurements would still be useful.

Any comprehensive treatment of procurements would fill a book, probably several. This chapter is purposely limited to discussion of what I consider to be important elements of the procurement process with regard to the nonfunctional elements: the quality of the requirements, sizing information, performance targets, hardware sizing by the bidders, hardware deployment and scalability, availability, and requirements for business continuity. There are some important topics that I do not cover here, such as security, systems management, and general operational considerations.

The procurement process can go under a host of different names, for example, Request For Proposal (RFP), Request For Quotation (RFQ), or Invitation To Tender (ITT). I use the term ITT.

4.3 THE PROBLEMS

I have been involved in the nonfunctional aspects of more than 250 ITTs. Although I have come across a number of first-rate sets of requirements, they tend to be scarce. Poor requirements frequently lead to a protracted and more expensive tendering process that can, and ultimately does, result in inappropriate solutions.

4.3.1 Authors of Requirements

Apart from price and general contractual minutiae, ITTs quite naturally tend to concentrate on the functional requirements of the proposed system. Looking at a small sample of six recent ITTs that I have dealt with, the split between functional and nonfunctional in terms of the number of pages in the ITT document is in the region of 85 to 90 percent for functional and 10 to 15 percent for nonfunctional elements (these figures specifically exclude general tendering information, contractual information, and acceptance criteria). It is therefore hardly surprising that the authors of ITTs tend to come from a business or IT development background. However, when they address the nonfunctional aspects they can often struggle.

A relatively common approach is to seek out a previous ITT and to copy and paste the nonfunctional requirements, in full or in part. The obvious danger here is that the requirements for one ITT may well be totally inappropriate for another ITT. The authors may rightly seek to involve somebody with a more technical background, either to verify the "copy and paste" method, or to develop the nonfunctional requirements from scratch. In the former case the resultant review or discussion is often short and unsatisfactory because the chosen person, perhaps from a service delivery background, has insufficient time to grasp the business requirements, and in the latter case she usually has insufficient time as this work has to fit it in with her "day job," and she will probably tend to resort to some form of copy and paste herself.

Whatever the approach, and whoever is doing it, unless the technologies are well understood, some research will probably be required. Once again, this is likely to be rushed, particularly as the Internet can allow you to find some information quite quickly. Without an understanding of what precisely is being sought, and without sufficient time to dig deep enough to uncover suitable technical material, it is more than likely that any unearthed information will have been heavily influenced by the sales and marketing arm of various vendors. The attendant danger is to happen on dubious claims that may persuade the unwary that high-performance, high-availability, and linearly scalable solutions are all *de rigueur*. The risk is that such claims are religiously copied into the ITT. A vendor that I was involved with shot himself in the foot by proffering wholly unrealistic availability figures to the client without even being asked. The vendor's technicians were mortified when they discovered that the client simply replayed the claimed figures in the contract that the vendor duly signed with the usual alacrity.

4.3.2 Poor Quality Requirements

The overall result of not concentrating sufficiently on the nonfunctional requirements is that they can easily be of poor quality in comparison to the rest of the document. Examples include the following.

4.3.2.1 Poorly Written Requirements

This can apply equally to functional requirements and is more likely to be found in larger ITTs where there are many authors. I remember being in a room with six other people discussing what we thought was being asked for in a particular section of an ITT and eventually admitting that we were all clueless. The requirement was repeated elsewhere in the ITT, and so the same assumptive words (there was no opportunity to get any clarification from the client) were inserted into multiple places in the proposal, as it is never clear if one person is evaluating all related aspects of the topic in question or if different individuals are evaluating different sections. The latter is assumed for obvious reasons, which makes for a verbose response that may not read particularly well.

4.3.2.2 Introducing Risk by Requesting Bleeding-Edge Technology

This can frequently be done by inference; where the choice of words leads the bidders to assume that the customer really wants this technology. I heard one organization clearly state that they had not dictated the use of any technology in their ITT, when in truth the wording positively dripped with signals of what technology was required.

4.3.2.3 Technically Unrealistic Requirements

For example, all response times must be subsecond. Notwithstanding what is technically feasible, it is amusing in a perverse sort of way that there is seldom any thought given to what response times might be appropriate for a given user/function, or to meet the general demands of the business.

4.3.2.4 Requirements That Bear No Resemblance to the Available Budget

For example, high availability is requested (possibly 24/7) when there is no budget to fund the infrastructure that will be needed to provide the necessary resilience. In one instance in a modest ITT, a company had asked for high availability and a warm disaster-recovery facility. Fortunately, one of the bidders had the courage to politely ask early in the tendering process if the company realized that the hardware infrastructure costs would be ~£1 m. The company's immediate reaction was not only to drop the high availability and business continuity requirements, but also to trim the basic volumetrics, reducing the likely hardware expenditure to £100 to 150 K, which presumably was more in keeping with the budget.

4.3.2.5 No Explanation of Any Ground Rules

This observation applies to situations where there is an existing IT infrastructure into which the proposed system must slot. If there are any potential constraints they should be stated. Examples include network bandwidth constraints, the use of existing servers where the available capacity is limited, the proposed geographic site for the servers, or office space constraints to house the equipment. Details of any existing problems should be included but many would balk at this degree of openness. I am thinking of one example where there was a performance problem relating to the infrastructure in local offices. The scope of supply was actually limited to the central server farm although end-to-end response time guarantees were being mandated. Notwithstanding the delicacy of the situation, it might have helped the company in the resolution or management of their problem if they had at least given details of the existing infrastructure, and asked the bidders to state how they could make best use of it.

4.3.2.6 Inadequate Sizing Information

This ranges from no volumetrics at all at one end of the spectrum, to sometimes comically ambitious figures at the other end. It is surprising how many ITTs, particularly very large ITTs, provide no meaningful volumetrics or information on working practices or peaks. At the ambitious end of the spectrum the dot.com boom provided many examples of fairly unhelpful information where a company thought that it would grow rapidly from a standing start.

4.3.2.7 Ambiguous and Even Contradictory Requirements

This is a particular danger when copying and pasting from other ITTs.

Table 4.1 provides a brief summary of observations on the six ITTs in the limited sample that I mentioned. "Size" refers to the estimated hardware capital expenditure: less than £250 K for small; ~£1 m for medium; £10 m plus for very large.

4.3.3 What Do They Want?

The effect on bidders of poor quality requirements is usually one of quiet bewilderment. Responses to requests for clarifications are often limited to minor, relatively noncontentious issues. Some bidders will be apprehensive about speaking their minds on matters that have significant cost implications in case they are ultimately considered to be noncompliant. All too

Table 4.1 Sample Summary of Nonfunctional Requirements from Six ITTs

Size	Type	Sizing Information	Scalability Requirements	Performance Requirements	Availability	Business Continuity
Small	Replacement	Good	Not mentioned	Slightly aggressive	None requested	Not mentioned
Small	New	Some data volumes but nothing on usage or frequency	Not mentioned	One part unrealistic, the other more important part from a business perspective has no requirements	99.999% (extremely unrealistic)	Surprisingly not mentioned given the availability figure
Medium	Replacement	Reasonable	Not mentioned	Slightly aggressive	"Continuous" (poorly worded)	Reasonably specified
Medium	New	Poor	Not mentioned	Unrealistic	100% inferred from the words	Not mentioned
V. Large	Partial replacement	Very poor	Specified (aggressive)	Unrealistic	99.95% (end-to-end) includes elements outside bidders' control	Unrealistically aggressive
V. Large	New	Almost non-existent	Inferred (poorly worded)	Unrealistic	99.9% end-to-end including WANs and remote LANs (unrealistic)	48 hours (generous given the nature of the business)

frequently, those bidders who do raise their heads above the parapet are either subjected to "we are looking for value for money" (often a lame excuse), or a general unwillingness to discuss the requirement (saving face?). The unfortunate result is that the bidders tend to go through hoops, trying desperately not to appear to be noncompliant. Their eventual responses can vary from "No problem at all," to general waffle and obfuscation, to a refusal to play the game by either not answering the question or putting their own spin on it.

4.3.4 And Now for Something Completely Different

When the initial proposals are received it becomes the turn of the ITT authors to become confused as they are faced with the task of trying to compare a range of solutions and costs from bidders who, at the very least, have had to invent assumptions. Not surprisingly, the company, having struggled to compare the solutions, is frequently forced to bring some belated order to the chaos by changing some/all of the requirements. A very common scenario is to discover that all the tenders are too expensive and therefore volumes are reduced (where they existed) or they are now invented, and availability/business continuity requirements are reduced. However, now that they have got their teeth into the subject there is a tendency to ask for lots of options, for example, provide costed solutions for 1000 users, 2000 users, and so on. This can mean significantly more work for the bidders, exacerbated by the fact that the company demands responses to the changed requirements within a very short period of time (sometimes a matter of days), as the tendering schedule is now running late. It is inevitable that quality is likely to suffer here, both in terms of the bidders' responses and the final solution.

It goes without saying that this situation is avoidable. The production of a sensible, realistic, and coherent set of nonfunctional requirements is eminently feasible. Furthermore, it can be achieved without necessarily sacrificing the Holy Grails of value for money and innovative solutions. Let us look at the main topics and attempt to draw out some of the key points.

4.4 SIZING INFORMATION

Any attempt to estimate the basic hardware requirements minimally requires some information on data volumes and likely system usage during peak periods. In my experience the majority of ITTs that provide satisfactory volumetrics tend to be replacement systems: the client has direct experience, and therefore access to actual figures that can be used as a basis for providing estimates for the replacement system. In the case of

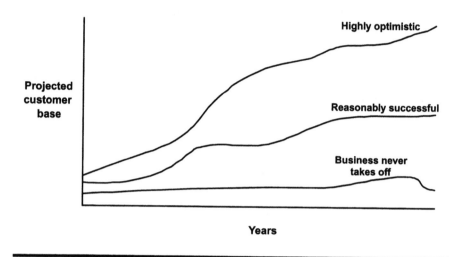

Figure 4.1 Possible Business Scenarios

new systems, particularly new business streams, reasonable volumetrics are seldom provided. More than once I have heard the haunting demand, "Look, we have no information. Can you just give us the answer." How can a company assess bids from competing vendors when they have made no attempt to establish a level playing field, unless of course they are just interested in the lowest assumptions and the cheapest solution? In truth, fear of the unknown, particularly for new business streams, is the primary reason for reticence to provide figures.

Although it may be challenging, it is far from impossible to produce a set of figures that can provide a firm basis for sizing. One anxiety that many people have is the perceived need to provide highly detailed information. More detail is preferable, however, it is not strictly necessary. In fact, it is frequently a hindrance. Individuals who are experienced in sizing can perform a reasonable job with a solid but rudimentary set of volumetrics:

- Key business metrics, for example, size of customer base, volume of business, and seasonal peaks
- Users of the system, the total number of registered users, and the estimated peak levels of concurrency, ideally by location for company employees

Estimates should be provided both for the initial implementation and for each subsequent year within the life of the system.

Apprehension frequently surrounds the choice of any given metric as individuals fret about getting it wrong (see Figure 4.1). This is natural but it can be overcome by producing a range of volumetrics (low, medium, and high) that reflects the range of views on the possible size and success of the business, and by asking the bidders to quote against each scenario in terms of (say) the size of the customer base and an associated level of concurrent usage.

It is essential not to get too carried away with this approach, as it is very easy to end up with too many scenarios. The idea is that as the procurement process proceeds a clearer picture tends to emerge of the actual functional and nonfunctional requirements, not to mention the cost implications; it may then be possible to home in on a smaller number of scenarios.

Another approach is to make use of bidders' enthusiasm to get involved before a tender is published as they consider (rightly or wrongly) that it may give them an inside track. If you are struggling to come up with any figures this may be an ideal opportunity to let the bidders give you the benefit of their experience in helping to formulate a set of volumetrics.

Further discussion on deriving sizing information can be found in Chapter 5.

4.5 PERFORMANCE REQUIREMENTS

Given the lack of volumetrics, reasonable definitions of peak throughput requirements are usually seldom found in ITTs. Requirements are often limited to expressions of the number of concurrent users, with no definition as to what a concurrent user actually is. The topic of peak throughput is covered in Chapter 5, Hardware Sizing: The Crystal Ball Gazing Act.

It is frequently difficult to understand how the authors of ITTs arrive at response time requirements. Have they investigated the different areas of the business, taking due account of the size of the customer base, the volume of business, the number of users in each area, workload patterns including daily or seasonal peaks, and so on? Inevitably, they frequently have not looked at any of these areas. Let us look at some of the factors that should ideally be taken into account when deciding on response time requirements.

Response times should be appropriate.

- Navigation of menus should ideally be subsecond, certainly less than two seconds.
- Front office operations, for example, call center agents, will require optimized performance, typically within two to three seconds for queries. Note that subsecond responses are often not necessary, particularly where there is not a strictly synchronous flow in a business process, for example, question/answer — transaction — question/answer — transaction, and so on. I have sat with an

efficient call center agent who would immediately ask for the customer's account number and then submit four or five queries, one after the other, to get an overall view of the customer and his dealings with the company, all this while spending 10 to 15 seconds getting the conversation with the customer underway.

■ Continuing with the call center theme, ideally any updating of the database should be done at the end of the call, or even after it has been completed, inasmuch as committing changes to the database usually takes significantly longer than queries.

■ Responses for back office operations will vary, depending on the tasks involved. High-volume, very repetitive tasks will necessitate fast response times, say under two seconds, but slightly more relaxed response times may be suitable for more ad hoc tasks.

■ As a general principle, response times should not be so consistently fast that the user feels as if the machine is driving her.

■ Conversely, the user should not feel as if the machine is slowing her down.

Users tend to understand instinctively when performance is satisfactory. For example, if a query is performed with a couple of commonly indexed criteria, and the result of the query contains up to (say) 20 hits, the user will expect a fairly snappy response in the range of one to three seconds. However, if a relatively infrequent query is performed, using nonindexed criteria on a large database, the user typically understands that significant processing is required, and he will usually be satisfied with a much longer response time, especially if the system can keep him informed of progress (e.g., by use of a progress bar showing the percentage completed).

The use of percentiles is a good method of ensuring consistent response times, for example, specifying that 95 percent of response times must be under three seconds. However, the actual percentile figures used in such requirements have tended to increase in recent years, and currently many ITTs insist that all response times are within the target. Notwithstanding the feasibility of a given response time, it is, statistically speaking, impossible to guarantee that 100 percent of responses can be within target. When I inform people of this, they magnanimously reduce their 100 percentile down to 99.9 percent! Without getting bogged down in statistics, as a very rough rule of thumb the 95th percentile response will typically be of the order of two to three times the mean response time and the 99th percentile will be three to five times the mean. Therefore, if the 99th percentile response time requirement is 2 seconds then the mean response time probably has to be in the range of 0.4 to 0.6 seconds. The range of response times is attributable to (a) the distribution of transactions over time (the rate at which they arrive), and (b) the distribution of processing complexity over time (some transactions consume more resources than others).

The scope of response times is often not defined. Does it span the user request to the servers and response back to the user (usually termed "end-to-end"), or is it limited to the time spent in the servers? The default interpretation is, unsurprisingly, end-to-end. This is particularly interesting in those situations where the bidders have little or no control over networks (LANs and WANs), or indeed sometimes over parts of the infrastructure in the data center, such as firewalls and traffic switches. Why should a bidder accept responsibility for elements of the overall system that are outside his control?

Response times can be affected by a number of factors, including the following.

- The complexity of the required processing. It should be blindingly obvious that a transaction that requires 50 database accesses will be slower than a transaction that only requires 5 accesses. Similarly, transactions that write to the database will be significantly slower than straightforward queries, often by an order of four or more. For these simple reasons, response time requirements should be split into categories that reflect the relative processing needs: simple, medium, and complex queries/updates. The use of a single, all-embracing response time requirement is very seldom appropriate.

- Complex user interfaces can add to system load. An example of this is the area of Web browser interfaces that are somewhat rudimentary in comparison to a standard graphical user interface (GUI). I have seen efforts to improve the user experience by heavy use of Java-Script, code that can be downloaded to the browser and executed. The functionality of this JavaScript can, unless it is carefully designed, adversely affect performance.

- The overall system design can have an impact on performance. Database design is frequently an area where the desire for absolute future flexibility results in a heavily normalized database that can adversely affect performance through the need for excessive database accessing.

- Design trade-offs. It is frequently the case that to provide optimal response times for one transaction the implementation has the knock-on effect of degrading the performance of another transaction: that is, you cannot necessarily "have your cake and eat it."

- A functional specification that has been agreed upon with the client can frequently contribute to poor performance by mandating the way in which functions have to be implemented. For example, it may insist on a business function being completed in a single complex step or interaction, when better response times may be obtained by splitting it into (say) two simple interactions.

■ The chosen technical architecture can affect performance. The current fashion may dictate that a request from a Web browser go through a firewall, possibly through a traffic switch that load balances requests across a number of Web servers, then onto an application server for business processing, once again possibly load balanced and optionally through another firewall, and finally onto a database server. The main functional work is actually carried out by the application and database servers that roughly equate to the older two-tier PC architectures with fat client and database server. The additional steps in our more modern multitier solution each impose some delay (a) for the network to get packets to/from these devices and (b) in the devices themselves. Although any individual delay may be small it all adds up. In our example above the multitier solution may add 0.5 second for a fairly straightforward request/response, possibly more where multiple responses are necessary to complete the transaction.

It is my strong opinion that requesting unrealistic response times is counterproductive, as it is simply encouraging bidders either to be economical with the truth, or to avoid the requirement. In truth, it is always difficult to be certain about performance targets until the design has been agreed upon and therefore, where possible, it is recommended that discussions on contractually binding targets should be delayed until that stage. ITTs should limit themselves to outlining the targets, and they should encourage the bidders to state what they consider they could provide for what price, and how they would ensure that the targets are achieved and maintained.

4.6 HARDWARE SIZING

I have spent time being critical of the authors of ITTs but this is an area where the focus is solely on the bidders. Many ITTs rightly ask for a system sizing to be performed. This means that the bidder is being asked to provide a coherent rationale behind the choice of the proposed hardware. Many proposals provide no rationale at all, merely stating the hardware that is required. To be pedantic, a statement of hardware (i.e., the deployment) follows from the sizing. See Chapter 5 for information on approaches to hardware sizing.

On some occasions bidders even struggle to quote hardware satisfactorily. "A Pentium server, ideally with dual processors" was one helpful example that I came across recently. The speed of a single Pentium processor can vary quite widely, particularly if you include older models (note that clients may well wish to make use of existing hardware). Without being too extreme, it is possible to see a three- or fourfold difference in processor speed. The addition of a second processor almost doubles the processing power. Therefore, we could be talking about a range in power of one to six or one to eight.

A second example was an ITT where the client had indicated that the database would reside on the company's SAN. One bidder seemed to take this as an invitation to ignore totally the amount of disk space that would be required to support his solution.

If a software product is being proposed to meet an application requirement, whether developed by the bidder or by a third party, there is no excuse for not providing detailed sizing information, as the product should be a known entity that presumably has been deployed many times before, and therefore there should be a reasonable amount of information on its performance characteristics. Even proposed bespoke systems should be sized although this is likely to be at a high level (user), rather than at a detailed level (transaction). Not least, hardware sizing will demonstrate that the bidder understands the requirements and the proposed technologies.

It would help if ITT authors explicitly requested to see a sizing rationale, either in the form of some rudimentary calculations or on the basis of previous experience with the same software/hardware. It is particularly important to ask to see estimates for any area of concern, such as network bandwidth constraints.

4.7 HARDWARE DEPLOYMENT AND SCALABILITY

Deployment is simply mapping the results of the hardware sizing onto a chosen hardware infrastructure. The main difficulty is how to cater for any future growth requirements that have been specified, or even how to make the solution "fully scalable" (another mantra of the moment) over the life of the system; ten to fifteen years appears to be a popular lifespan for larger systems.

4.7.1 Deployment Approaches

The first question is "must the initial solution be fully scalable?" that is, be readily expandable over the life of the system to meet growth requirements. Well, there are a number of issues to be considered here. First, hardware technology has been changing at a rapid pace. One of the results of rapid change is that hardware becomes obsolete much sooner than it used to. Many people recognize this and take the view that today's hardware is unlikely to last for ten years. Therefore, they will build in the need to perform a partial or complete technology refresh at some point. This usually occurs between years four and seven and really depends on (a) your view of how quickly obsolescence may occur, and (b) your willingness to spend money sooner rather than later. From a hardware perspective, if you are going to cater to a technology refresh then the initial solution may not necessarily need to be as scalable, and hence it may be cheaper.

To take a simple example, a Sun 4800 is a medium-sized server that can house up to 12 CPUs. The next model up the range is the more expensive 6800 that can house 24 CPUs. Let us say that only 4 CPUs are needed on day one, growing to 16 CPUs by the end of year four, and to 28 CPUs by the end of year seven. If the preferred approach is to avoid budgeting for a technology refresh then it may be necessary to plump for a 6800 up front, assuming that there will be at least one increase in processor speed during the seven years in order that the 24-CPU limit not be broken. However, if a refresh is catered for it is more sensible to deploy a 4800 initially. It will last until year four. If there have been increases in the power of CPUs during those four years they may usefully increase the life of the 4800 beyond year four. Alternatively, there may be replacement models by that time that constitute better value for money with a product life that is guaranteed to take you up to and possibly beyond the ten-year mark. In the final analysis it is always possible to resort to a 6800 upgrade, although this is arguably the least likely option.

4.7.2 Software Scalability

Second, scalability is not just about hardware. It is also, and arguably more importantly, about the design and implementation of the software solution. Designing and building inherently scalable software solutions is hard, despite what vendors may wish you to believe. Therefore, is scalability really necessary? Beware the danger of overengineering the solution with the obvious cost and possible complex maintenance implications. Some expansion can usually be provided by the hardware, as discussed above, by upgrading the capacity of an individual server. However, the point may be reached when a single server is insufficient either because even more capacity is required, or because the software is designed in such a way that it cannot make use of additional capacity on a single server, such as extra CPUs. For example, I have come across Web servers that do not scale well when more CPUs are added. One solution is to split the workload over multiple servers. Advances have been made by vendors in a number of areas to provide support for this type of scaling (out). Examples include firewalls, Web servers, and occasionally application servers. However, it pays to check that such scaling is effective. If the introduction of a second server only increases throughput by 20 to 30 percent it may not be an effective solution. If bespoke software has to be developed without the aid of off-the-shelf middleware it may be complex and costly to provide scalability both within server(s) and between server(s).

Database scalability beyond a single server can be the most difficult area. If the data can be partitioned such that there is no requirement to share information between the partitions (i.e., they are effectively self-contained), it is usually fairly straightforward to employ a predominantly hardware-based solution by having multiple systems, one per partition or group of partitions. A company that is organized by area across the country where each area has its own discrete customer base is an example of this type of "hard" partitioning. However, if the majority of the data is shared (i.e., the partitions form what is to all intents and purposes a single data repository), multiple systems are not appropriate. For a single system that spans multiple database servers, issues such as data integrity and recoverability have to be addressed, while at the same time not sacrificing performance. Database vendors have been working in this area for quite some time and solutions have improved, but we are still some way from seeing a totally acceptable, seamless, yet performant solution at high volumes. Solutions are achievable but they require careful application design.

4.8 AVAILABILITY

This subject is a potential minefield.

4.8.1 General Observations

A hardware vendor may make claims for a server of (say) 99.9 percent. Any figure, whether claimed or quoted, relates to the number of failures in a year. However, I have seen many ITTs that will take the claimed figure and say that they want this figure quarterly, monthly, or weekly. I have even seen one ITT where they wanted it daily! In the majority of cases this is simply a lack of understanding that 99.9 percent for a year converts into larger figures for shorter timespans, for example, ~99.99 percent for a month.

If the system consists of multiple hardware components such as an application server and a database server, statistically the overall availability will be less than for a single server because there are two components that can each fail and thereby make the application unusable. It follows that the more components there are the less the overall availability may be, without some form of resilience.

The next observation covers the different interpretations of availability between vendors/bidders and the client. Figures from hardware vendors will normally cover the hardware components, and the operating system if the vendor provides and supports it. If the operating system is provided by a third party, for example, Microsoft, the vendor figure will probably only cover the hardware components. Historically, availability figures were commonly understood, unless explicitly stated, to cover hardware, operating system, and other systems software components. In the last ten years or so when the subject of availability has assumed greater importance, there seems to be a perception among many ITT authors that availability encompasses the whole solution, that is, not only hardware and systems software components, but also the application software. I use the word "perception" because in the majority of ITTs there is no precise definition of availability.

There are undoubtedly systems where application availability is crucial, such as a safety-critical system, but the majority, certainly of commercial systems, tends not to fit into that category. The greater part of standard application software contains little or no resilience features that may help to provide high availability. If hardware/systems software for a simple server can provide over 99.5 percent availability, when applications software is added the figure will frequently be reduced, probably to less than 98 percent if the definition states that availability means that the application software must be usable and performant. For example, if the database has become corrupted such that it cannot be used until it has been repaired that constitutes unavailability even though the DBMS may be loaded. It is an interesting observation that software vendors (DBMSs, middleware, application products, etc.) do not quote availability figures for their products. For the remainder of this discussion it is assumed that availability excludes application software.

Another area that is frequently murky is the term "planned downtime." It seems fairly obvious that if a fault develops in our server that requires an engineer to fix it, that is unplanned downtime, and the system may be unavailable until it is repaired. Conversely, planned downtime is scheduled in advance and typically covers preventive maintenance and the implementation of required changes in hardware and software. Few ITTs make it clear if planned maintenance is viewed as unavailability or if it is to be excluded from any availability calculations. The latter is more normal although it is equally important that the amount of planned downtime per instance and per measurement period is agreed upon to avoid possible abuse.

4.8.2 Building in Resilience

A single server with reasonable resilience features built in (e.g., redundant power supplies, redundant fans, and resilient disks [RAID]) can usually achieve a minimum of 99.5 percent availability, possibly slightly more depending on the vendor and the precise configuration. Be wary of claims that 99.9x percent is eminently feasible and that there are lots of sites that achieve even better figures. Of course, if a vendor is supremely confident they will sign up to their claimed figures! If higher resilience is really required it will be necessary to configure additional hardware to provide the increased resilience. Inherently fault-tolerant systems with full redundancy built in can be purchased but they are not cheap and they are usually found in niche areas within the finance, telecom, or military sectors rather than being used as general-purpose machines. A more popular method in the commercial world is to configure two or more servers as a fail-over cluster. In its simplest form, this means that if one server fails, another server can automatically take over the running of the workload that the failed server was handling. This fail-over is usually not instantaneous, particularly where any application recovery is necessary. In this case, it is possible that the system may be unavailable for ten to fifteen minutes. There are ways to reduce the amount of downtime but it is seldom likely to be seamless to the user unless the servers are stateless; that is, no application data is maintained and hence no recovery is required. In terms of availability, a two-server cluster should provide in excess of 99.9 percent.

I remain to be convinced that anything higher than 99.95 percent (4 hours 23 minutes downtime per year) is currently achievable in a cost-effective manner. One of the current mantras is "five nines," that is, 99.999 percent. This equates to approximately five minutes downtime per year. Ignoring such fanciful claims, solid high availability figures can be achieved, but they come with a price tag. In addition to the obvious cost of the additional hardware, other cost implications include: software licenses (for running on multiple servers), increased maintenance costs to reduce the call-out time or even to house permanent engineers, space to hold on-site spares, and staff costs (e.g., who will let the engineer into the data center in the middle of the night and do any necessary recovery and restarting of workloads).

The examples in this discussion have primarily related to server farms but if availability is important to an organization the whole infrastructure has to be considered. This includes the wide area network (WAN) including the terminations at each end and the local area network (LAN) including cable infrastructure, file servers, printers, and so on.

In the final analysis, highly available systems come with a commensurate price tag.

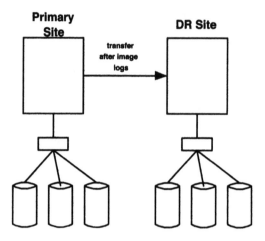

Figure 4.2   Warm Disaster Facility

4.9   THE NEED FOR BUSINESS CONTINUITY

There are several ways of addressing serious long-term problems, such as fire, where the data center may be out of action for a lengthy period. The first step is to estimate the cost to the business of not having the system, or a particular subsystem, for an hour, a day, a week, or a month. This will provide the business case for the budget to meet the cost of the required level of disaster recovery (DR). It should be realized that there may be other non-IT related costs depending on the type of disaster. For example, office accommodation and other associated overheads may come into play if members of staff are in the same building as the servers, and they also have to be moved.

The simplest and cheapest solution is to decide that the system is not business critical, accept the risk of a disaster, and hence come to the conclusion that disaster recovery is not required.

If some form of business continuity is deemed necessary there are certain key questions that have to be tackled. First, what elements of the system are considered to be business critical? For example, MIS (Management Information Systems) is frequently considered not to be business critical. Second, how quickly does the system have to be working again? If the company can afford to be out of action for a week or more then it may be possible to make do with a cold DR site where backup tapes are used to reconstruct the environment and databases. There may even be time to commission replacement hardware rather than have it all sitting there ready. If the system needs to be working again within 48 hours a warm DR site will be required (see Figure 4.2) where equipment and software are already installed and there are copies of the production

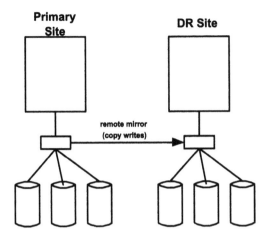

Figure 4.3   Remote Mirroring Across Sites

databases that are updated periodically (every ten minutes, every hour, or whatever) during the day with logs of changes that have occurred on the primary system. These logs are usually sent via a communications link. It follows that the DR center is always slightly behind and indeed the latest set of changes may well be lost in the case of a disaster.

Finally, if the system has to be working as soon as possible (within the hour, although this target is extremely aggressive) it may be necessary to consider a hot DR site where techniques such as remote mirroring (see Figure 4.3) are used to help keep the two sites in sync. Remote mirroring simply replicates any disk writes on the primary system over to the secondary system via a fast communications link such as fiber. It should be noted that there are no foolproof methods of ensuring that the secondary site does not get corrupted in the course of a disaster.

The third question is how much capacity and resilience is required on the DR system. It is possible to take the view that disasters only occur very infrequently and that it is therefore reasonable to configure reduced server capacity (possibly 50 percent) with minimal resilience features, for example, no fail-over clusters. This is obviously a calculated risk. Alternatively, you may take the view that you should faithfully replicate the components on the primary site to provide comprehensive capacity and resilience. This approach provides you with the opportunity to flip the production system periodically between the primary and secondary sites. A number of sites adopt this approach as a means of ensuring that the DR site is ready. It is a perennial problem trying to ensure that a DR site is up to date (in terms of hardware and software changes) and ready to take over the mantle.

There is an alternative approach that can combine high availability and disaster recovery. It is sometimes called campus clustering. As the name implies it is only suitable for data centers that are relatively close, say no more than ten kilometers apart. In this system each server in our simple two-node cluster resides in a separate data center along with some storage. Data is replicated using mirroring across the two sites. If a server or a site fails, the system fails over to the other site. If it is a real disaster rather than a temporary problem such as a power problem you only have 50 percent of the total capacity and no clustering capability.

It can be seen that there are a number of ways to tackle business continuity. However, it should be apparent that if a company is serious about the subject any solution is likely to have significant cost implications. Business continuity requirements should only be included in an ITT if the business considers that they really need it. If business continuity is required there will presumably be some clear ideas of its relative importance. These ideas should be conveyed clearly in the ITT, and not left to the bidder's imagination.

4.10 SUMMARY

The main points of this chapter are as follows.

- Ideally, an individual who has experience of application development, technical architectures, and general service delivery working should be actively involved in both the production and evaluation of the nonfunctional aspects of the procurement. The emphasis is on the word "active," as opposed to "passive" where an experienced person may be periodically consulted. I have come across several instances where after award of contract a company's service delivery personnel have unintentionally, but somewhat embarrassingly, sided with the chosen bidder on the infeasibility of the requirements, mainly because they had not been fully consulted during the procurement.

- To adhere to the tendering and implementation schedule it is absolutely imperative that a level playing field is produced that will allow the relative merits of opposing solutions to be assessed in a single iteration. The basic prerequisites are a set of realistic requirements and an agreed-upon set of basic sizing information. For new businesses you may have two to three discrete business scenarios: the business never really takes off, it is reasonably successful, or it is an outstanding success. Sizing information is then produced for each scenario. For each scenario request solutions and costings for a basic approach (no high resilience), high availability, and business continuity. Do not ask for options just for the sake of it; for example, do not ask for a basic solution if you know that that you need high availability. I do not accept the excuse that the procurer needs to see all the relative costs before deciding on the approach. To be candid the company should have a reasonable idea of the likely solutions and costs before it sees any tender responses. By all means request any innovative approaches/solutions but they should be in addition to responding to your stated requirements not instead of them.

- Requirements should be realistic unless a lengthy tendering cycle, not to mention a painful development and acceptance process, is considered acceptable.
- Finally, and this is a general comment on ITTs, please allow sufficient time for the bidders to produce responses of reasonable quality. I have witnessed some extremely silly timescales, for example, two weeks to produce an initial proposal for a very large over-£100m system. It is appreciated that in some cases there is already a preferred supplier and the company is just going through the motions, using the other vendors merely as "bid fodder." However, in other cases they seem to misguidedly think that keeping the vendors on their toes is somehow beneficial and demonstrates their mettle. At the other end of the spectrum some ITTs go on interminably, either because the company has not decided on the requirements or because they perceive that the requirements will ultimately be better by making use of this "free consultancy" that the bidders provide. As with many things in life, the better approach usually lies somewhere in the middle ground.

5

HARDWARE SIZING: THE CRYSTAL BALL GAZING ACT

5.1 ABSTRACT

Unless an established application software package is being used where adequate sizing information is available, hardware sizing during the early stages of the system lifecycle is frequently impeded by the scarcity of information. As the task tends to consist more of judgment than science, many people are discouraged from attempting to size the proposed system, although it is important that it should be tackled at this time to provide capacity and cost estimates.

Despite the apparent problems, there are a number of ways to tackle the subject when information is scarce. The simplest but least reliable method, given the rate of technological change, is to base the sizing on an existing application. A popular approach is to ask the main hardware or software vendor to tackle the problem for you. Apart from a potential conflict of interest, the usual problem is that vendors often have access to even less information on the proposed system, as they are seldom treated as being an integral part of the project team. In-house attempts at sizing can fall foul of the perceived requirement to perform a very detailed sizing, even though the amount and quality of available information does not warrant such an approach. Where there is limited information to work with, a higher-level sizing is often more successful.

This chapter summarizes the possible approaches and walks through a high-level sizing methodology, discussing the main issues. For people who are involved in procurements this chapter should be read in conjunction with Chapter 4.

5.2 THE CHALLENGE

As the title of the chapter implies, the emphasis is on those situations where there is minimal information with which to work. This frequently occurs during the early stages of the lifecycle, particularly at the feasibility or bid stage. Nobody likes to tackle estimation, whether it is the nation's economy, business growth, project planning and costing, or hardware sizing. The obvious reason for this reticence is fear of the unknown. Hardware sizing has to deal with factors such as:

- Assumptions that may not be valid
- The likelihood that the goalposts will be moved
- Business people who are not keen to provide sizing information in case they give the wrong information
- A hazy understanding of the business requirements

There is seldom much information that is tangible, and most people are only comfortable when they can, in IT terminology, feel and touch the bits and the bytes. It follows that many initial hardware-sizing exercises are ultimately 90 percent judgment and 10 percent science; they cannot possibly be anything else. Occasionally, it is 100 percent judgment. As mentioned elsewhere there have been a couple of occasions when I have been informed that there is no point in my fishing for information because there is none; and so, can I just give them the answer now! You may think that I am exaggerating for effect here, but I can assure you that I am not. Judgment is based on an understanding of the technologies being proposed, the vendors, the development toolsets, as well as general IT knowledge and experience.

The objectives of hardware sizing during the early stages of the system lifecycle are:

- To simply be in the right ballpark. A level of accuracy of plus or minus 20 to 30 percent at this stage is good going. What needs to be avoided is the recommendation of a workgroup server when a mainframe server is required, or vice versa.
- To provide sufficient capacity to allow the developers a realistic chance of designing and implementing a system that will perform satisfactorily.
- To provide a foundation that will cater for any growth and scalability requirements.
- To *avoid* any response time calculations unless there is lots of detailed information with which to work.

The sizer may be lucky to discover existing sizing tools that will significantly simplify the task. This is most likely when large, well-established products such as SAP and Oracle Financials are being used. However, even here judgment is still required in estimating data volumes and transaction rates; remember GIGO (Garbage In Garbage Out).

It is assumed for the purposes of discussion that there is no suitable sizing tool available.

5.3 SUMMARY OF HARDWARE SIZING APPROACHES

Five possible approaches are discussed.

5.3.1 By Simple Analogy

This is a seemingly attractive method whereby an assumption is made that the proposed application is similar to an existing application. It is seductive because it appears to be relatively quick and painless. Needless to say, it can be very speculative. The sizer may be right, in which case she will be hailed as a genius, but she may equally be wrong, exceedingly wrong. It is most likely to be successful when the proposed application is using the same technologies as the existing application. This method was more feasible up to the mid-1990s when technologies were, relatively speaking, more stable. The approach is less useful given the current rate of technological change, particularly in the software area. Of course, if the proposed application will be using the same technologies there is in theory much useful performance information that could be extracted from the existing application and used in a more coherent set of sizing calculations. My experience of happening on the use of this approach tends to indicate that roughly one in five can be regarded as reasonably accurate. Arguably the main reason for inaccuracy is the failure to take account of the different functional requirements and likely designs of the systems. For large organizations with many systems that use the same technology, the levels of accuracy may be greater.

5.3.2 Vendor Sizing

The approach here is to ask the vendor to perform the hardware sizing. This may be the main software vendor or hardware vendor. Beware that many software product vendors, particularly smaller companies or companies with immature products, may lack sufficient understanding of the performance characteristics to size the system adequately.

Having got past that issue, the next question here is do you have sufficient confidence that the vendor can be trusted to be dispassionate? There are dangers of undersizing if the vendor considers that there are cost constraints, particularly in a competitive bid situation, or oversizing if there is no effective competition or the vendor is totally risk averse. The next issue is that although a vendor may be able to provide sizing expertise that your organization does not have access to, the only way that it is likely to be successful is if the person(s) who is responsible for the sizing is a fully fledged member of the project team for the duration of the exercise. In the majority of projects where I have witnessed vendor sizing, the usual approach is to expect the vendor to complete the process quickly, either by analogy or by performing the exercise in almost total isolation from the project. The success rate of either approach tends not to be great. This lack of active participation naturally encourages vendors to attach many caveats to their conclusions, which can render their conclusions almost worthless. The solution to this problem is to agree upon a sensible approach to an ongoing vendor involvement on the project to refine the initial sizing and work through any caveats. Naturally, greater responsibility for the accuracy of the results comes with increased participation. However, beware of vendors with an ingrained aversion to risk who are loath to commit themselves despite greater participation.

5.3.3 Using Benchmarks

Except for the simplest applications it is seldom likely that a single benchmark can be used to size an entire system. Either multiple benchmarks are required or a benchmark has to be used alongside other sizing techniques. As stated in Chapter 3, industry benchmarks from TPC and SPEC tend to be more reliable, although far from infallible, whereas the watchwords with in-house and vendor benchmarks are "handle with extreme care." The problem with any benchmark is how to equate its complexity (or more usually its lack thereof) with the proposed application. This topic is discussed later in the high-level sizing methodology where in the simple sizing example use is made of a vendor's benchmark for a firewall and the SPECWeb99 benchmark for Web servers.

For in-house benchmarks the approach of the client that was mentioned in Chapter 3 could be adopted. He mandated a custom-built benchmark that could deliver 20 times his actual requirement to give him the necessary confidence that the actual application would perform. Twentyfold may be somewhat extravagant for an in-house benchmark but as a rough rule of thumb I would want to see a minimum of five to six times the requirement, and possibly more, depending on my level of confidence in how representative the benchmark was.

5.3.4 Detailed Transaction-Level Hardware Sizing

Unless there is the utmost confidence that genuine, credible, detailed information exists, as opposed to a stack of assumptions, this approach should not be used. Remember that we are talking about the early project stages when there is usually a dearth of information. In almost all the cases that I have witnessed, any detailed sizing has been precariously perched on top of layer upon layer of ever more dubious assumptions, and only a small percentage of such exercises produced satisfactory results. If time permits, one approach is to concentrate on a small number of key transactions, typically three to four, that are perceived to be the most frequently used. Working through the likely design for these transactions can yield useful input to the sizing calculations. Let us say that they constitute 50 percent of the expected transaction load; the remaining 50 percent could be treated as a single item and assigned a capacity factor based on judgment of the likely complexity relative to the identified transactions. For example, it may be decided that on balance the remainder of the load will use 30 percent more hardware resources than the identified transactions.

Detailed sizing needs detailed metrics that can be difficult to obtain without a great deal of work. I have seen a highly experienced performance analyst who used the TPC-C sample programs to derive a set of basic SQL hardware resource costs on a bid for a medium-sized project (~£4 m). He took six weeks to complete the task with a moderate degree of success. The problem here is knowing what the actual SQL is likely to be so early in the lifecycle, so that use can be made of such TPC-C derived figures. In the vast majority of cases that I have witnessed there is insufficient information and insufficient time to attempt a detailed sizing so early in the lifecycle.

5.3.5 High-Level Sizing

This approach sometimes goes under the title of "back of the envelope" sizing. The term is misleading in that it implies that the sizing is done quickly and with minimum effort, which is not the case. If a detailed sizing is performed at the individual transaction or message level, a high-level sizing is typically performed at the user or message-type level. The rationale is that a high-level sizing will use hardware resource costs that are based on the observation of actual production systems plus general sizing experience. The gross nature of such costs tends to compensate for omissions and invalid assumptions that occur in more detailed sizing exercises. This is the approach that I employ most of the time, supplementing any lack of resource usage metrics with information from focused benchmarks, or by taking a view of appropriate vendor benchmarks. It is this approach that we discuss in further detail.

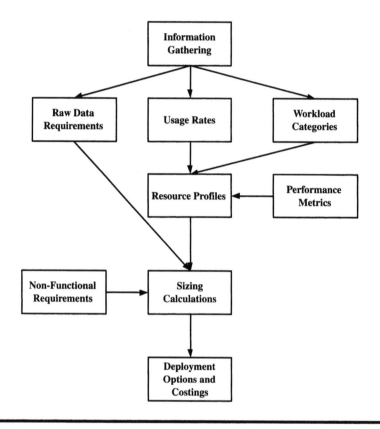

Figure 5.1   High-Level Sizing Methodology

5.4   HIGH-LEVEL SIZING METHOD

This section describes the general approach (Figure 5.1) that is adopted, although the precise method naturally varies from project to project, depending on the information that is available. It should be regarded simply as a framework. The minutiae of the calculations that are used may differ from project to project, and indeed from sizer to sizer, according to personal taste.

5.4.1   Step 1: Information Gathering

Because there is typically minimal relevant information in the early stages of the lifecycle it is important to seek out whatever nuggets may be hiding in dark corners. Persistence may be required to uncover previously unknown sources. On a large case management bid that I worked on, the ITT provided limited information on the number of cases handled per annum, the total number of printed pages, and the number of registered users. When the resultant project got underway we unearthed a chap who maintained a whole host of detailed and extremely useful information on types of cases, working practices, and peak loads, information that would have been invaluable during the bid. I guess that we failed to push hard enough in our quest for information during the bid process.

5.4.1.1 Raw Data Volumes

The easiest volumetric data to get a handle on is usually the raw data requirement. There is frequently sufficient information available on the major data entities, possibly in the form of entity relationship diagrams, to allow estimates of the raw data requirement to be calculated. Even where there is no explicit data, business analysts find it feasible, with some helpful prodding from the sizer, to visualize and estimate data requirements using rudimentary information such as the likely size of the customer base and the number of transactions per customer per year.

5.4.1.2 Peak Period

The objective of any sizing exercise is to handle an agreed-upon peak period. This will typically be a daily, weekly, or monthly peak. Organizations where trade is seasonal (e.g., 35 to 45 percent of annual turnover occurs pre-Christmas during November and December) will probably base the sizing on a typical daily peak during this period. Having decided on the type of peak, it is necessary to understand at what time of day it occurs. This is not necessarily straightforward. One client thought that his peak occurred over the lunchtime period when customers came into branches. In fact, the system peak turned out to be at the beginning of the working day when the mail was being handled. Therefore, it pays to talk through the working day to understand precisely when different categories of users are busy. As a broad generalization, the typical office system may have two peaks, one during the mid to late morning and the second during the mid to late afternoon. They are sometimes referred to as "the camel's humps" (see Figure 5.2). Customer-facing systems, particularly call centers, tend to be busier on a Monday morning, as people often decide over a weekend that they must contact you.

5.4.1.3 Identify Workloads and Users

The next step is to understand the discrete workloads that comprise the overall system. The workload split may be along business area lines or by job category. Each user in a specified workload should have similar frequency of usage characteristics. For example, in a document management

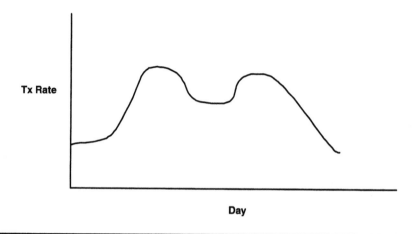

Figure 5.2   Camel's Humps

system there may be contributors and consumers. Contributors write and edit documents and may be classed as heavy users with respect to both the complexity and frequency of transactions. Consumers simply browse/read documents and will be less demanding in their requirements. However, from a frequency perspective there may be speedreaders who glance at many pages in quick succession and may be classified as medium users, whereas slower readers who are taking in every word may be classified as light users. The terms heavy, medium, and light users are often found to describe either the functional complexity or the rate of usage in sizing calculations. It is important that these generalized, seemingly nonspecific terms have defined meanings within the context of a particular sizing exercise.

Each workload requires an estimate of the load that it will put on the overall system. For user-based systems, the first step in this process is to assess the number of concurrent users in the peak period. Take account of the fact that different classes of user may be busy at different times of the day. The term "concurrent user" denotes a person who is actively using the system, such as typing, reading the contents of a screen, or thinking. A person who is simply logged on but is not actually using the system in any way is not a concurrent user in this context. Where user sessions are short and sharp (say ten to fifteen minutes), the level of concurrency, expressed as a percentage of the total registered user population, may be quite low, 10 to 20 percent. Where user sessions are long (over three hours), for example, call center operatives, the level of concurrency will be significantly higher, possibly 70 to 80 percent.

It can be difficult to obtain information on concurrent usage from the business, particularly for new, as opposed to replacement, applications.

Fear of the unknown and the apprehension of providing figures that subsequently prove to be inaccurate are natural inhibitors. There are several ways to circumvent these fears. First, the sizer can assure them that their views will remain anonymous. Second, the sizer should avoid asking for precise figures. It is better to seek opinions rather than to ask for precise numbers, and indeed any figures that are provided may ultimately be adjusted, or even ignored, by the sizer. Request a range of numbers, for example, low (business is poor), best guess, and high (business is better than expected); or best guess plus or minus 20 percent; or state the degree of confidence in a given number. In my experience, estimates on usage rates that are provided by the business tend to err on the high side by as much as 100 to 200 percent, usually because contingency is added to combat the fear factor. When working at the detailed transaction level, rather than at the user level, beware that there is sometimes a tendency for business people and analysts to focus on the important areas of capturing the business, that is, typically the functions that write to/update the database, with the attendant danger that queries, which may well form a significant part of the overall load, are glossed over.

5.4.1.4 Transaction Rates

Ultimately, user concurrency must be converted into a transaction rate per second (or whatever unit of time is being used in the calculations). The definition of a transaction in this context is a single request–response interaction between the user and the system. A complete business transaction will typically consist of multiple interactions. Note: it is imperative that everybody agree on the definition of terms such as transaction; I have seen too many systems where confusion reigned because some people thought that a transaction was at the business level, whereas others thought that it was at the level of a single user–system interaction.

The rate at which users access the system will vary, depending on the tasks being performed. Examples include:

- Call center operatives, other front-office staff, and bulk data entry clerks are typically busy users, possibly averaging a transaction every 15 to 20 seconds.
- Back-office staff may be slightly less demanding users, for example, one transaction every 30 to 40 seconds.
- Staff who spend more time analyzing transaction output may only submit a transaction every one to two minutes.
- Message-based systems will usually derive their workload transaction rates from estimates on the daily, weekly, and monthly business volumes.

For Internet-based systems, there are at least four types of activity, possibly more depending on the type of system:

- Passersby who may inadvertently arrive as the result of a search, click on a couple of pages, and disappear when they realize that the site contains nothing of particular interest to them.
- Surfers who are there by choice and view material for several minutes, possibly issuing four to five requests per minute.
- Serious users who may be purchasing items, issuing more complex requests but possibly at a slower rate, say two to three requests per minute.
- File downloads or video transmission where the transaction rate may be negligible although a steady stream of data will be sent from the server.

The really difficult question is how many users of each type are likely to hit the system at peak times. There was a tendency during the dot.com boom towards the view that the whole planet, well, at least the part that was actually awake, might descend on your site. Ideas that a peak hit rate should be calculated and multiplied by a magic factor (ten seemed to be a popular number) to cater for spikes in usage were common, perhaps not so much now that a degree of normality has been restored. There is a fair amount of material on traffic patterns available on the Web itself that may help the sizer, from overall hits by time of day to more detailed information from individual sites. In addition, there is useful material on Web mining techniques. However, ultimately it comes down to market analysis and a commercial decision: just how much business is out there and how much the company is prepared to invest so that a satisfactory experience can be provided to users. My approach to estimating peak Internet activity is to calculate daily hit rates, and then to use my understanding of the requirement to calculate a peak hour requirement (usually 15 to 20 percent of the daily figure), and to double that figure to cater for spikes. This is far from an infallible approach but it frequently seems to fit in with what businesses are prepared to agree to initially, until there is an opportunity to see how successful the site becomes.

5.4.2 Step 2: Assess the Credibility of the Available Information

This is where experience is particularly important. The easy way, as it affords a degree of self-protection, is simply to accept the information that has been gathered and to base the calculations on them. In my opinion, the sizer should assess the credibility of the information, and adjust or even ignore information where it is considered appropriate to do so.

- Basic business forecasts are frequently over-egged, due to misplaced optimism, although the cynical sizer may regard this favorably as it can provide a welcome degree of contingency.
- Similarly, as stated above, there is a tendency to overstate concurrent usage. The fear factor encourages many people to say that all registered users will be concurrently active at peak periods, which is extremely unlikely.
- Decision support systems are a classic example of overstating the number of concurrent users that are likely to run ad hoc queries. It can take just a couple of users to bring even large servers to their knees when running complex ad hoc queries, particularly when the queries can be parallelized. The danger is that too much hardware will be configured to support such activity when many users may be happy with pre-canned reports that are run overnight.

We have discussed some of the problems that are connected with the collection of volumetrics. They pale into insignificance when compared to getting a handle on the relative processing complexity of transactions, which tends to be underestimated by a wide margin; underestimates by factors of ten or greater are not uncommon. The reasons can vary from business people omitting queries as they concentrate on those transactions that capture the business, to developers failing to understand the impact on the design of the technologies that will be used, and to the more fundamental problem of both the business and the development analysts having difficulty in envisaging the full scope of the system and the impact of the requirements on the hardware that will be required to support them.

A particularly glaring example of understating the problem was a bid for a small system where the inexperienced person who was investigating the functional solution considered that the system would only have two data entities! If true, this would have resulted in an extremely simple system. I chose to ignore his thoughts and, after considering the overall requirement, I eventually assumed 20 entities for the purposes of sizing, which resulted in a system of medium complexity. The actual figure turned out to be 17 entities and the sizing turned out to be in the right ballpark.

It is difficult to advise just how to assess the credibility of information relating to processing complexity:

- Try to gauge the degree of confidence in how well the requirements are understood.

■ Assess the number of unknown factors.
■ Consider the likelihood that the goalposts will be moved.

As indicated, processing complexity is almost always underestimated, usually by a minimum factor of two to three; it is the sizer's responsibility to assess the level of confidence that she has in the available information, to consider how far the goalposts may be moved, and to factor them into the sizing.

5.4.3 Step 3: Establish the Resource Profiles

Deciding on the workload categories and the levels of usage is arguably the easy part. The really difficult element is to decide on the hardware usage metrics that equate to a given workload category. The term "resource profile" is used to describe the hardware usage per transaction for a workload. It typically includes CPU usage, disk IO traffic, memory, and network bandwidth for each component in the proposed solution.

5.4.3.1 Magic Numbers

The actual usage metrics in a resource profile are sometimes referred to as "magic numbers" because people do not know how to obtain them but they perceive them to be invaluable. In essence, the best figures are simply obtained by observing and analyzing production systems. If time permits, the next best figures are obtained by using focused in-house benchmark figures. External benchmarks can be used but, as discussed elsewhere, access is required to detailed benchmark reports so that the necessary detailed metrics can be extracted, and adjusted if necessary, based on an assessment of how well or badly the benchmark fits the proposed system.

The example sizing calculations in Step 4 use a mixture of observed metrics (application and DB server) and adjusted benchmark figures (firewall and Web server). Let us look at the benchmark-derived figures.

5.4.3.2 Use of Benchmark Figures

The firewall figures are fictitious in that they are based on a mythical vendor benchmark. See the Firewalls taster (Chapter 25) for information on benchmarks. It claims to support 1000 Mbps on a single uniprocessor system but there is no information on latency, that is, the time for a packet to get through the firewall. It is decided that the proposed usage of the firewall (e.g., the number of rules and the firewall functionality that will be employed) will be more complex than that used in the vendor benchmark. In addition, it is decided that any latency must be minimized so that overall response times are not significantly affected. The conclusion is that the utilization of an individual firewall should be kept low to ensure good performance, and a figure of 20 percent is chosen.

For the Web servers, the SPECWeb99 industry benchmark is used. This contains a mix of 70 percent static content (with files of varying sizes) and 30 percent dynamic content. The key output from the benchmark is the number of concurrent "sessions" or connections that are supported by a Web server on a specified hardware configuration. Additional reported information includes throughput operations and kilobits per second. The values that are used in the calculations, while they are in SPECWeb99 terms, are actually based on the observation of production systems and reflect the fact that real-world systems typically use significantly more resources than benchmarks. I do not like to drive Web servers at more than 40 to 50 percent CPU utilization, as I am dubious about scalability; 40 percent is used as the utilization threshold in the sizing calculations.

The sizing example also includes the use of an application server and a database server. The figures that are used for them are based on experience, although adjusted benchmark figures could have been employed. For example, SPECjAppServer2002 could be used for Java-based systems, although at the time of writing there are few submitted sets of results. TPC-C could be used for the DB server. Introduced in 1992, TPC-C is an Order Entry OLTP benchmark that expresses its results both in terms of the number of new order transactions completed in a minute and the monetary cost of the system per new order. The complexity of database implementations has increased inexorably over time as hardware speeds have increased. This means that any TPC-C values used in sizing calculations have to be continually reviewed and adjusted, as appropriate.

The resource profiles that are used in the sizing example are inevitably general figures. In reality, some products perform better than others. Similarly, a rough rule of thumb for the ratio of CPU power required across Web, application, and database tiers is 0.7:2:1, but these figures can be affected by the features that are used and by the design; for example, heavy use of XML may inflate the application figure by as much as 100 percent. The overall message here is — do not use figures blindly.

5.4.3.3 New Software Technology

The most difficult assessment with respect to resource profiles is for new software technology where there are no published or in-house benchmarks. This can be a 100 percent judgment call, and it is tricky to give any specific advice other than to involve the vendor, search out any scraps of relevant sizing information, and consider the use of a sizing specialist.

5.4.3.4 Adjusting Resource Profiles

Finally, it may be necessary to adjust the resource profiles to reflect your particular situation. Barry Boehm's COCOMO technique for project estimating caters for adjustments to be made to take account of the general experience of the project team, the maturity of the technology, time constraints, and so on. There is no reason why the resource profiles should not be similarly adjusted. A recent project heavily used C++ with a team that had limited relevant experience. Neither the development effort estimates nor the original hardware sizing made allowance for this fact.

5.4.4 Step 4: Sizing Calculations

The calculations in this section are illustrated by a simple example for an interactive system. Do not regard the specific resource profiles and utilization thresholds that are used as definitive figures. The main objective in quoting them is to illustrate the method. Although they are considered to be reasonable for a modern system (plus or minus 20 percent), they should be treated with great care. They are no substitute for your own observations and experience on a given assignment. I never use my own metrics and thresholds "parrot-fashion," typically adapting them to suit the needs of the particular exercise that I am undertaking.

5.4.4.1 The System to Be Sized

The sizing example is a mythical OLTP system for a simplistic financial portfolio system with a Web interface. To protect the innocent no product names are mentioned. All users are on an intranet and their requests go through a single firewall layer, to a Web server layer, on to an applications server layer where the majority of the business logic resides, and finally on to a DB server. It is assumed that some business logic is also executed on the DB server, mostly in the form of stored procedures. There are 2 million customers and 700 concurrent users at peak periods. There are several types of user:

1. *Heavy* — high frequency, one complex transaction every 15 seconds with frequent DB writes (in general, DB writes are more expensive than reads by a factor of two to three)
2. *Medium* — one transaction every 30 seconds (less DB writes)
3. *Light* — one transaction per minute (query only)
4. *Very light* — one transaction every minute (simple queries only)

The example is covered in stages:

- The first stage is to estimate the basic disk capacity that will be required, primarily by the DB server, as the results will be used later to calculate the number of disks required.
- The second stage is to produce the individual categories of usage, with the number of concurrent users in each category, along with their associated resource profiles.
- The third stage comprises the main calculations.
- The fourth stage summarizes the outline deployment configurations.

5.4.4.2 Disk Capacity: Stage 1

DB server disk space (see Table 5.1) is arguably the easiest component to size. As previously mentioned, there is usually sufficient information for designers to derive rough raw data entity sizes and an estimated number of occurrences per entity. Multiplying the two items together produces a raw capacity figure for each entity.

There are many overheads for which we need to account. They include column and row overheads, indexes, space lost due to the page size, spare space to cater for insertions, any log files or journals, and audit trails. They are usually accounted for by multiplying the total raw data figure by a multiplication factor. My multiplier for a typical relational DBMS is usually in the range of two to four, depending on the type of system and the level of information that is available. For example, for a DBMS I might use a factor of two if there is a reasonable amount of credible information on the proposed database, or four if there is extremely limited information in which I have little confidence.

A quick note on audit trails: beware of any unrealistic requirements. It is not unusual to find requests that everything that moves is to be audited, without taking account of the possible effects on performance. I once worked on a system where they wanted to audit calculations performed during large batch programs, presumably to check that they were correct. It was estimated that it could require 70 GB per day. Quite how anybody was ever going to plow through 70 GB was never explained. Fortunately, the requirement was significantly reduced when the figure of 70 GB was mentioned.

In addition, specific allowance should be made for a systems disk plus any other dedicated disks that may be warranted by the software that will be used, for example, DB before and after images, transaction logs, and so on. Note that additional spare space will usually be required for housekeeping tasks such as database reorganizations.

Table 5.1 assumes the use of 36-GB disks and it produces a basic requirement of 8 disks. This is purely from a capacity perspective. There

Table 5.1   DB Server Disk Capacity Estimates

Entity	Raw Row Size (bytes)	Occurrences	Raw Total (MB)	Notes
Type of product	500	30	0.02	
Sector	200	50	0.01	
Product	1200	5000000	6,000.00	Assumes 2.5 products per customer
Deal	250	75000000	18,750.00	Assumes 15 deals per product
Receipt	250	25000000	6,250.00	Assumes 5 distributions per product
History	300	168000000	50,400.00	History kept for 84 months
Diary	200	100000000	20,000.00	Assumes 50 diary items per customer
Total Raw Row Size			**101,400.03**	
Apply Multiplier Factor of 2			**202,800.05**	Allowance for indexes, spare space, page size, before images, etc.
			Disks	
Basic number of 36 GB disks			6	
Plus additional disks			2	One for after images and one for systems disk
Basic Number of Disks Required for Capacity Purposes			**8**	

Table 5.2   Resource Profiles

		Processor Usage/Sec			
User Category	Users	Firewall	Web	Apps	DB
		Mbps	SPECWeb99	SPECint2000	SPECint2000
Very light	35	0.003	0.166	0.5	0.25
Light	105	0.006	0.33	1	0.5
Medium	210	0.015	1	3	1.5
Heavy	350	0.03	2.33	7	3.5

		Disk IO (physical IOs/sec)			
User Category	Users	Firewall	Web	Apps	DB
Very light	35	n/a	0.02	0.01	0.1
Light	105	n/a	0.04	0.02	0.2
Medium	210	n/a	0.1	0.06	0.4
Heavy	350	n/a	0.2	0.125	1

		Network Bandwidth (megabits/sec)	
User Category	Users	Network	Server LAN
Very light	35	0.003	0.025
Light	105	0.006	0.05
Medium	210	0.015	0.15
Heavy	350	0.03	0.4

is also a need to assess how many disks are required from a performance perspective. Too few disks, although they will satisfy the capacity requirement, may result in bottlenecks that affect response times as users queue for them. This topic is covered in Stage 3.

With respect to the other servers, three disks are assumed per Web server: systems disk, static HTML files, and logs. For an application server two disks are assumed: systems disk and space for logs.

5.4.4.3   Resource Profiles: Stage 2

The following subsections comment on various elements of the resource profiles in Table 5.2. Note that the unit of time for the calculations is one second.

5.4.4.3.1 Processor

Using the estimated network bandwidth figures and applying the adjusted benchmark figures that were discussed previously, the firewall and Web server figures are derived.

For the application and DB servers the figures that are used are based on experience of recent systems (2003). They have been converted into SPECint2000 units for use in the calculations. For commercial systems the CPU usage is often driven by the amount of data accessing and manipulation that is involved in a transaction.

5.4.4.3.2 Memory

Note that the resource profiles in Table 5.2 do not contain any memory figures. It was common, and still is to a degree, to find vendors quoting detailed memory figures such as allowances for the base operating system, base product, per concurrent user, per concurrent stream of work, cache, and so on. The advent of object-oriented systems, memory heaps, and dynamic file system cache sizes makes it much more difficult to provide detailed memory figures. The availability of cheaper memory allows a simpler method to be employed, a memory allowance per CPU. Here are some very rough rules of thumb per CPU that are no substitute for your own observations: Web server (0.5 to 1 GB), apps servers (1 to 2 GB), and DB server (1 to 2 GB). Remember that more memory is always better. Modern operating systems can always make use of any spare memory for the file system cache and thus aid performance by minimizing physical disk IO traffic. One caveat with this approach is the application where individuals may be logged on all day but make little or no use of the system. If large numbers of users are involved, it may be necessary to make a specific per user allowance on the applications server, possibly on the order of 100 to 200 KB depending on the technology being used.

5.4.4.3.3 Network Bandwidth

It is sometimes possible to obtain typical network bandwidth figures from software vendors. Here are some rough rules of thumb in lieu of any specific information: client/server (4 to 15 kbits/sec) and Web-based (3 to 30 kbits/sec). The lower end equates to very light users and the high end equates to heavy users.

Information from software vendors on the usage of the server LAN(s) is likely to be very scarce. In fact, I have only seen one vendor who was prepared to provide any figures. Once again, in lieu of any specific information I would allow in the range of 50 kbps to 400 kbps per concurrent user for a straightforward three-tier architecture.

5.4.4.4 Main Calculations: Stage 3

Table 5.3 shows the processor, disk IO, and network calculations.

The first step is to multiply the individual resource items in the resource profiles by the respective number of concurrent users to produce resource totals. Note that disk IO traffic is subsequently converted from units of physical IOs to busy time by assuming an average service time per IO (seven milliseconds in the example).

The initial resource totals are then adjusted to account for contingency (30 percent is added in the example). Contingency can take two forms: the optional form caters for any specific doubts that there may be concerning the processing complexity, and the other form is general project-level contingency that may need to be factored in, for example, on a fixed price proposal. An optional additional factor (not shown in the example) would be to include any specific growth requirements.

The next step is to apply the utilization thresholds. This step is an indirect method of addressing response times. Individual hardware components cannot run at 100 percent utilization without seriously affecting performance. As shown in Figure 5.3, queueing increases as the utilization grows, and adversely affects performance after it reaches a certain point (sometimes called the knee of the curve). Therefore, to minimize queueing and to avoid unnecessary bottlenecks, a utilization threshold is built in. Individual hardware components have their own typical utilization thresholds, for example, CPU (60 to 80 percent), Ethernet (30 to 40 percent), WAN (60 to 70 percent), memory (80 percent), disk (30 to 40 percent), and disk controller (20 to 30 percent). In Table 5.3, it can be noticed that different servers have their own utilization thresholds. In the case of the firewall and the Web server, benchmark figures are being used rather than raw CPU figures, and here the low utilization thresholds limit the use of these servers, in line with the judgment on how the usage in the application will differ from the benchmark, as discussed previously.

CPU utilization thresholds also need to take account of other factors. *Potential software bottlenecks.* If information relating to the software has been obtained from a benchmark on a comparable configuration this may not be an issue. If not, it is possible to find that the CPUs cannot in fact be driven at the hardware threshold figure, never mind higher than that. Perhaps the application design will not scale up to the required number of CPUs, or perhaps the software design may inhibit the use of any of the CPUs. I have seen a software product that could support multiple CPUs but failed to drive any of them above 20 percent, arguably, although I was never given a reason, due to its client/server implementation. Similarly, I have witnessed a benchmark for a custom publish and subscribe mechanism that failed to drive a server with four CPUs above 25 percent utilization due to its software design. Reducing the CPU

Table 5.3 Processor, Disk IO, and Network Calculations

		Processor Usage/sec				
	Users	Firewall	Web	Apps	DB	Notes
		Throughput benchmark	SPECWeb99	SPECint2000	SPECint2000	Firewall uses vendor throughput benchmark. Web is based on SPECWeb99. App and DB are CPU usage figures based on observation, expressed in SPECint2000
V. light	35	0.105	5.81	17.5	8.75	
Light	105	0.63	34.65	105	52.5	
Medium	210	3.15	210	630	315	
Heavy	350	10.5	815.5	2450	1225	
Total	700	14.385	1065.96	3202.5	1601.25	
Apply 30% contingency		18.70	1365.75	4163.25	2081.63	Add general project level contingency
Utilization thresholds to be used		20%	40%	60%	60%	
Apply utilization threshold		93.50	3464.37	6938.75	3469.38	Applied thresholds are: firewall 20%; Web server 40%; Apps server 60%; DB server 60%
Base CPU value		1000	800	600	600	Firewall CPU = 1000 Mbps; Web CPU = SPECWeb99 rating of 800; App/DB = SPECint2000 rating of 600
Estimated CPUs required		1	5	12	6	

Disk IO Traffic (IOs/sec)

	Users	Firewall	Web	Apps	DB	Notes
V. light	35	n/a	1.4	0.7	7	
Light	105	n/a	4.2	2.1	21	
Medium	210	n/a	21	12.6	84	
Heavy	350	n/a	70	43.75	350	
Total IOs per sec			96.6	59.15	462	
Total busy time (%) (IOs * 7 ms per IO)			0.68	0.41	3.23	Multiply by average disk service time
Apply 30% contingency			0.88	0.54	4.20	Add general project level contingency
Apply 40% utilization threshold			2.20	1.35	10.51	General disk util. threshold of 40%
Total disks required (performance)			3	2	11	Total disks required from a performance perspective
Total disks required (capacity)			3	2	8	Total disks required from a capacity perspective
Total disks to be configured			**3**	**2**	**11**	Pick the larger from capacity/performance perspectives

Table 5.3 Processor, Disk IO, and Network Calculations (Continued)

	Users	Network	Server LAN	Notes
		Network Bandwidth (megabits/sec)		
V. light	35	0.21	1.75	
Light	105	0.63	5.25	
Medium	210	1.26	10.5	
Heavy	350	10.5	140	
Total		12.6	157.5	
Apply 30% contingency		16.38	204.75	Add general project level contingency
Utilization thresholds to be used		50%	30%	
Apply utilization threshold		**32.76**	**683**	Network util. threshold 50%; data center LAN util. threshold 30%

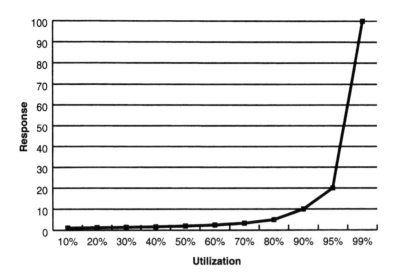

Figure 5.3   Response Time Versus Utilization

utilization threshold to cater for possible software bottlenecks is a judgment call. Dedicated DBMS servers tend not to suffer from this type of bottleneck. It is more likely to occur at the Web and application layers. If (say) the application server is a cause for concern, but there is a struggle to come up with a number, I would suggest reducing the threshold from 60 percent to 40 percent threshold in lieu of any specific information.

Multiprocessor overheads. Apart from the ability of the software to exploit CPUs effectively, allowance must be made for low-level multiprocessor overheads, where appropriate, unless they have already been accounted for in the metrics, for example, from a comparable benchmark. As CPUs are added to a server, more behind-the-scenes work is required to look after them. The overall overhead per CPU can be a modest ~5 percent on a two-processor system, growing to ~15 to 20 percent on a four-processor system. Note that the overheads on a four-processor system can be significantly greater than 20 percent per CPU on certain hardware/operating system environments. The overheads on even larger multiprocessor systems can be extremely onerous, depending on the implementation. In the example, the utilization threshold of the apps and DB servers are set at 60 percent, the lower end of my rule-of-thumb range for CPUs, to cater for multiprocessor overheads.

In the case of the processor calculations, the total figures after the utilization thresholds have been applied are divided by either the target SPECint2000 rating (in the case of the application and DB servers) or by the benchmark figures (in the case of the firewall and Web server) to produce the estimated number of CPUs that are required. The proposed Web server

CPU has a SPECWeb99 rating of 800, whereas the CPU that will be used for both the application and DB servers has a SPECint2000 rating of 600.

In the case of the disk IO calculations, the estimate of the total number of disks is solely from a performance perspective. This figure is then compared with the number of disks that are required from a capacity perspective, as calculated earlier in Stage 1. The greater of the two values is then used in the configuration. In the example, more disks are required on the DB server from a performance perspective. Note that in this situation any apparently spare capacity can always be used. An adapted version of Parkinson's Law applies to disk space: however much there is, it will all be used. If specific allowance has not already been made for them, spare space can always be used to cater for any necessary database reorganizations, or for logs and audit trails.

5.4.5 Step 5: Consider Deployment Options

Unless high availability and business continuity have been specifically mandated it is easier to start with a basic solution that includes adequate resilience, for example, redundant power supplies, redundant fans, and RAID disks. High availability and business continuity can always be added later, as costed options.

5.4.5.1 Issues

The answers to many of the following points revolve around debates on cost versus performance and management issues. There are no hard and fast pieces of advice. They depend on cost constraints and local conditions.

The first step is to decide how to map the various elements of the solution onto hardware servers. For example, should the application and database layers reside on the same server or should they be on separate servers? The same question may be asked of the Web and application layers. If there is a shared file system (NFS-based or similar) should it have its own dedicated server that will provide good performance but may possibly be a waste of CPU resources, or should it coreside with another server? In this particular example it is decided to deploy the Web, application, and DB servers on separate servers.

The second step is to incorporate any growth requirements into the equation. They can influence the server model that is proposed. For example, the DB server could be housed on a server that can take up to eight CPUs on day one. This may be adequate for the first year or two. The preference may be to go down this route to keep the costs down and to replace it with a larger model when necessary, or to configure a larger server on day one. As no growth requirements have been specified, we will stick to an eight-CPU model.

The choice of disk subsystem may also be affected by growth. Modestly priced, limited-growth, rudimentary subsystems may be adequate. Alternatively, more sophisticated, expandable, and higher-performance subsystems may be more appropriate. With respect to resilience the choices are typically between mirroring (RAID 1) and parity (RAID 5). RAID 5 is cheaper as there are fewer spindles, but mirroring will perform better, particularly for write-intensive applications. See the Hard Disk Basics technology taster (Chapter 17) for further information.

The results from the sizing example are carried through to Table 5.4. Here, it is decided: how many CPUs to configure per node, for example, four processor nodes for the apps servers; if high availability (HA) is required, and if so, configuring a spare node; and the choice between mirroring RAID 1 and RAID 5 disks. Outline configurations are then produced from this information. Note that the DB server assumes four disks per RAID 5 array and includes the provision of two hot spares.

There may be ancillary questions that need to be addressed, such as backup and recovery. Will the timing and volume of data to be backed up necessitate a dedicated backup server LAN to avoid interfering with production performance?

5.4.5.2 Other Environments

We have focused on the production environment but what are the requirements for other environments, for example, development, system testing, acceptance, performance, and support? Decisions on the provision of dedicated environments are invariably based on cost considerations. The bare minimum is a combined development and testing environment, but this may seriously hinder testing. Much debate usually surrounds the provision of a dedicated performance environment. It is frequently assumed that performance testing will be run on the production environment before the system goes live. This may be satisfactory if performance testing is actually completed before the "go live" date, except that it is frequently not completed. The obvious supplementary question is what hardware will be used when performance tests are required on release 2 of the system?

5.5   BATCH PROCESSING CONSIDERATIONS

Batch processes are inherently more difficult to size. This is an area where detailed sizing is preferable. The ideal information consists of transaction volumes and CRUD matrices (estimated number of Creates, Reads, Updates, and Deletes per function). Even then, the sizer needs suitable low-level

Table 5.4 Outline Deployment

	CPUs Estimated	Preferred Max. CPUs/ Node	Disks Estimated	Resilience	RAID	Outline Configuration
Firewall	1			HA		2 node model xyz firewall cluster
Web	5	2	3	HA	RAID5	4 servers, each with 2 CPUs, 2 GB of memory and 4 × 36 GB disks
Apps	12	4	2	HA	RAID1	4 servers, each with 4 CPUs, 4 GB of memory and 4 × 36 GB disks
DB	6	8	11		RAID5	1 server, with 8 CPUs, 8 GB of memory and 18 × 36 GB disks

Required Network Capacity = 33 Mbps

Required Data Center LAN Capacity = 683 Mbps

Table 5.5   Simple Overnight Batch Estimation Steps

Batch Window Calculations

Overnight window =	6 hours	2200–0400
Reduce by half to cater for re-runs =	3 hours	
Contingency allowance =	1 hour	
Total time available for processing =	2 hours	
Transactions per night =	20,000	
Number of program steps =	4	
Throughput per second per stream	8.75	Assumes 3 complex (@ 5/sec) and 1 simple (@ 20/sec) step
Estimated seconds required	9142.857	
Number of streams required	2	

CPU usage metrics for each type of access to make use of this information. However, it is unlikely that this level of information will be available at the bid or feasibility stage.

5.5.1   Simple Background Batch

For batch work that runs in the background alongside online work it may be sufficient to estimate the number of concurrent batch streams that will be required, and make an allowance of 0.5 to 1.0 CPUs per stream, depending on how CPU-intensive the processing is considered to be. With respect to disk IO traffic, batch processing tends to perform significantly more disk IO than online tasks. This may simply be handled by allowing higher disk utilization thresholds, say up to 60 to 70 percent, although this may affect online response times. Alternatively, as a first cut, it can be assumed that on a per-CPU basis, batch will perform five times more disk IO than the interactive work. This means that if 4 CPUs are estimated for online usage and 1 for batch, add 125 percent ((1/4) * 5) to the online disk IO calculations.

5.5.2   Overnight Batch

For overnight batch runs, where there is no accompanying online work, the following rudimentary approach, which is summarized in Table 5.5, can be used.

■ For each program, assess the likely complexity of the processing and estimate how many batch transactions per second can be supported. This could be done by running a focused benchmark, or by using previous experience. In lieu of any hard information use (with extreme care), 5 per second for complex (significant validation and updates), 10 per second for medium (moderate validation and updating), and 20 per second for light (read-only reports).

▪ Calculate the length of time taken to complete the program by dividing the transaction volume by the estimated throughput. Repeat this process for each program to produce a total elapsed time.

▪ The next step is to decide how many concurrent streams are required to complete all processing within the window of time that is available for overnight processing. Start by estimating the size of the window. Remember to reduce the size of the window by the time that is required for backups and other management tasks that cannot run alongside production work. If six hours are available, you will probably want to allow time for reruns if there are problems, and therefore reduce the window by half, that is, three hours. Make an allowance for contingency, (say) one hour, thus resulting in a window of two hours.

▪ Divide the previously calculated total elapsed time by the window size to estimate the number of streams that will be required. As above, allow 0.5 to 1.0 CPU per stream. Allow two to three disks per stream for disk IO accesses.

It should be apparent that this is a simplistic approach but it provides a reasonable first pass. The main danger is the assumption that multiple streaming is always possible. There is usually some point in even the best-designed systems when the processing has to be single-threaded. The sizer needs to assess the likelihood of this situation and build it in to the calculations, possibly in the form of contingency.

5.6 SIZING SOFTWARE PRODUCTS

The software product vendor has to be relied upon to provide adequate sizing information, of the sort that has been described in the previous section. With the notable exceptions of SAP, Oracle Financials, and several others, it usually ends up being something of a struggle to obtain satisfactory information. Although some vendors positively seek to hide sizing data, presumably on the basis that the figures are not very impressive, it is readily apparent that far too many vendors know little or nothing with respect to the performance characteristics of their products. This is more likely to be the case when a product has not been deployed on any large scale. For those companies who are considering such a product for large-scale deployment, any lack of sizing and performance data should ring large warning bells. If time permits, and usually it does not, consider benchmarking the product to obtain the necessary information.

5.7 SIZING REVIEWS

5.7.1 The Battleground

Hardware sizing is just another form of estimation. Management will naturally want to review the estimates, particularly if the results are likely to jeopardize the budget, or if when bidding, it is perceived that it makes the solution too expensive. If the cost is seen to be excessive, expect lots of pressure from all quarters, viz. project or bid management, sales and marketing (your own and the hardware/software vendor's), and middle and even senior management. Frequently, the normal attendees at bid or project reviews will have no experience of hardware sizing. Unfortunately, if the agenda is to beat the price down, discussions can get quite heated. Most reviewers can grasp the rationale behind functional estimates because many of them come from a development background. Nonfunctional matters are typically more difficult for them to grasp, with the result that their lines of argument tend to degenerate quite quickly. The speed and depth of degeneration is usually directly proportional to the amount of money involved: the greater the sum, the quicker that tempers can fray. Wild claims can be made that a similar system that they were involved in could support 100 users on a little ol' 286 PC, and there was still sufficient room to produce all the management reports that anyone could ever want!

5.7.2 Productive Approach

A common problem is the frequent insistence on tying technical and commercial issues together. I fully accept that management may wish to go forward with a particular offer that they consider will be attractive to the decision makers. However, browbeating the messenger is not a productive method. A preferable approach is to divorce the technical and commercial aspects in the first instance.

The starting point may be a peer review. I am generally not in favor of peer reviews. The reason is that if the sizing is 90 percent judgment and 10 percent science its conclusions are underpinned by assumptions, and changing a couple of assumptions can quite easily alter the results. This plays into the hands of those who are looking for simple ways to drive the price down. A preferable approach is where two independent sizing exercises are performed, and their relative merits are subsequently assessed.

Prudent sizers will pre-empt commercially driven questions by sizing and roughly costing a range of solutions. For example, there may be several basic scenarios, optimistic (low cost), medium, and pessimistic (high cost), which reflect the possible success of the business. Each scenario may be further split into minimal resilience, high availability, and high availability plus disaster recovery. When I say rough costs, I really do mean rough (say to the nearest £100 to 200 K for a large system). If your company is used to getting regular quotes from hardware and software vendors there may be sufficient information to perform a rough first-pass cost estimate without having recourse to the vendor(s). The first step is to discuss and agree on a limited number of scenarios that will be short-listed as potential candidates for the official solution. The sizer should obviously promote his preferred scenario although it is naturally management's prerogative to have the ultimate decision on the proposed solution and its associated costs. However, any serious disagreements should be documented, for example, reducing volumes or limited scalability, along with an assessment of the associated risks, including any potential cost implications. When agreement has been reached it will be time to request detailed quotes from the vendors. There are opportunities at this stage for commercial discussions with vendors.

5.7.3 Unproductive Approaches

One vivid example in my memory from 15 years ago was a client who was developing a new business. His business case included a provision of ~£1 m for hardware. Unfortunately, my estimate came in at ~£2.5 m. He exploded fairly quickly. He insisted on changing all the volumetrics and key assumptions until the answer fit his business case. What actually happened was that, within 18 months of going live, the hardware cost was ~£3 m. I had in fact underestimated by 20 percent. In retrospect, I did not handle the situation very well as I did not present a range of options, notwithstanding my strongly held belief that the probable solution would be considerably more expensive.

This particular incident highlights certain points of note. The first point is the impenetrable wall syndrome (see Figure 5.4) from which bid reviewers often suffer. Here, the sizer's conclusions are assumed to be worst case. Management takes the view that the truth, a.k.a. the acceptable cost position, lies somewhere between their best-case scenario, a.k.a. the budget, and the position of the sizer (the wall), usually somewhere very close to the budget position. The idea that the answer may possibly lie over the wall (beyond the sizer's position) never seems to occur to the participants.

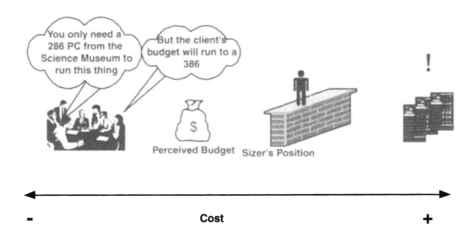

Figure 5.4   The Impenetrable Wall Syndrome

The second point is more universal. There is a tendency for people or companies who are pushing to get the initial go-ahead for projects to pitch their estimate at a level that will be palatable to the decision makers. It is interesting just how often the actual cost comes out somewhere around three times the original estimate. I am not just talking about IT projects. I take an interest in reading stories about the latest large building or infrastructure project that went way over budget, and I never cease to be amazed at how often the overspend is around the threefold mark. It is almost as if there is a subconscious threshold that people use, taking into account what they may subsequently have to defend. It would appear that excuses about problems with the technology, the business requirements being greater and more complex than previously understood, changes that have had to be adopted, and delays caused by third parties can all be used to justify an eventual tripling of the cost. This seems to be a subconscious limit, as if anything greater than three is unjustifiable and smacks of incompetence, not to mention financial lunacy.

A perennial claim by management is that any allowances in the sizing for the use of inexperienced staff or problems with an immature technology should be removed as the A team will be on the case. The A team is invariably a very busy team as they get proposed on at least three new projects every month. In fact, they are so busy that you may well never actually get to meet any of them.

A more laid-back comment came from the technical ambassador of a large software house, who proclaimed, and this was about 15 years ago, that hardware was now so fast that there was no excuse for performance problems. I wonder if he observed how the performance of various versions of Microsoft Word altered over time as faster PCs were introduced. One of my personal mantras, alias Wirth's Law, is that software gets slower quicker than the hardware gets faster. This means that as software techniques evolve developers are always pushing against the speed and limitations of the current hardware technology, and they will continue to do so for the foreseeable future. Examples include: significantly more complex databases now in comparison to five years ago, extravagant use of network bandwidth to stream video, and much more exotic HTML pages than five years ago.

5.8 DELIVERABLES

In addition to the contributions that will be made to the official proposal or feasibility study it is important that all findings be documented. This is mainly for the benefit of the project team that will follow, as nobody ever remembers the rationale and the caveats; they just remember the bottom line. A suggested layout comprises:

- Summary of findings
- Scope/omissions (e.g., only minimal resilience features included, overnight processing not addressed)
- Key assumptions
- Method employed
- Sizing calculations (may just summarize a sizing spreadsheet)
- Hardware deployment
- Risk assessment, including estimates of the likely effects of false assumptions on the solution
- Chosen solution (after the reviews have been completed) with rationale

All volumetric and sizing models must be retained and made available to the project team.

5.9 HARDWARE SIZING REVISITED

When the project gets underway it might be assumed that a fined understanding of the requirements will result in the availability of more concrete information that will permit a much more detailed sizing exercise to be performed in the middle and later stages of the project. Improved information will certainly appear but it may be a very gradual process. I have often been asked at what stage the 90 percent judgment and 10 percent science ratio is reversed; that is, when does it become 10 percent judgment and 90 percent science. The standard answer is that it is hardly ever fully reversed. Even on the day before a system goes into production, it would be good going to have reached 40:60, mainly because there is still likely to be lots of uncertainty surrounding the actual usage of the system. Functions that were perceived to be useful, and hence frequently used, may in fact be difficult to use or they may be extremely poor performers, with the result that users avoid them. I performed a post-implementation study on a call center system where the profile of usage was totally different from the assumptions that had been made during development. Many more queries were performed per call, and conversely slightly fewer updates, than the developers and indeed the client had forecast.

Up to the early to mid-1990s it was usually beneficial to attempt to construct a detailed sizing model at the design stage, as there was usually sufficient information to warrant it. However, the current tendency of the requirements and functional specification stages to continue well into the project means that the design stage has to commence with less information than it used to have. This can make the benefits of detailed modeling at the design stage problematic. On a very large project that I witnessed recently, a comprehensive volumetrics model was produced over a period of six to eight weeks. This was a successful and very useful piece of work, not least because there was access to detailed and meaningful statistics that the client maintained. The resultant volumetrics were then used to construct a detailed transaction-level sizing model over a period of five to six weeks. Unfortunately, detailed design work was hampered by ongoing requirements and functional specification work. This meant that many speculative assumptions and judgments had to be made on the scope of individual tasks, their database access requirements, and the complexity of the user interface. The benefits of the detailed task model were questionable and a preferable approach, given the lack of information, might have been to revisit the original high-level sizing model and refine it. The message here is not to be in a rush to produce a detailed sizing if the level of information does not warrant it.

5.10 CHANGE

While discussing the topic of revisiting the hardware sizing, it is important to stress the need to review, and where necessary, refine the sizing to cater for agreed changes in functional requirements. On the development side, projects are usually on the ball when it comes to assessing the additional development effort and cost that is required to implement agreed-upon changes. However, I have lost track of the number of projects where the impact of change on hardware and performance has been forgotten. It is also important to remember that a single minor change may have a negligible impact, but multiple minor changes, possibly spread over a lengthy period of time may ultimately have a noticeable impact, so it is important to be vigilant.

5.11 SUMMARY

The main points of this chapter are as follows.

- Hardware sizing, similar to any form of forecasting, is difficult when there is limited information. It should still be tackled even though it may well be 90 percent judgment and 10 percent science.
- The secret is not to be tempted into detailed sizing (transaction level) unless there is sufficient information to warrant it. High-level sizing (user/message type level) tends to produce more accurate results.
- There are a number of approaches to high-level sizing, ranging from the use of sizing tools where they exist, similarity to an existing application, use or adaptation of benchmarks, to custom calculations.
- The primary technical objective should be to provide sufficient capacity for the designers and developers to produce a satisfactory solution without undue constraints. Other technical objectives may include the provision of a resilient and scalable infrastructure, if required.
- Response times can seldom be estimated at this stage due to the lack of information. The subject is typically addressed indirectly by using hardware component utilization thresholds to minimize physical and perceived software bottlenecks.
- Divorcing commercial and technical matters can help to ensure that sizing reviews are productive.
- The proposed solution must be cost effective. Test the waters at the earliest opportunity by submitting broad costs for a range of scenarios, in an attempt to seek agreement for a scenario that is palatable to all.
- Sizing should be revisited at appropriate points in the lifecycle, particularly at the design stage and in the wake of functional change.

6

BID LOGISTICS

6.1 ABSTRACT

This chapter applies almost entirely to the bid process where a company is responding to an ITT that has been issued by another organization, although there may be some elements that are applicable to feasibility studies. The emphasis is on those bids where the vendor is proposing a new solution for the first time, that is, where it is not a straightforward regurgitation of a frequently proposed solution with a few cosmetic changes.

The fundamental problem is that work in the early to middle stages of a bid tends to be sequential; functional comes before technical, comes before hardware sizing. This can put undue pressure on the person who is responsible for the sizing and those people who are responsible for putting together hardware configurations, as they are at the end of the solution chain.

This chapter suggests proactive approaches to hardware sizing during the bid process to minimize the likelihood of rushed work at the eleventh hour.

6.2 THE CHALLENGE

Work on new solutions tends, by and large, to proceed sequentially during the early and middle stages of the bid. Investigations eventually lead to a proposed functional solution, and thence on to a technical solution. With this *modus operandi* the hardware sizing activity frequently does not get underway until a first-pass functional and technical solution is in place because nobody who is working on the solution wants to commit herself until she feels relatively confident of the solution. This can leave limited time for the hardware sizing activity, and even less time for hardware vendors and third-party software vendors to turn around configuration and licensing quotations. Bid changes, refinements, and price tinkering, or even wholesale butchery, frequently continue right up to the last possible moment, and are an inevitable fact of life. They necessitate changes to the hardware sizing, configurations, and licensing that must be completed in almost no time at all. In short, bids can be stressful, particularly when you are near the end of the solution pipeline.

The situation is being exacerbated by a general shift to shorter procurement cycles. Although there still continue to be some overly long procurements that can last for a year or more, the majority are getting shorter, a number of which are frankly suicidal. If it was previously difficult when the hardware sizer waited for a solution, it is now becoming virtually impossible. He has to hit the ground running at the start of the bid; a proactive approach to sizing is becoming a necessity.

6.3   BID QUALIFICATION

Some form of bid qualification usually takes place when the ITT arrives, if only to decide if the company is going to bid. Members of the bid team will read the supplied documents initially to establish the scope and practicality of the proposed system, and to identify areas of vagueness and ambiguities. There is an understandable fervent desire to fire as many questions back at the client as soon as possible so that a clear picture of the requirement can emerge, and work on the solution can proceed unimpeded. Unfortunately, there is seldom any degree of priority attached to individual questions. High-level and minutely detailed questions are all lumped together in the rush. When multiplied by the number of bidders, the volume of questions that the client may be faced with can be quite daunting. For this very reason many clients tend to answer questions only in writing, shying away from meetings, particularly when there are a large number of bidders. This can delay feedback on important questions. I prefer to see a system where the first round of questions is limited to important items, that is, those with a significant cost impact. The objective should be to submit these questions in the first day or two and to receive prompt feedback from the client by the end of the first week at the latest. More detailed questions can be dealt with in an agreed-upon series of iterations.

From the hardware sizing perspective, the important questions will cover:

■ Clues on the likely budget, as this can help to shape the proposed system. This is the client's view of the budget, as opposed to what your salesperson thinks may be acceptable to the client.

- High-level volumetrics, for example, the likely user population, the size of business, or the volume of transactions, will provide useful indicators of the potential size of the system.
- The importance to the business of high availability and business continuity in case of disaster. More important, does the budget match the client's view of their importance?
- The hours of service. Long hours of service (e.g., 24/7), may necessitate sophisticated and potentially expensive backup solutions. Is 24/7 actually required, or is it just unthinking use of a currently popular mantra?
- In addition to the production environment how many other environments are implicit in the ITT as written, such as development, integration testing, system testing, performance, and acceptance? Obviously the more environments there are, the greater the cost.

6.4 THE POLITICAL DIMENSION

ITTs are not necessarily all that they seem. A company may be considering a move into a new business area, usually an area that has already been shown to be lucrative, but they may be reticent to make the necessary investment. Putting out an ITT is a method of trying to attract sufficient interest and competition to drive down the price and then to decide if the business is likely to be viable. If the price is too high it is likely that the idea will be dropped.

A slightly more Machiavellian illustration is the case where part of an organization is convinced that it is not feasible to ask for a fully functional solution, again on cost grounds, but it goes through the ITT process simply to confirm that fact either by the prices that are submitted or by the fact that most, if not all, of the potential vendors withdraw. The result is to force a rethink inside the organization, which was the original objective.

From a bidder's perspective the secret is to uncover such machinations. This is really a job for the sales and marketing/commercial people. Ultimately, a collective view is required on how to respond: simply adhere to the ITT, go for a lower cost solution, or have two (or more) solutions ready. The decision must be communicated to all members of the bid team so that they can plan their activities accordingly. Unfortunately, this is seldom the case.

6.5 TEAMING

The problems of establishing effective communications within a bid team are hugely compounded when the team is actually a consortium. This subject is covered in Chapter 11. For the moment, it is sufficient to say that a workable *modus operandi* must be agreed upon on day one to avoid untenable delays, which can introduce yet more difficulties to those individuals who are near the end of the solution chain.

6.6 DEALING WITH HARDWARE AND SOFTWARE VENDORS

Planning is a key activity when dealing with hardware and software vendors, particularly on bids that have to be completed in a relatively short period of time, say up to six weeks.

The first step is to decide if quotes are required from multiple vendors in any area. This is usually more of a commercial question, unless there are specific issues that may affect the technical solution. Initial bids of four weeks or less do not have the luxury of seeking multiple quotes, and it is still questionable for bids of up to six weeks. This subject should be discussed with bid management, procurement, and commercial departments at bid start-up. I have come across ITTs where two and sometimes three vendors have been asked in the early stages to quote for the hardware, usually by a bidder, but occasionally by the client. The key point is that they were involved from the beginning and there was something approaching a level playing field. This is obviously the sensible approach where time permits, and where there is no preferred supplier.

However, I have also been involved in ITTs where a single supplier was dealt with until the eleventh hour when it was then decided to ask a second supplier for a set of quotes. The second vendor is invariably adept at realizing that his company is probably there to force the original vendor to reduce its price. Having got half a foot in the door, he is going to do all that he can to stay there by undermining the original vendor. The typical method is to state that there is no time to perform an independent sizing and configuration (which is true) but that they can quote against the original vendor if you can provide details of what they quoted. Not surprisingly, the second vendor claims that he can do it cheaper and with less hardware. This is a total distraction at the moment in the bid process when you can least afford it. I well remember one account executive trying valiantly, and at tiresome length, to persuade me that his company's 8-CPU server was the equal of the other vendor's 64-CPU server offering. There are other ways to tackle commercial issues without resorting to such eleventh-hour gamesmanship.

Hardware vendors should be contacted as soon as possible. They should be provided with a sufficient outline of the requirements, and where possible with some idea of the likely type of equipment, for example, mid-range servers. The requirement for any meetings should be agreed upon, for example, to understand recent product announcements. Secrecy for secrecy's sake should be avoided. I have seen a number of counterproductive bids where the bidder has steadfastly refused to provide any information, including the name of the client or even the market sector. Finally, vendors should be given the dates when first-pass quotations will be required. Be aware that it can take time to configure large and complex systems, particularly where server clusters are required. For example, the bidder might say that it will be two weeks before she has sufficient information for a server vendor to configure a system, and it is expected that two further iterations may be required over the following ten days, as the solution is refined. This approach should ensure that the bidder receives timely and reasonable service from the vendor. Do not ring her for the first time at 4 P.M. on a Wednesday afternoon, two thirds of the way through the bid, demanding a host of configurations by early the next morning!

I remember a vendor employee telling me that he had received such a request from a person in a major software house. He informed the requester that he already had four sets of configurations to do for other people and that he would be unable to meet the timescale. He was subjected to a tirade that revolved around how large and important the project was, and more important, did he realize what an important customer his company was to the vendor. The vendor employee said that he did not doubt the importance of the bid. He was also well aware of just how important the software house was to the vendor, indeed the four other bids that he was working on were all for the said software house!

Similarly, any meetings with software vendors whose products are being considered should be planned, agreeing upon timescales, agendas for meetings, and most important, the skills of the people who will be required to attend these meetings. It is imperative that introduction-only meetings are avoided where time is of the essence. The software vendor should be provided with sufficient background information ahead of the first meeting to avoid wasting time. A bid that I was involved in demonstrated just how not to do things. The software vendor was a medium-sized, international company. They were given no background information prior to the meeting. The sales director, technical director, and a pre-sales support person attended the initial meeting. The main objective on our side was to understand how the product could meet some fairly exacting functional and technical requirements, and to understand what sizing information they could provide. After it became apparent that they were unprepared for this type of meeting it ended up as the standard introductory affair, where our side spent several hours explaining the requirement and they made some positive, but not particularly confident noises, and gave a demonstration.

It was agreed that a second, more technically oriented meeting was required. Due to other commitments that the software vendor had, there was a delay of five days before the second meeting that was held at their offices. At this meeting they had a functional specialist; so good progress was made in this area. However, they were struggling on the technical side until they managed to rustle up a technical specialist for 30 to 45 minutes (this highlights a good reason for going to them rather than expecting them to come to you). This satisfied some of the technical concerns, but not all of them. With respect to sizing, he knew of a document that he would e-mail to us. It failed to arrive. It transpired that everybody had gone off to some company get-together for several days. The sizing document arrived a week later. It was one of the better sizing documents that I have seen, but it begged quite a lot of questions, including the fact that it did not cover replication of data between geographically disparate systems, a key requirement. He could not answer the sizing questions except to say that there was an updated version of the document that would probably answer my questions, which begs the question of why he gave me an old version. The new document did not arrive. I could not wait any longer and had to proceed with the available information and use my judgment to adjust the figures to cater for the replication.

6.7 ITERATIVE SIZING

An embryonic solution is required early in the bid stage to allow an initial rough sizing to be completed with associated broad-brush costs. I suggest that this should be done after ten days to two weeks on a short-to-medium length bid. It may sound impossible, particularly on those bids where you sometimes consider that you are going backwards for the first half of the bid, but it is feasible even if it feels as if it consists of 100 per cent assumptions. It pays initially to err on the pessimistic side, for example, to assume a more complex system than initial gut-feel may indicate. I tend to find that the overall solution gradually increases in complexity as the bid progresses, simply because the other bid members are progressively beginning to get a better understanding of the scope of the ITT. The simple objective of this initial sizing is to understand roughly what ballpark you are in, and to flush out any early cost objections. It may be beneficial to have a short informal bid review within the team to discuss any implications of the embryonic solution, issues that may require further investigation, and the shape of the rest of the bid.

At this point the hardware vendor is asked to produce initial quotations. There is a tendency to ask for highly detailed quotations, right down to the last interface board, even when the available information is quite skimpy. There is no particular need for such detail at the first iteration. If the eventual hardware costs are in the region of £1 m it is sufficient to be plus or minus ten percent at this stage. If you have access to pricing information from other recent bids, it may be possible to derive your own rough costing, although it is best to check with the vendor that the prices have not changed.

Review and refine the initial sizing at appropriate intervals, minimally once per week. If the solution appears to change dramatically overnight, usually it becomes much more complex; it is better to sit on the information for a couple of days rather than immediately get on the phone and request revised quotations. Perceived, hugely increased complexity can disappear just as quickly as it arrived, or it can turn out to be a more modest increase. Large swings in perception are a common bid phenomenon. Any wild swings in hardware requirements without associated changes in the complexity of the solution (e.g., a workgroup server solution at the end of week one transformed into a mainframe server solution a week later) are usually indicative of a lack of sizing experience. It may be useful to use a consultant to assist if the bid team lacks confidence in the area of sizing.

6.8   BID REVIEWS

The hardware sizer should not go into an initial bid review with a single solution unless he is a masochist who enjoys being beaten up! It is preferable to put forward a range of solutions, such as low cost, medium, and high cost, with views on the assumptions and risks that underpin each scenario and broad costs. For example, low cost may have minimal resilience features or a conservative estimate on the number of concurrent users. Be prepared for the "What can I have for a buck?" question. The objective in the initial bid review should be to home in on an agreed-upon scenario, or set of scenarios.

The functional and technical solution will invariably continue to change after the first bid review. Refine the sizing, including feedback from the bid review, and go back to the vendors for detailed quotations. There may be several such iterations depending on the size of the bid and the number of bid reviews. This stresses the importance of planning ahead and getting dates in people's diaries for the production of quotations, as there is usually limited time available for these iterations.

6.9   PROTOTYPES

Longer procurements are usually split into phases where the number of bidders is gradually whittled down to two or three. At this stage a prototype or proof of solution is requested. The resultant prototype, which is almost always limited to functionality, can introduce two problems:

- "Not the solution," a Heath Robinson job, a quickly put together but satisfactory prototype demonstrates feasibility and instills confidence, but it invariably gives the customer ideas that the solution is straightforward and will require less hardware
- The sexy alluring prototype that requires additional hardware and is unlikely to perform

This stage requires somebody to play devil's advocate and ensure that a delicate balance of appeal and credibility is maintained in order that the original sizing and performance projections are not totally undermined.

6.10 BAFO

Many procurements now include a BAFO (Best and Final Offer) stage. There are typically two variants: providing all the requirements but at reduced cost, and providing a reduced solution at reduced cost. The driver in this situation is frequently that the customer's budget does not match their requirements. If a range of options has been sized and costed during the bid they can provide useful input to this process. However, beware that this is the time when your own side can come up with some really wacky ideas. "How about, instead of the large multimillion-dollar server, we do a deal with the Science Museum and take as many 286 PCs off their hands as possible and connect them together using that wonderful super-scalable software glue that has just been announced?" The majority of radically alternative technical solutions have risks attached to them and it is important that they are clearly spelled out to the decision makers.

6.11 DOCUMENTATION

The danger with delaying any views on the solution until late in the bid process is that the production of the proposal document can also be delayed. This makes life difficult not only for the hardware sizer, but also for document reviewers and polishers. Documentation should be started as soon as possible. The first step is to agree with the bid management team as to what aspects of the hardware sizing will be included in the proposal document and what aspects will be excluded. The proposal may be limited to a summary of the results, with no underlying explanation. The hardware sizer should still produce a detailed internal report, even if it only sits in the bid file, along with any sizing models. See Chapter 5 for suggestions on the format of a report.

Also, a short memo should be drafted to the incoming project team (assuming that you win) that explains the options that were explored during the bid, the reasons for the final choice, the risks that may be inherent in that decision, and any other background information that the eventual project team might find useful.

6.12 SUMMARY

The key points are:

- Plan the approach, even though there are many unknowns
- Concentrate on the big questions (largest cost items) during bid qualification
- Discuss and agree upon sizing scenarios during the first two weeks of the bid
- As part of the bid start-up process line up vendors for meetings, pricing, and so on at appropriate points in the bid cycle
- Perform sizing iteratively over the course of the bid, even if there is limited information
- Where possible, present options at bid reviews
- Get documentation underway as early as possible.

7

DESIGNING FOR PERFORMANCE, SCALABILITY, AND RESILIENCE

7.1 ABSTRACT

The design stage is the defining moment for addressing performance. Retrofitting performance, resilience, and scalability into a design is frequently expensive and time consuming. It is preferable, not to say cheaper, to build it in from the beginning.

Good design is based on a sound understanding of current hardware and software technologies, the use of best practice in their deployment, and an appreciation of the underlying resource costs that are attributable to them. The ability to partition the overall problem will often allow best use to be made of the available capacity and it will contribute to better throughput, superior response times, and the capability of enhanced scalability.

A proactive approach to design and implementation will help to produce a better product, one that not only performs better and exhibits superior scalability and resilience, but also one that is ultimately easier to maintain.

7.2 INITIAL OBSERVATIONS

7.2.1 Understanding the Work Done in Previous Stages

The first step should be to review the work that was done during the bid/feasibility stages and to understand the rationale of the solution at that time. Where there has been no continuity of team members there is

117

a tendency to ride roughshod over the earlier approach, frequently ignoring or changing fundamental assumptions. There are undoubtedly occasions when such an approach is warranted, typically when the scope of the problem was not well understood in the previous stages. Equally, there are many occasions when there were strong cost or technology reasons behind the earlier solution, and it is important that the designers understand the reasoning behind the original decisions. Other frequent reasons for wholesale changes in the design include the propensity of enthusiastic designers to overengineer the solution, out of a desire to produce a clean and aesthetically pleasing solution, or to use the latest technology. A review of the poor performance of one project showed that part of the solution, which handled large volumes of incoming data, had been developed in Java and had made heavy use of XML, both of which had an impact on the hardware requirements, yet neither were mentioned in the original proposal. It requires a strong pragmatist to insist on a design that is fit for purpose and that matches the original assumptions. For example, if it is considered extremely unlikely that the system will have to support large volumes it is highly questionable that the additional effort and cost that is required to incorporate scalability into a design will be justified.

7.2.2 Nirvana

Vendors, particularly software vendors, have a natural tendency to talk up the performance and scalability potential of their products. The frequent inference is that developers can concentrate on the business functionality, secure in the knowledge that the nonfunctional aspects will be handled without much effort on their part. Developers tend by nature to be optimists, and many are only too ready to accept such claims. They frequently exhibit a "can do" mentality. This is laudable but the question is more "how can do?" On larger systems, in-house design techniques assume greater importance as the limits of what current technology offerings are capable of are reached. I was forcibly reminded of this fact on a recent bid for an extremely large system that would require very careful design. One otherwise bright young man stated that if vendor X said that their product could handle the volumes unaided (i.e., with no need for careful design), perhaps we should accept their claim. Every design team needs at least one person to play devil's advocate, to identify when that point is likely to be reached, and to question the validity of simply relying on standard features in the software to build the system.

Be extremely wary of new or immature features in the development toolset that promise to reduce development timescales by allowing the developer to concentrate on the business functionality. Check out the claims before committing yourself to using them. I have encountered such features that could be deemed suitable for small systems, but were inappropriate for larger systems. One particular promise to hide all the intricacies of a database from the developers was implemented behind the scenes by writing all data to a single table in a relational database, not a particularly clever idea for any reasonably sized system. Where it is necessary to develop any customized code in place of immature product features, attempt to design and build the feature in such a way that it can be replaced with the toolset version when it has matured sufficiently.

Will nirvana be reached in the near future? I do not think so. The voracious appetite of the software industry to invent new technologies almost certainly means that attempts to provide inbuilt scalability into products and toolsets are doomed to be playing catch-up for the foreseeable future.

7.2.3 Does It Cost More?

Some people view designing for performance, scalability, and resilience as an element of overengineering. They perceive that it equates to significant effort and cost. If major benchmarking exercises are embarked upon, or the basic design principles were not sound and the design has to go through a number of iterations, there may well be additional effort and cost. However, I have been involved in designs for large systems with stringent performance and scalability requirements that incurred no significant additional development costs. The secret is to understand what the issues are likely to be and to circumvent them. Some examples are provided later.

7.2.4 QA

I am not a particularly keen fan of design reviews, mainly because they frequently take place near the end of the design stage. Unfortunately, if the designers have spent significant effort on the task in hand they tend not to be predisposed to accepting any major observations, such as "this will not perform." To avoid the inevitable arguments, not to mention any necessary rework and subsequent delay, short, focused wipeboard sessions early in the design to thrash out issues are preferable, to agree on the basic design principles, or at least to identify areas that need further investigation. Designers are much more receptive to suggestions before the passage of time has entrenched them in their views, and therefore such sessions are generally productive. Using this approach, reviews near the end of the stage, accepting that they have to be done, tend to be much more of a formality.

7.2.5 In-House Benchmarks

Custom-built benchmarks can be a useful method of resolving any areas of the design where there are question marks over the feasibility of the approach. However, they have to be extremely focused, as time and cost pressures are often constraining factors. If the benchmarking activity is struggling to get anywhere near the required level of throughput or performance, do not be afraid to pull the plug on it and to rethink the strategy. I have seen several benchmarks that went on far too long in vain attempts to succeed. As discussed in Chapter 3, be careful in the conclusions that are ultimately drawn from a benchmarking exercise. It is very easy to be seduced by the seemingly promising results that are produced by a rudimentary benchmark, and to overestimate the likely effect that the approach will have on the real system.

7.2.6 Change

This point was made in Chapter 5, on hardware sizing. I make no apologies for reiterating the message. All investigations into the development effort and cost of making requested functional changes should include the effects on the nonfunctional aspects. Unfortunately, the nonfunctional side is frequently forgotten.

7.3 BASIC DESIGN PRINCIPLES

Before discussing individual design topics, a brief description of the main basic principles can help to set the scene.

7.3.1 Understanding Resource Usage Costs

The primary prerequisite is to understand the likely impact of design or implementation decisions on the use of hardware resources, and therefore on performance. Casual or overambitious design/coding can result in the profligate use of hardware resources. The simple expediency of following the standard performance guidelines for a specific programming language, development tool, or software product can frequently result in considerable savings in resource usage. However, ultimately a solid understanding of the resource costs that are likely to be incurred by using certain approaches, coupled with solid design techniques, will help to avoid excessive use of hardware resources, to minimize latency, and to achieve satisfactory performance. As a very rough rule of thumb, the quicker the design and implementation, the more extravagant the use of hardware resources is likely to be.

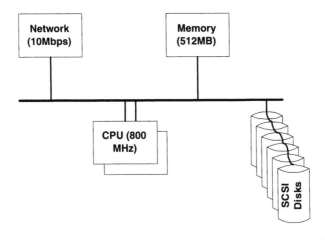

Figure 7.1   Questionable DB Server Configuration

7.3.2   Balanced Hardware Configurations

A balanced hardware configuration is one where each component is capable of contributing towards the satisfactory support of a specified load; that is, no component becomes an obvious bottleneck that will have an adverse impact on performance. The use of this technique is one of the cornerstones of infrastructure design.

Figure 7.1 shows a simple example of a potentially unbalanced DB server configuration, although to what degree it may be an issue will depend on the processing load.

- There are two reasonably powered CPUs. They could well support more than 250 concurrent users on an interactive system. In terms of the potential workload that can be processed, they dominate this configuration. Even if the transactions happen to be highly CPU intensive it may not be an issue.
- The LAN connection is a modest 10 mbps. It will be able to support ~4 mbps before it may start to become a bottleneck. If the LAN utilization is greater than 50 percent it may well constrain the throughput capability of the DB server. With more than 250 heavy concurrent users it may struggle to cope.
- 512 MB of memory is quite modest to support more than 250 concurrent users. At the very least it is likely to limit the size of the various DB memory caches that can significantly improve performance, thereby putting more pressure on the disk subsystem. This is arguably the weakest link in the configuration, that is, the component that is most likely to become the initial bottleneck.

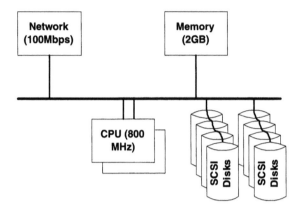

Figure 7.2   More Balanced DB Server Configuration

- The disk subsystem consists of a single daisy-chained set of six disks that is connected via a single interface. Although there is the question of whether six disks are sufficient to support the disk IO load that more than 250 users may generate, the main issue may surround the fact that they are all sharing a single interface and it may become a bottleneck, particularly if the lack of memory results in additional disk IO.

Assuming that the CPUs need to be fully exploited, a more balanced configuration (Figure 7.2) would have, in order of priority: 1 to 2 GB of memory rather than 512 MB; additional disks, split across two disk interfaces; and a 100 Mbps LAN interface.

7.3.3   Partitioning

Partitioning is a mechanism that allows the available capacity on a single hardware server to be fully exploited (scaling up), and that affords a method of providing scalability over multiple hardware servers (scaling out). In Figure 7.3 the objective is to exploit the available capacity and to increase throughput by having multiple batch processes on a single hardware server that can operate on the data in parallel.

This approach is most successful when the data can be naturally partitioned in some way, for example, by area, department, or similar means. Ideally, the data partitions are physically separated on the disk subsystem to minimize any cross-partition contention. There are two CPUs in this example. It is assumed for the sake of the example that the processing is roughly 40 percent CPU and 60 percent disk access. This means that each CPU is capable of supporting two batch processes. The

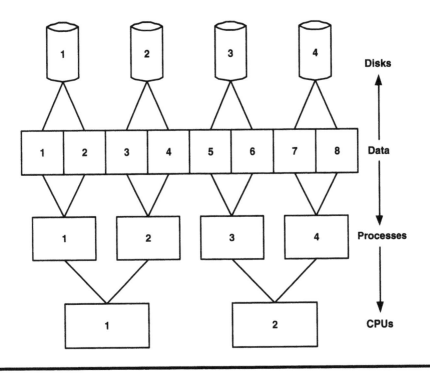

Figure 7.3 Partitioning Batch on a Single Server

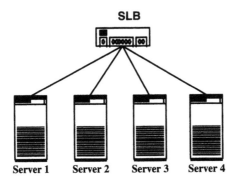

Figure 7.4 Server Partitioning Using a Server Load Balancer

diagram shows a fairly optimal setup where four concurrent processes can operate with minimal contention for CPU and disk resources, thus allowing maximum performance.

Figure 7.4 shows a simple hardware method of partitioning an interactive workload across multiple hardware servers. A server load balancer

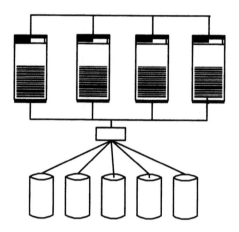

Figure 7.5 Share Disk

(SLB), sometimes called a network load balancer or a traffic switch, is used to partition the inbound requests across four servers. This method is particularly suitable for servers that hold no persistent data (e.g., firewalls), or servers that have no sophisticated requirements to read and write shared data (e.g., Web servers and occasionally application servers). There are also a number of software-based approaches to load balancing, as described in Chapter 26.

Servers that share volatile data present greater problems, as there is a need to ensure that data integrity is maintained, for example, by preventing two servers modifying the same record at the same time. Standard network file systems such as NFS or CIFS can be used, although vanilla-flavored implementations are unlikely to be suitable where high disk access rates need to be supported. A single large DBMS server may also be sufficient. More scalable approaches include cluster file systems, a relatively recent phenomenon, and DBMS products that support a multinode database. Cluster file system implementations vary but typically involve one of the nodes acting as a master either for all metadata changes and possibly for all writes.

A multinode database is typically implemented using one of two standard approaches, share all (Figure 7.5) or share nothing (Figure 7.6). In either case interserver synchronization is required to ensure data integrity, and this can significantly affect performance. Whatever approach is adopted, the secret is to minimize the amount of interserver synchronization. For example, the share nothing approach in Figure 7.6 will perform better if the majority of accesses can be made to disks on the local server, rather than from the other server.

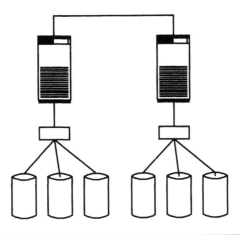

Figure 7.6   Share Nothing

7.3.4   Resilience

A single server can be made resilient in a number of ways. First, there are in-built, or optional add-on features such as redundant power supplies, redundant fans, and an uninterrupted power supply. The disk subsystem can be made resilient through the configuration of redundant controllers, redundant host connections, and RAID disks (typically using mirroring (RAID 1) or parity (RAID 5)). Similarly, additional CPU, memory, and network interfaces can provide further resilience, although the degree of resilience and the possible need for a reboot when a failure occurs will depend on the individual hardware and operating system features.

Resilience across multiple servers can be achieved in several ways. For servers that do not store data, and hence do not require any application recovery procedures, a simple deployment of $N + 1$ servers may be sufficient as long as the software that decides which server to use is capable of understanding that a server has failed and can ignore it until it has been repaired. An alternative approach is to use standard clustering software where the overall workload is split into services, each consisting of a mixture of hardware and software resources plus host IP address. When a service fails, due to a software or hardware failure, the cluster software can simply attempt to restart the service or to move it, along with its host IP address, to another server within the cluster. The other server may be an idle standby server (Figure 7.7), or it may be a server that is already running another service(s) (Figure 7.8). Some cluster products provide the ability to move services between clusters, for example, in a disaster situation where service(s) are moved to another site.

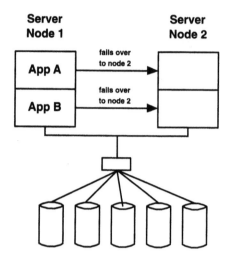

Figure 7.7   Fail-Over to Standby Node

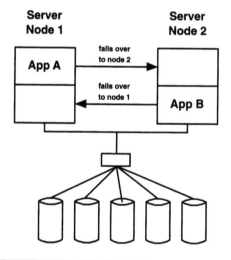

Figure 7.8   Fail-Over to Working Node

7.4   GENERAL THOUGHTS AND GUIDELINES

This section contains discussions on a variety of design topics. The simple objective is to highlight issues that designers may need to consider.

7.4.1   Threads

Marketing material from any vendor will intimate that threads are much better performers than processes, particularly when their product uses threads. Is this true? Well, the answer is yes and no. From a simple low-level operating system perspective, the answer is yes. Processes have more baggage that has to be handled during process creation, deletion, or context switching (switching from one process to another), whereas threads are more lightweight. However, it is not as straightforward as that. Consideration has to be given to how the threads are actually used. There is a tendency to keep threads small and thus make them easier to maintain. Indeed, in some cases the developer may have limited control over the granularity and the deployment of threads. The possible disadvantage of having many threads is that they are more likely to result in significant interthread communication. The mechanisms used by modern development toolsets to support procedure calls between threads can be relatively expensive in performance terms, even within the confines of a common process, and they can be more costly where the calling and called threads reside in different processes, even though they are on the same server. It pays to check how interthread communication is implemented if large-scale use is likely to be made of the facility.

Thread-based systems may generate significant synchronization overheads to maintain integrity. In addition, it is important to understand how effective the environment is, be it the operating system or a threads package, in dispatching and executing threads. For example, in a system with two CPUs the objective is to make maximum use of both of them by dispatching a thread per CPU. In some environments, there may be constraints that may inhibit the full exploitation of the available CPUs.

In summary, threads can provide superior performance, particularly where low-level custom design and code are used and the developer has full control over the granularity and deployment of threads. Modern development toolsets can simplify the development process but the overheads may prove to be as onerous in performance terms as an equivalent process model, if not more so. Finally, the environment may inhibit the achievable physical multi-threading level.

7.4.2 Communication Between Software Components

Extending the theme of interthread communication to general application-level communication (Figure 7.9), it is important to understand that the farther the "distance" between two communicating items of software, the greater the resource overheads are likely to be, and the greater the latency. By distance, I mean the number of software and hardware hops between the caller and the procedure. The infrastructure design can have an impact on the latency. Examples include: servers that reside on different LAN segments thus introducing additional hops for the bridge or switch involved, firewalls, and/or load balancers that may have to be traversed to reach the procedure.

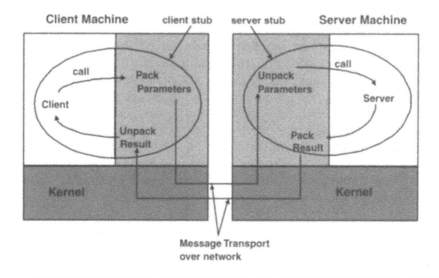

Figure 7.9   Simple Remote Procedure Call Across Servers

On a platform that supports threads, interthread communication within a common process should perform better than interthread communication across processes within a single server, which should in turn perform better than interthread communication across processes that reside on different hardware servers. Remote procedure calls, as they are sometimes called — I use the term in a generic sense — have significantly extended the flexibility of software architectures. However, it can be wasteful if the designers forget about the overheads and use the facilities extravagantly, without thinking through the costs. Where feasible, the remote procedure (or a copy of it) should be sited as near to the caller as possible. Another approach is to minimize the number of calls that are made to the remote procedure so that the overheads of communication and latency may be minimized. For example, it may be beneficial to extract all required data from an external source in a single call, rather than in (say) four discrete bite-sized calls that may reflect the different types of data that are required. A database stored procedure is an obvious example: a client process makes a single logical call to the database server which runs (say) six SQL statements and returns the extracted data, in preference to the client process submitting each SQL statement separately.

7.4.3   Minimizing Overheads

System overheads that are directly attributable to the design and implementation can have a severe impact on performance if they are overused.

Examples include the creation/destruction of processes, threads, and object containers, and the opening/closing of network connections and files. In the case of processes, threads, and object containers, it is preferable to create a pool of them at system start-up and then to keep them alive, reusing them when they become free. Network connections can be onerous to set up and tear down, and they also benefit from the concept of a pool of reusable connections. DB software products often use this technique. When talking about the evolution of a software product or application, pooling is a technique that seldom appears in V1.0.

We have spoken about reusing what are essentially containers that house functionality. It would also be useful to reuse data, where possible. Memory-caching techniques have always been a staple way of improving performance, as disk performance is significantly slower than memory performance. Well-established products, particularly DBMSs, tend to have effective caching mechanisms. Where possible, data should also be cached on the client machine to minimize the need to request the data again from the database. This is relatively straightforward where the data is either read-only or limited to the confines of a single database transaction. It becomes much more difficult where the data is volatile and any change on the server has to invalidate the client's cached version.

The majority of custom memory-caching mechanisms that I have come across in the commercial world tend to be simple lists that are accessed sequentially. However, the advent of greater memory sizes brings the potential for having much larger caches where sequential access may result in unsatisfactory performance. More sophisticated storage and retrieval techniques may be required, including a binary chop, balanced tree structure, indexing or hashing techniques, or partitioning.

7.4.4 Going with the Flow

It is always beneficial for an application design to "go with the flow," that is, to take into account the likely case. One system received many thousands of daily transactions, which it used to update its database at the end of the day. These input transactions were stored in a single database table. On completion of the daily processing cycle, transactions that had been successfully updated were individually deleted from this table. Typically, only two to three percent contained errors and they were retained for subsequent correction. This nightly deletion run took in excess of two hours to run, time that could not be afforded. A quicker approach was to extract the two to three percent that were still required and use it to re-create the transaction table and populate it.

7.4.5 The Only Transaction in the World

This is concerned with how designers view the likely performance of an area of design. There is a tendency to look at performance from the perspective of a single transaction, considering methods to optimize the response time of that transaction, often by using some degree of parallel processing. This could be through inbuilt parallel processing, or a database parallel query feature, or the use of RAID disk array features to perform parallel disk IOs. The general idea is to make use of multiple CPUs or multiple disks to shorten the response time. This is perfectly laudable when the transaction is either the only one that is resident in the system at the time, or it is one of a small number of coresident transactions. If the number of coresident transactions is not modest there is a greater chance that all these "selfish" transactions will simply get in each other's way and result in unsatisfactory response times for everybody. Therefore, it is important to get the balance right among the load on the system, the available hardware resources, and the degree of parallel processing that can be supported, that is, to view the system as a whole, not just from the perspective of a single transaction.

7.4.6 Under the Covers

It is sometimes important to understand what precisely is going on behind the scenes of a seemingly attractive feature if it is going to be heavily used. A possible example could be a client process with a scrolling facility that will aid access to a set of query results from a database. Scrolling forward may be a simple matter of requesting subsequent rows. However, scrolling backward may involve the underlying software in going back to the top of the list and reading down until the desired point is reached or, even worse, asking the database to rerun the query and to send another set of results.

7.4.7 Relational Databases

There is a plethora of books available on database design and performance. I limit myself to a small number of key points.

- It is important to decide where to pitch camp on the normalization/denormalization line. Some DB authorities prefer to start with the flexibility of a fully normalized design and wait to see how it performs, only introducing denormalization in identified areas when forced. This is a luxury that is difficult to justify nowadays with the pressures to deliver quickly and effectively. It is usually possible to identify performance-critical areas during design and to make reasonably informed decisions on those entities that are most likely to benefit from denormalization.

■ The use of bind variables rather than literals should be used in dynamic SQL statements. Parsing of SQL statements is a considerable overhead. It is extremely beneficial if a parsed statement can be retained in memory and reused when the statement is encountered again, as the parsing does not need to be repeated. However, the software may be quite pedantic, considering SELECT WHERE NAME = "FRED" to be different from SELECT WHERE NAME = "JOHN." If a bind variable CHRISTIAN_NAME is used to store the name (FRED, JOHN, or whatever) the statement SELECT WHERE NAME = CHRISTIAN_NAME is used in both cases and it can be parsed once, stored in memory, and subsequently reused.

■ Where appropriate, batch processing, sometimes called array processing, will provide superior performance for bulk processing. For example, if 100 rows need to be written to the same table, an array can be set up with the necessary 100 entries that are sent to the DB server along with a single INSERT statement. This is in preference to sending 100 separately executable INSERT statements. This is another example of effectively minimizing the number of calls between a client and a server process.

■ The effectiveness of caching techniques is a primary driver for DB performance. We have spoken above about an SQL statement cache. There are other caches, including data dictionary, object, and data. The data variant, sometimes called a buffer cache, is the one that is usually most visible. It can significantly reduce the need for physical disk IOs. Most DB products have mature and effective caching mechanisms if they are given enough memory with which to work.

■ JOINs are a powerful means of combining data elements from different tables. However, they can also be resource intensive depending on the number of tables that are joined in a single SQL statement and the number of rows that are initially accessed. Large joins over as few as five tables can lead to poor performance.

■ Ensure that highly hit files do not become bottlenecks. For example, at the system level, transaction logs, before images, and after images are important files that must not encounter delays if overall performance is to be satisfactory. They may need to be on dedicated or lightly loaded disks.

7.4.8 Database Transactions

Transaction mechanisms help to ensure the integrity of the database. From a performance perspective, the potential disadvantages are the length of time that data items are locked (thus preventing other transactions from accessing them) and the expensive cost of committing changes to the database. The COMMIT statement causes database changes to be irrevocably written to the database. It is the final step in a transaction. If a transaction fails before the COMMIT is reached the database can be rolled back to its state at the start of the transaction. Committing database changes is typically onerous in performance terms.

There appears to be a general move towards a greater number of smaller transactions. The advantage is that the length of time that any locks are held will be shortened. The downside is that it means more commits and hence more resource costs. This is a judgment call. In general, a smaller number of transactions are preferable. An effective commit strategy can be vital for long overnight batch runs, where it is usually preferable to limit the number of commits, for example, to every 100 or 200 iterations of a transaction loop.

Transaction Managers (TM) have become an accepted method of controlling database access and updates. The detailed architecture of such products tends to be a closely guarded secret. The key questions for high-volume systems are how much of an overhead do TMs impose, and just how far does a single TM scale. One of the key features tends to be support for distributed transactions (where multiple databases are to be updated), typically by using a two-phase commit. As the name implies, there are two phases to the commit: the TM issues a prepare command to each database; if none of the databases objects then the TM issues a commit. It follows that there is an overhead of additional messages between the various parties and additional log writes (each party maintains a log of activity). Ideally, two-phase commits should not be used if they are not absolutely necessary. I have seen systems with a single central database that were using two-phase commits, although this is sometimes due to the fact that the relevant ODBC or JDBC driver only supports two-phase commits. In addition, be wary of being too adventurous with distributed transactions; the larger the number of databases involved, the greater the performance degradation is likely to be, even more so if WANs are required to access any of the databases.

7.4.9 File Handling

File access software can affect performance. For example, on UNIX systems there is the choice of the standard buffered file system, raw IO, and direct IO. A standard file system is easy to use but vanilla-flavored versions rarely perform very well at high access rates, particularly on heavy update systems where journaling is used to aid recovery. The use of facilities that minimize the overhead of journaling (e.g., by allowing parallel access to both journal and data) can produce noteworthy performance gains.

Raw IO allows the developer to bypass the file system and use in-house developed file access software. This is not something about which many organizations even think. Raw IO is most likely to be found in a product, particularly one that runs on multiple platforms, such as DBMS software. Raw IO can outperform a standard file system by 20 to 25 percent, although it obviously depends on the implementation.

Direct IO allows the file system to be used to physically access data, but it bypasses the file system buffering and caching techniques. Once again, this is more likely to be used in a product where it is considered that its caching techniques either outperform the file system, or that there is too much overhead in going through both the product's and the file system's caches.

Where some form of cluster file system is being considered on a multinode system it is important to check precisely how the product works to ensure that the mechanisms that are employed to ensure the integrity of the file system are not likely to cause any performance problems. See Chapter 23.

7.4.10 Network Performance

Network resources are precious commodities and they should not be used extravagantly. See Chapter 24 for more detailed information.

- Where possible, reuse network connections.
- Where possible, use a smaller number of larger messages to cut down communication overheads.
- Compress data before sending it, as long as it does not adversely affect CPU performance.
- Cache data locally to reduce traffic.
- Carefully consider the effects of XML on network performance before committing to using it extensively. One closed system was considering it for capturing over 500 readings per second from outstations. The actual data content was modest, ~30 to 40 bytes per reading. The XML version was close to 500 bytes.

7.4.11 Publish and Subscribe

Publish and subscribe mechanisms have become popular, not least because they can allow a loose coupling of applications; the application that is publishing does not need to be aware of the existence of an application that is subscribing to and receiving the data. Extravagant claims are made for the throughput that can be achieved using this technology. Assuming a reasonable design, the level of achievable throughput depends on the need to persist messages (store them on disk) at the subscriber end before they are processed, as part of the means of guaranteeing delivery. For example, if share price changes are being published it is possible that the volume of updates could be on the order of hundreds, possibly even thousands, per second at peak periods. A careful and scalable design may cope with such volumes, but not if all the data has to be persisted to disk at the subscriber end (it is obviously assumed here that the subscriber is interested in all share price changes). The performance of a system where messages are persisted is likely to be significantly inferior, on the order of tens rather than hundreds per second. The design may have to take account of this fact, possibly partitioning the data over multiple publish and subscribe mechanisms, or possibly simply accepting that instances of highly volatile data items, where replacement values may arrive within a second or two, can be "lost" if the subscriber is struggling to keep up.

7.4.12 Gluing Software

The growing use of off-the-shelf software products for discrete elements of an overall system leads to a greater requirement to "glue" products together or to glue bespoke software and product to provide a comparatively seamless interface between them.

File conversions of bulk data are arguably the easiest to handle. I have seen a number of successful hub implementations. A hub in this context accepts data from a source application and passes it on to one or more target applications, performing any necessary transformation of the data in the process. These systems were implemented using simple file transfer or a messaging product, coupled with a parameter-driven software product that performed the necessary pass-through or transformations. The asynchronous bulk nature of such systems means that they seldom cause performance problems. From a performance perspective the key criteria when assessing the suitability of products in this area are (a) their throughput capability, particularly when transformations are required, and (b) their ability to support multiple parallel streams.

The gluing of synchronous online components is the potentially difficult area and it pays to investigate what effects there may be on performance and throughput. The fewest problems are likely to occur where both sides are using the same technology, and one side is acting as a passive server, fielding requests and sending back responses. Greater difficulties are likely to be encountered when both sides are active; that is, they can submit requests to each other. Finally, the worst performers are likely to be those where each side is using a totally different technology; such gluing frequently goes under the titles of "gateway" or "bridge."

7.4.13   Data Replication

There are various ways of replicating data across servers.

- At the database level, the cheapest and frequently the most effective option to maintain a copy of the database on another machine for resilience purposes is to periodically transfer transaction or after image logs from the primary server to the standby server over a network, using the logs to update the standby database.
- At the disk, file system, or file level, disk writes can be replicated at the system level from a primary to a secondary node. This can be done either in software or in hardware. Software-based replication will typically work asynchronously. The infrastructure design needs to account for the overheads of replication on the servers (CPU and memory), the disk subsystems, and the network between the servers. Hardware-based replication, usually found on more sophisticated disk subsystems, can be done synchronously or asynchronously. There are a number of questions that have to be addressed when deciding on the use of synchronous or asynchronous replication. The distance between the disk subsystems may play a factor, particularly on disk remote mirroring where any noticeable latency (say more than two milliseconds) may be totally unacceptable and thus render synchronous working a nonstarter.
- Asynchronous replication will typically need to use part of the disk controller memory cache to identify outstanding blocks that are still to be replicated. The design needs to account for this usage in any cache sizing calculations. Using either synchronous or asynchronous hardware-based replication, allowance needs to be made for disk subsystem overheads plus the bandwidth and network interfaces that are required to support the estimated volume of replication. There are always risks of possible data corruption using either method, plus questions surrounding the ease (or otherwise) with which it can be repaired or worked around.
- Transaction-level software replication that is built into an application or product can add 30 to 50 percent to the overall hardware resource costs, possibly more, and it may significantly increase response times if it is performed synchronously.

7.4.14   Partitioning the Problem

Arguably the single most effective design technique for large systems is to partition the problem so that it can be tackled by parallel tasks that are running on one or more servers. Product vendors have been working on partitioning for some time with some degree of success. If you wish to rely solely on vendor solutions it is important to be confident that they can provide satisfactory performance at the required volumes. The larger the volume is, the more likely it is that pure vendor-based load balancing or partitioning will prove to be unsatisfactory.

To be clear, really successful partitioning depends on effective data segregation. This section illustrates an example of custom partitioning.

About five years ago, the design of a large system in the utilities sector had to support very high data volumes, up to 20 million occurrences of the primary entity and in the region of 400 to 500 million database rows in total. The key processes were batch. On a normal day 5 to 10 computation runs were required to be completed in a six- to eight-hour period where each run would involve reading through most of the database. However, the peak, which occurred twice a year, was extremely onerous, as up to 25 business runs were required within the same time window. The documentation in the earlier stages of the project (under the auspices of a different company) had been based on the use of the SSADM methodology. It was decided to continue with SSADM, which splits the design into two stages, logical and physical. On many projects, time pressures mean that the physical design stage is often limited to crossing out the word "logical," and replacing it with the word "physical"! Such an approach would have been suicidal on this particular project.

Two views were formed: trawling through the database 25 times in such a short time was not feasible; and using a relational database for all data accessing was going to be too expensive. Note that all other operations, such as maintaining and updating the database, could be and were satisfactorily handled by the DBMS, as the volumes were not so onerous. The agreed-upon design solution (see Figure 7.10) was to:

- Scan the database once and extract the information that would be required for all the runs that were required on that day.
- Partition the database (which was feasible — sometimes it is not so easy) so that multiple parallel processes could each scan one partition at a time.
- Build in a mechanism to limit the number of parallel processes to a level with which a given hardware configuration could cope.
- Write the extracted data to flat files (less expensive than a relational database).
- Four to five intermediate processes use the same parallel process concept, all working with flat files.
- When all computations were completed the penultimate process wrote the results back to the relational database.
- The final process, which was not partitioned, sent the summarized results (a modest several thousand rows) to another system.

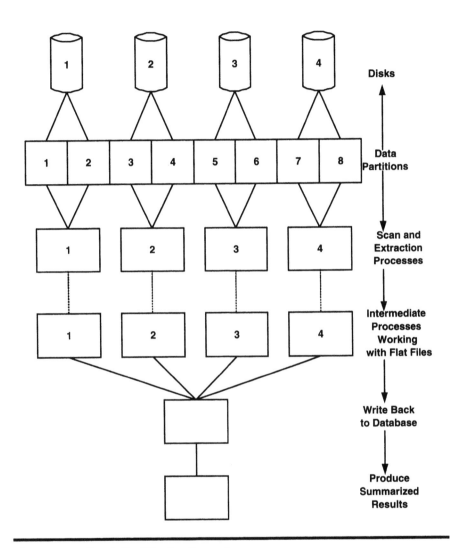

Figure 7.10 Batch Partitioning Example

This framework was agreed upon fairly quickly, in a matter of days, early in the design stage. It did not delay the design, and no additional effort or cost was incurred either during the design or implementation. Performance and scalability targets were met.

7.4.15 Some Basic Hardware Considerations

Here are several basic hardware considerations. More detailed information can be found in the various tasters.

- There are invariably factors at the hardware, operating system, and more particularly at the application level that will affect the performance of a system that runs on a server containing multiple CPUs. As a generalization, with a given aggregate amount of CPU power, a smaller number of faster CPUs will perform better than a larger number of slower CPUs.
- Do not skimp on memory. Object-based systems in particular tend to devour memory. Any excess memory can frequently be used for memory caching, for example, by the file system.
- Despite the best endeavors of vendors to talk up the performance of RAID 5 in comparison to RAID 1, I remain to be convinced. I accept that it is possible to improve RAID 5 write performance by the use of techniques such as staging, but this is likely to be at the expense of memory in a disk controller that could otherwise be used as a cache to improve IO performance. My view is that RAID 5 is fine for read-intensive applications, but it is unsuitable for write-intensive applications.
- Switches, whether used in LANs or SANs, are preferable to hubs from a performance perspective.
- Effective LAN design is hugely important but it sometimes does not get the attention that it warrants. Reliability, resilience, and scalability are the key prerequisites. There is little point in building these features into server configurations if the plumbing is not similarly architected.

7.4.16 Server-Side Batch Processing

There is a tendency to run batch processes in client/server mode where the two elements reside on separate hardware servers. This may not be an issue for processes that handle modest volumes, or for noncrucial tasks. For high-volume, time-critical tasks the overheads of shipping SQL statements and responses across a network, albeit a fast LAN, can be a problem. Although I accept that there are situations where it may be preferable to run in client/server mode, there are often occasions where a batch process can be run on the server, thus eliminating the client/server overheads. I recollect a system where the daily billing run was run in client/server mode, the client-side residing on a PC in an office that was more than 50 miles away from the server, connected by a less-than-desirable corporate network. Running the jobs during normal office hours when the network was at its busiest, supporting large online user populations, exacerbated the situation. As can be imagined, performance was not good. Some general network improvements helped in the short term but the real breakthrough came when the processes were converted to run solely on the server. This is obviously an extreme example but it does help to illustrate the point.

7.4.17 Application Resilience

Although additional hardware may have been configured to provide resilience this is not going to help with problems at the application level, for example, if a process fails or hangs. There are software products that provide facilities that will allow individual processes to be monitored and for failures to be reported. However, taking specific actions on process failures, except for restarting, is not something that a product can do easily. For systems where high availability is crucial, custom code will usually be required to decide on questions such as whether to simply restart the process and attempt the transaction again, or whether to log and remove the offending data or transaction.

7.4.18 Security Implications

Effective security is essential. However, the degree of security that is necessary may come with a price tag. Requirements or recommendations are sometimes almost suffocating, including excessive auditing, complex authorization and access control mechanisms, and encryption of nontext data that would be difficult to make sense of in the first place. I have seen systems where the cost of the hardware would have doubled if all the security recommendations had been implemented. Unfortunately, security is often considered to be "in the price," even though the detailed solution may not be produced until after the price is agreed upon. The preferable approach is that the proposed solution is discussed and agreed upon with the business up front, including the cost of additional hardware and the acceptance of any degraded performance.

7.4.19 Evaluating Design Approaches

Precisely how to divide up processing can require some thought. On one project the team that was designing a subsystem that had to handle a large volume of inbound documents initially decided on a functional pipeline approach (see the top diagram in Figure 7.11).

The elements consisted of basic validation, securing the document, sending a response to sender that it had been received, unzipping documents (if necessary), parsing the document, and finally processing the document. The initial thinking was that each function would reside on a separate server and that a configurable number of instances should be possible to allow each server to handle multiple documents. The issues

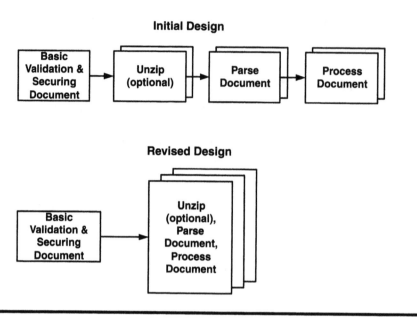

Figure 7.11   Design Approaches

with this approach were that the documents (in their various forms) and their related status information had to be passed along the pipeline from server to server, typically by using a shared file system such as NFS or CIFS. As an agreed-upon design objective was to support a sustained peak of 50 documents per second and it was expected to take 15 to 20 seconds to traverse the pipeline, there was the potential for up to 1000 documents to be in the pipeline, requiring a possible IO rate of several thousand IOs per second. This was not considered to be feasible or indeed desirable. The second potential problem was that it would not necessarily make the best use of the available server capacity. For example, the unzipping server may spend a lot of its time with no work to do.

Taking account of the issues the design was modified so that the main functions of unzipping, parsing, and processing were combined into a single "process" that would run on one server. There were a pool of servers and a configurable number of instances on each server. An instance effectively picked up a document and handled all its processing. This approach drastically reduced the disk IO and network traffic, and it made more effective use of the available capacity.

7.4.20   Something for the Back Pocket

If there is any lack of confidence about an area of the design, or if it is considered that it may need to be redesigned in the future to support higher volumes, it is preferable to have an alternative design in your back pocket, just in case. A simple recent example involved the evaluation of products to provide a data repository for documents. All the products contained many features that were not required, which as a result made it expensive in monetary terms. However, the main concern, given the high volumes that had to be supported, was their performance throughput. It was considered that custom software could be developed at a significantly cheaper cost to provide a better performing, scalable, lightweight solution for quickly storing and retrieving documents. There was some apprehension that the claims for the custom approach may have been unfounded. Successful benchmarking of a prototype provided the necessary degree of confidence. However, the overall design framework was structured in such a way that if the custom software turned out to be unsuccessful it would still be possible to replace it with one of the products with minimum impact on the rest of the design.

7.4.21　Data Migration

This is an unglamorous topic that is seldom accorded the necessary respect, whether it is the development effort required or the performance implications. The volume of data that has to be migrated and the time that is available to complete the migration should dictate the care that is taken over the design from a performance perspective.

The normal data migration is from old to new system. However, I have seen large systems where the solution changed sufficiently between phases to force a data migration. In one particularly severe case, the volume of data precluded any thoughts of a removal of the service for a weekend (or slightly longer) while the migration took place. A more sophisticated drip-feed migration that could take many months to complete had to be considered.

Returning to more typical migrations, I have seen programs that have been developed quickly that managed to migrate three to four customers per second. In one instance, there was a requirement to migrate a customer base of two million over a weekend. At four per second it was going to take close to six days to complete the migration. The main pointers for heavy-duty migration are as follows.

- Where possible, design the migration so that multiple streams can be run in parallel to improve throughput. For designers of new systems this is a case of "do as you would be done by." One of the byproducts of thoughtful data partitioning during system design is that the eventual demise and replacement of the system will be smoother, as the data will be able to be migrated more quickly.

- The use of software products that can transform data in a user-defined manner is frequently attractive, as they minimize the development effort required. Check the throughput capabilities of such products before committing to such an approach.
- Make maximum use of standard loading utilities, for example, relational DB loaders, as they will invariably perform better than quickly developed custom code.
- Where custom code is developed, use any bulk processing performance features. For example, in a relational database make use of bulk writes, minimize the number of commits, and create indexes after the data has been migrated rather than as part of the process.

7.4.22 Backup and Recovery

The time window that is available to perform backups will frequently drive the solution. Where time is limited, it may be possible to run backups asynchronously by copying the data to disk and subsequently writing the copied data to tape in a more leisurely fashion. More sophisticated techniques, such as the use of point-in-time copies can achieve the same end. However, in many systems it is the time taken to restore previously backed up data after a failure or data corruption that is more important, as it is usually the subject of Service Level Agreements (SLAs). Requirements to complete the recovery as quickly as possible may entail a more expensive solution.

Whether synchronous or asynchronous, the time taken to back up or recover will be driven by two factors, bandwidth and parallel streaming. Bandwidth is particularly important for those backup and recovery solutions that run over a production LAN. If a backup is running in the middle of the night when the production LAN is lightly loaded it may be acceptable to use this LAN. However, if crucial production work is running at the same time as the backup, the LAN may well become a bottleneck and a separate, dedicated backup LAN(s) may be required to ensure satisfactory performance.

Running parallel streams can shorten the time taken to complete backup or recovery. This can be achieved by running multiple backups of different file systems or DB table spaces alongside each other, or by making use of the features in certain products that allow a single backup/recovery to read/write in parallel across an array of tapes. To drive the tapes at maximum speed: ensure that there are sufficient tape controllers (in lieu of any better information allow one controller per two tape drives), use available data compression techniques, and once again, in lieu of any better information, allow 0.5 CPU per tape drive in the server that is running the backup/recovery software.

7.4.23 Archiving

Archiving is probably the number one target for de-scoping on development projects. I have lost track of the number of projects that I have seen where it is replanned for the current release + 1. From a technical perspective, the infrastructure designers should be wary that the business, and even members of the project team, might assume that the necessary infrastructure is in place to implement archiving, even though the development has been deferred.

Application-aware archiving is far from straightforward to develop, and it can be time consuming to run on large systems that run into hundreds of gigabytes, or even several terabytes. There are techniques such as partitioning databases over time where an entire partition can be archived at one point in time. This is fine if time is the only archiving criterion, but frequently it is not.

HSM (Hierarchical Storage Management) systems that handle nondatabase files have been around in various guises for over 20 years and are relatively mature. Once again, they tend to work on a time basis, transferring files across multiple hierarchy layers, usually ending up on a cheap but slower medium such as optical disk or tape. When calculating the number of drives in the tape library or jukebox it is important to make allowances for retrievals as well as archiving, and drives will also be required for management tasks (e.g., copying media for off-site storage) or as part of a renewal cycle. The trend towards the use of such media may be bucked by improvements in disk technology that see the gradual introduction of cost-effective, high-capacity drives (180 GB at the time of this writing although even larger drives will eventually appear). It is important to assess when archiving can be treated as backup. For example, some application products that contain archiving features will copy new data to the archive as soon as it arrives in the system. Where possible, it is obviously preferable not to archive and back up the same data.

Where there is a hot disaster-recovery system that data is replicated to, archiving presents a serious challenge; products typically do not support coherent archiving across two sites.

7.5 CODING AND TESTING

A carefully thought-through design can sometimes be undermined by thoughtless coding and implementation. It pays for the designers to pass on useful information that they have gleaned, or any general experience, to the developers. I am a fan of performance guidelines that can, if preferred, form part of the general coding guidelines. I have seen several excellent examples of guidelines for developing efficient DB applications. The secret is to keep them short and punchy.

Time pressures may prevent performance from being comprehensively addressed during this stage. One solution is to concentrate on the main bread and butter functions. In many systems there are usually a modest number of functions that account for the majority of the overall usage. Comprehensive reviews and early performance testing will pay dividends. Coding reviews should include performance aspects, such as adherence to general design principles and to coding guidelines. Early testing is imperative for key functions to provide crucial feedback on both the design and coding. Results can be used to refine any performance model.

7.6   SUMMARY

The key points in the area of design are to:

- Avoid the temptation to overengineer the solution. In particular, technologies that have not been costed into the solution should not be used.
- Check out vendor claims on scalability. The larger the system the less likely you will be able to rely solely on vendors to provide the necessary scalability.
- Appreciate that several days spent at the beginning of the design stage assessing the possible approaches to performance and scalability, and getting the basic design infrastructure right, can frequently save much heartache and cost.
- Effective design requires
  - An understanding of the advantages and disadvantages of the technologies that are being used
  - The need for balanced infrastructures to avoid unnecessary bottlenecks
  - The advantages that can be gained from partitioning the overall problem into smaller, more manageable chunks
- Early testing of key transactions is essential to identify potential performance issues as soon as possible.

8

AWARENESS OF QUEUES

8.1 ABSTRACT

Delays that are caused by the sharing of hardware and software resources can greatly affect performance if they are not addressed adequately during development. Before the reader is frightened off by the thought of lots of complex mathematical formulae let me say that this chapter is a queueing theory free zone. There are plenty of books that go into great detail on the subject for those who have a particular interest in the subject. The simple objective here is to make the reader aware of queues and their effect on performance, particularly a network of queues. Where time permits, modeling techniques, using analytic or simulation modeling tools, can be useful in identifying and understanding delays that are attributable to queueing.

8.2 QUEUES

Queues form wherever a resource is shared. A resource can be a piece of hardware (e.g., a CPU, a disk, or a network link), or it can be a software component (e.g., a process, a thread, or a procedure). Shared resources may not be self-contained. They may make use of other resources, which are in their turn shared. Therefore, a delay in accessing one resource may well have a knock-on effect in other resources.

Let us start with a simple example to illustrate the potential effect of queues. In Figure 8.1 there is a single software service P. To make the example easier to explain it is assumed that it runs alone on its own dedicated hardware server. It executes instructions on the CPU and reads/writes to three disks. There are four hardware resources: the CPU (a uniprocessor) and the three disks. Each invocation of P uses 150 ms of CPU time and performs 5 IOs on each disk, each IO having an average

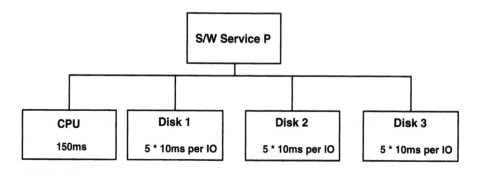

Figure 8.1   Simple Example of a Software Service

Table 8.1   Software Service P Under Various Load Conditions

CPU	Copies of P	Invocations of P (sec)	Est. Mean Time/Invocation (sec)	CPU Util. (%)	Avg. Disk Util. (%)
Uniprocessor	1	3	0.42	45	15
	2	4	0.38	60	20
	3	6	0.52	90	30
Double Speed	3	6	0.31	45	30
	4	8	0.36	60	40
	5	10	0.44	75	50
	6	12	0.60	90	60

service time of 10 ms. Therefore, the total disk service time is also 150 ms (5 × 10 × 3).

Table 8.1 illustrates various scenarios in the use of software service P. It is assumed that requests to use P can arrive randomly.

One invocation of P will have a service time of 300 ms (150 ms CPU and 150 ms disk IO). With a single instance of P the only queueing is to use P itself. Once processing gets underway, there is no subsequent queueing for the CPU or the disks. Note that in the real world this is not quite true, as there will be system tasks vying for use of the CPU and disks, but it serves our purpose for the sake of clarity.

This single instance of P can only support 3 invocations per second (3 × 300 ms) although the overall CPU and disk usage is moderate at this rate, 45 percent utilization for the CPU and 15 percent for each disk. The single-threaded nature of P prevents any higher rate from being achieved.

For example, the CPU cannot be used when disk IOs are being performed, and vice versa.

A higher rate of invocation can only be supported if it is possible to have multiple instances of P that can operate in parallel. This will allow us to exploit the available hardware capacity better, reaching six invocations per second with three parallel instances, before the CPU eventually runs out of steam and prevents any higher throughput from being achieved. The average disk device utilization is still reasonable at 45 percent.

If the CPU were to be upgraded to double its speed, it would only be using 75 ms per invocation rather than 150 ms, and it would then be possible to reach 12 invocations per second with six instances of P. At this point both the higher-speed CPU is running out of steam again and the disk utilization is also starting to become a problem. Even higher call rates would only be possible by deploying more CPU horsepower (a faster CPU or alternatively multiple CPUs), spreading the disk load over a larger number of devices, and by increasing the instances of P.

In summary, the software service P is the bottleneck initially as there is only a single instance. It is only by having multiple instances that the available hardware capacity can be exploited more effectively.

Moving on to a slightly more complex example, Figure 8.2 shows a mixture of hardware and intercommunicating software resources. There are three software services, A, B, and C. Each service performs some local processing by using the hardware resources CPU and disk, and each calls another software service Y to perform a common service. Service Y is similar in that it performs local processing and makes use of service Z. Service Z is also called by service C. Each software service and each hardware resource is a queueing point. If it is assumed that Y and Z are both single instances, it can be seen that unless they use a negligible amount of hardware resources they may well become bottlenecks. Pressure on Z will affect the time spent in Y, which in turn will affect the time spent in the top layer services A, B, and C. This percolation of delays up the hierarchy is often a reason for the inability of a software design to exploit hardware resources fully.

8.3 LOCKS

Apart from queues the other major item of delay is the software lock. Locks are mostly used to protect the data integrity of a part of the system. They typically ensure that only one caller can use part or all of a service or resource at a time, as the presence of multiple callers operating in parallel would lead to data corruption/loss of integrity. Databases are examples of software products where locks are used. Assessing the

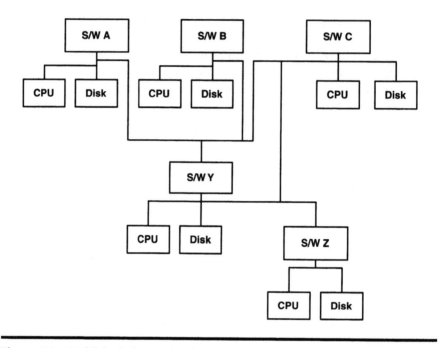

Figure 8.2 Multiple Software Services Example

potential impact of a lock on performance can be difficult without detailed information on the rate at which lock requests are likely to be made and the length of time that the lock is held. I prefer to concentrate on reducing the number of locks that are necessary by ensuring that the design avoids sharing a resource wherever possible. Naturally, there may be low-level software locks that are outside your control.

8.4 TACKLING DELAYS

The most effective way to handle queues is to pre-empt them as much as possible by the use of solid design techniques. Data partitioning and the use of multiple software instances, whether processes or threads, are fundamental techniques for minimizing software queues. Hardware queues can be minimized by ensuring that resources are not used wantonly, typically by using the performance guidelines in any given area, and by using the appropriate utilization thresholds to avoid any significant queueing.

8.5 ANALYTIC AND SIMULATION MODELING TOOLS

The advantages of modeling techniques during design are that they can highlight queues and their effects on performance. They were extremely popular in the 1980s and early to mid-1990s when systems were more straightforward, with only one or two tiers, and there was sufficient time to create and run the models.

Analytic models use queueing theory equations to estimate performance whereas simulation models view a system as progressing through time from one event to another. Both analytic and simulation models can be time consuming to create. In the case of analytic models there is the problem of obtaining sufficiently detailed performance metrics to populate the model. During design this may have to come from focused in-house benchmarks. The term "angiotrace" is used to convey the ability to capture detailed trace data for a transaction across threads, processes, and servers. I have yet to see this seemingly attractive facility deployed on a typical commercial system. Wherever the metrics come from, the key point is that the level of detail in an analytic model is determined by the granularity of the performance metrics; process level metrics preclude modeling at the procedure level. The obvious danger is that if the modeling level is too high queues that form at a lower level will not be detected. In the case of simulation models, the development of a complex model showing the individual paths of a transaction through the system will frequently be even more time consuming to develop unless pre-built components are available from the vendor to lighten the task.

Each approach has its advantages and disadvantages. The analytic approach is typically quicker, but it may be less accurate as assumptions have to be used in detailed areas such as handling passive resources, for example, memory or locks, priorities, and interrupts. In my experience, analytic modeling tended to be favored for commercial systems and simulation techniques were more popular for designing networks and for low-level hardware and software design.

The ultimate question is whether there is time during the design stage to use these techniques. I am far from being a typical performance person but with the increasing pressure on the design stage I have only managed to build one (analytic) model in the last four years. Perhaps you may be in a luckier position.

8.6 ALTERNATIVE APPROACHES

The dilemma is what to do if there is insufficient time for detailed modeling. I have seen "quick" models that have been produced where lots of assumptions were made in lieu of any concrete information. This approach is not recommended, as it is extremely risky. An alternative method is to limit any detailed modeling or queueing calculations to that part of the system about which you are most concerned. The obvious danger here is that unless the subsystem being modeled is fairly self-contained the results may be unsound.

With respect to software products, modeling is virtually impossible unless the product vendor provides a model, which is rare, or where the design is simple enough to grasp and it is possible to attempt it with the help of the output of benchmarks.

As I seldom have the luxury of being able to model in detail, I tend to stick with my high-level sizing approach from the bid or feasibility stage, using the latest information to refine the metrics and the utilization thresholds that I use to address queueing indirectly (see Chapter 5). I rely on solid design techniques to minimize the likelihood of any significant queueing, using focused benchmarks to provide additional information in any areas of concern. Where necessary, I perform some rudimentary queueing theory calculations, typically using spreadsheets.

8.7 SUMMARY

The key points are that:

- It is important to understand where queues are likely to form.
- Software queues are invariably more troublesome than hardware queues.
- Sound design techniques can help to minimize queues.
- Modeling tools can be useful if there is time to make effective use of them.

9

NONFUNCTIONAL ACCEPTANCE

9.1 ABSTRACT

There are various forms of testing that come under this banner. Stress testing is necessary to confirm that the application will meet the performance targets under the required peak load conditions. If addressed comprehensively, it can require significant effort to prepare and run the tests. This can be an issue for those projects where the development is squeezed into a relatively short space of time and there is little time left for stress testing. The objective of soak testing, which follows stress testing, is to detect problems such as memory leaks that can occur when the application has been running continuously for many hours, or possibly days. Operational-readiness testing is vitally important to ensure that all features function correctly, for example, failing the software over to a standby node, remote mirroring, and backup and recovery.

9.2 THE ISSUES

Although technologies change and the established testing tool vendors have to play catch-up on occasion, the testing tool market is relatively mature in the provision of functional, nonfunctional, and test management products. The frequent sales pitch with respect to performance testing is not to wait until the stress testing stage but to commence it during development. Needless to say the vendors frequently have products that will assist in this early testing process. It should be obvious from the rest of this book that I am a keen adherent of pre-empting problems, and that I strongly endorse the idea of early testing. However, the gradual compression over recent years of the time available for the design, code, and unit test stages is making it ever more difficult to attempt any performance testing. For those projects where there is sufficient time, the use of tools that allow performance testing at the unit test stage is to be encouraged, particularly for the key transactions.

This problem of a lack of time is even extending itself to the common load or stress test that is carried out before the system goes into production. I have seen two large projects where the time that was originally allocated for stress testing disappeared totally. On the first occasion the time was eaten up by the need to modify and test significant changes to the technical infrastructure that were required late in the project, plus problems were encountered with the functional testing. On the second occasion it was quite simply the aggressive compression of the design and coding phases. It may seem that the obvious answer in these situations would have been to start stress testing earlier. In fact, this did happen. However, both systems simply hit the insuperable problem of code that was not stable enough to withstand stress testing, and it turned out to be mostly unproductive. There was no question of delaying the launch date in either case. This exacerbated the problem, as an underlying assumption had been that both systems would use the production environment for stress testing. The testing was curtailed so that operational-readiness testing could be completed. Ideas about stress testing after the launch date, but before the user population had been ramped up to the full production numbers, were faced with logistical problems such as getting time on the production environment — "it is available for testing from midnight Saturday to 2 A.M. Sunday morning," and finding the necessary disk space to load the stress test databases and file systems.

9.3   STRESS TESTING

Chapter 3 on Benchmarks, which includes advice on the set-up and running of tests, supplements the information in this section.

9.3.1   Scope and Logistics

In light of the above comments, and the fact that stress testing can take significant effort to prepare and run, the first question has to be, "Is it strictly necessary?" This is obviously a judgment call. I have seen several software-only procurements where the client was absolutely insistent that stress testing be carried out, even though mature and proven application software products were being deployed. Although it is accepted that there are occasions when a degree of uncertainty may surround particular customizations, these procurements were simply adopting the checkbox approach without really thinking through the need.

If stress testing is required, can its scope be limited to the area of maximum concern? Once again, it is accepted that one part of the system may affect the performance of another part and therefore it would be wise to cover all parts. However, it is a question of risk versus the cost of comprehensive testing, versus the possibility of failing to complete the testing.

The other key questions surround what happens if the time available for stress testing is squeezed. Can the launch date be delayed? If not, can stress testing be continued after the launch? Is there a suitable environment to carry out any post-launch testing? Limited access to the production environment may not be satisfactory, as it frequently happens that a test may quickly fail with a code or data problem and it is not possible to rectify it in the allotted time slot. A dedicated performance environment would be preferable although it is likely to be prohibitively expensive unless it is acceptable to run tests on a limited subset of hardware. An alternative approach may be to arrange to use a hardware vendor's benchmarking center although there will be a cost involved, and there may be problems in replicating the production infrastructure, particularly in cases where hardware from a range of vendors is employed.

9.3.2 Planning

Thorough planning is absolutely essential. Arguably, the secrets of success are (a) the understanding of how much effort is required in the preparation and running of stress tests, and (b) the need to be brutal when deciding on the test scenarios. There is a general tendency to be optimistic and overestimate what can be achieved.

9.3.3 Tools

With the possible exception of batch testing and low user population online testing some form of automation will be required to drive the tests. Online tests that use real people sitting at real devices are often difficult to orchestrate, and even more difficult to repeat (as stress tests invariably have to be). In some instances it may be possible to develop an in-house test harness, particularly for batch or messaging systems. However, for user-based online systems of any size it is likely that a stress-testing product will be required. None of the tools in this area are absolutely perfect but typically they are eminently capable of doing a satisfactory job. There are many criteria that should be used to assess the suitability of a stress-testing tool, but I limit my observations to particularly notable items.

■ It is important to understand precisely what elements the tool is simulating, and importantly, what it is not covering. A tool for a fat client/server system will typically send and receive SQL traffic. It will not reflect the vast majority of the processing on the PC. Similarly, on a system with a Web interface a tool may be mainly working at the HTTP traffic level, thus not reflecting browser-run Java or JavaScript code.

■ Look for tools that simplify the capture of user scripts that will be used in the test and contain comprehensive and flexible methods of customizing these scripts. One important customization is the ability to vary the data that is submitted every time a captured script is used to submit a user request. It will not be very representative if each time that a captured transaction is replayed it uses the same customer ID or account number.

■ It should be possible to set up a test that reflects a representative mix of transactions, usually by creating discrete workloads from one or more scripts, and assigning a specified number of simulated users to each workload. For example, a call center test may reflect pools of agents, where each pool is handling a different type of call, such as general queries, payments, and new business. It should be possible to define the frequency with which a user in a specified workload submits transactions by specifying some form of pacing or think-type time.

■ Many tests require a warm-up period, for example, while all users log on to the system. Facilities that allow "users" to log on in tranches, but then wait until all users have logged on before the test proper is allowed to commence, are useful.

■ Many people take the approach that functional testing has been completed by this stage and that stress and soak testing can therefore ignore functionality and simply concentrate on performance. I disagree with this view, having seen examples of functional problems that only came to light under a certain load, and therefore they were not found during functional testing. It is preferable that some form of nominal validation should be performed on each response to check that it is reasonable. It may be that a simple check that the right sort of page has been returned is sufficient. A variation of this requirement is that the tool should wait for a response to a specific simulated user before submitting another request from that same user. There are some tools that simply plow on regardless!

■ Where there are hundreds or even thousands of simulated users it is important that the hardware that is driving the test, submitting requests, and receiving server responses does not become a bottleneck. Lack of memory is a frequent culprit although CPU power and network interface capacity can also be causes. This comment is equally applicable to home-built harnesses. Reasonable tools will provide facilities to allow multiple machines to act as test drivers, all being controlled by a master process, which could reside on a standard PC or laptop.

■ If some stress testing is started early in the overall testing phase there is the danger that the user interface or general design may be changed sufficiently that it is necessary to recapture scripts and to reapply any customizations. Any features that help to minimize the reworking of customizations would be very helpful.

■ The analysis of test results, whether the test was successful or not, can be time consuming. It is usually not sufficient just to analyze the response times that a tool will readily collect. It is usually necessary to scrutinize the various hardware and software performance metrics from each hardware server in the system to understand the general performance characteristics, any bottlenecks, and the potential scalability of the system. Some vendors have put significant effort into collecting performance metrics from the various hardware and software platforms during the test. For example, there may be firewall statistics, Windows 2000 metrics for the Web servers, UNIX metrics for the application and DB servers, and detailed metrics from the DBMS product. Graphs of specified items can be created, for example, throughput versus DB server CPU utilization. These features can significantly reduce the effort that is required to fully analyze the test results.

■ Some tools offer a "quicker" method of testing. They concentrate on allowing changes to be made very quickly to key drivers such as the user population, transaction rate per second, and user thinking/typing times. The objective is to quickly ramp up the load to the point where bottlenecks are encountered. This type of tool can be useful where time is limited, as they can quickly home in on bottlenecks. Their disadvantage is that they lack some of the features that are necessary for comprehensive testing, and they may present a misleading picture of performance and the points at which degradation occurs. It is ultimately a judgment call as to which type of tool is more appropriate in a given situation.

9.3.4 Workloads

The workloads that comprise a stress test should strike a balance between the assumed representative mix of transactions and the effort that is required to set up that mix. I have seen tests at either end of the spectrum: small, totally unrepresentative mixes of one to three transactions where there was either insufficient time or a general unwillingness to put adequate effort in, and fully representative transaction mixes that took too long to set up and to maintain. The most frequently used transactions should be at the head of the queue, followed by any other transactions that are particularly important to the business, followed by any transactions over which you have particular concerns. As a very rough rule of thumb, on a high-volume system, transactions that have a rate of less than one every five seconds should be omitted unless there are other reasons for their inclusion. There is a tendency for lengthy debates on which transactions should be included. I deliberately used the phrase "assumed representative mix" above because I have seen many systems where the actual use of the system differed significantly from the views of the business and the project team, particularly for online systems. I have observed several call center systems where the actual usage was radically different from the profiles of calls that had been agreed upon during development. Users may avoid specific transactions, for myriad reasons, for example, unsatisfactory performance from their perspective (although it may seem satisfactory to you), difficult or unwieldy to use, or not particularly useful. There is no magic answer here; these are often functional issues that should have been sorted out during the requirements stage. From a testing viewpoint, do not waste too much time fruitlessly arguing over the transaction mix.

The usual objective in a test is to reflect the estimated peak activity. This may be a daily, weekly, or, less likely, a monthly peak. I have come across extremely fanciful projected peaks for Internet-based systems where estimated peaks are multiplied by some factor (ten, say) to make allowances for a site launch where the world descends on you and will never return if performance is unsatisfactory or nonexistent. The fear that is stoked up about a possible failure of service is usually contrary to the budget that is available for hardware to support this mass invasion. If the business case and budget cater for extraordinary usage then the estimated peak should already account for that usage. There should be no reason to multiply by large factors to cater for a solitary spike. It is prudent to run a number of test iterations where the load is gradually ramped up, say from average to peak usage, to understand how the system performs and behaves as the load increases.

9.3.5 Data

The main objective is to ensure that there are sufficient unique instances of individual data items, ideally representative of the actual system, to avoid the likelihood that all items end up in a memory cache and help to produce excellent response times that are unlikely to be achieved in the production system. However, the setting up of representative databases or file systems where there is no existing data to work with, possibly hundreds of gigabytes on a large system, can be a very time-consuming and often infeasible exercise. As a rough rule of thumb, test databases that are 25 to 30 percent of the production size are usually sufficient to ensure a reasonable approximation in performance. It is usually large enough to highlight any poor access techniques, such as the use of whole or partial table scans (heavy-duty sequential access) where indexed access would provide better performance. The disadvantage of using a reduced database is that it may prevent an understanding of the effect on performance of increased database sizes.

9.3.6 Test Environment

The ideal environment is one that mirrors the production environment. For applications that will run on new hardware, it may be possible to use the production environment before the launch date. Subsequent stress tests for V2 and the like may not be able to use the production environment. A frequently used alternative is to rent a similar facility at a vendor's benchmarking center. Another, albeit less ideal, option is to use a smaller, but more readily available environment. If this latter approach is adopted, consideration should be given to scaling down the stress test in line with the scaling down of the hardware in an attempt to produce a mini-environment that is more likely to identify some of the problems that will be found in the production environment. For example, if the size of the database server is the main problem and it is only possible to have a four-CPU server rather than an eight-CPU server, it would be preferable to reduce the memory and disks on the database server by half as well. Similarly, the overall capacity on the rest of the environment should be halved, for example, firewalls, Web servers, application servers, and network bandwidth. Naturally, the size of the stress test will be similarly reduced. This is obviously not ideal but it may constitute a pragmatic approach.

9.3.7 Preparation

As discussed earlier, the largest tasks are (a) data creation and either (b) the capture and customization of scripts, where a stress-testing tool is being used or (c) the development of test harnesses where a proprietary tool is not being used. It is imperative that adequate resources are available in a timely manner to address these tasks. If early versions of code are to be performance tested, time should be set aside to consider how to minimize the reworking of scripts, particularly their customization, to handle future versions where the input formats have changed.

Where a testing tool is being used for the first time it is sensible to set up and run a mini-pilot at the earliest opportunity to ensure that the tool does precisely what you expect it to on your system.

Ensure that the code is ready for performance testing. Do not shoot yourself in the foot. Check that traces, extraneous logging, and any other debugging aids are removed. Wherever possible, perform early testing on key transactions to identify and fix obvious performance problems. This should ideally be done during coding and unit testing, or alternatively in parallel with integration testing.

Ensure that the disk subsystem is set up sensibly, as if it were the actual production environment. For example, where dedicated disks or arrays are required for performance reasons, such as the DB after images log, make sure that this is done.

Ensure that all necessary performance monitors are available and working.

9.3.8 Test Logistics

Decide on any required actions between tests. Examples may include:

- Ensuring that memory caches are flushed to avoid the next test from achieving unrepresentative performance;
- Reloading software components to avoid any benefits that may accrue from them being in a warm state;
- Reboot servers between tests.

Decide on the need for a warm-up period to avoid unrepresentative overheads. For example, it is unlikely that 1000 users will log on at the same time and immediately start a peak period of activity. It would be more realistic to have the majority logging on gradually during the warm-up period and the test proper starting when the log-ons are completed. Note that if wholesale logging on at start of day, or after a failure, is considered to be a potential problem then consider a separate log-on test to understand what level of concurrency the system can support.

The length of the test should be long enough to ensure that any effects that may arise from repeated use can be seen. As a rough rule of thumb, the length of the test proper should be in the range of 10 to 60 minutes.

Consider how to minimize the time gap between tests, which is attributable to restoring the database to its original state. For small- to medium-sized systems it may be satisfactory to simply restore the data from a backup. This may be inappropriate for large databases where it may be necessary to think up more sophisticated software-driven methods.

9.3.9 Analyzing Results

The key indicators are response times, or elapsed times for batch work, and throughput. Irrespective of the comparative success or failure of a specific test, it is prudent to inspect the performance metrics for the key hardware and software components of the system to assess any actual or potential bottlenecks. For example, a simple check of the utilizations of major hardware components such as CPU, disk, memory, and network will reveal any high figures that may indicate a potential problem. This is where tools that contain comprehensive performance metric collection and reporting are advantageous, as they remove the need for onerous manual collection and analysis.

It is often possible to tell after a couple of tests just what the hardware is capable of supporting without upgrades or improvements to the software. However, it is extremely difficult to use the metrics to assess where and when software queues or locks may become a problem. Ramping up the transaction rate is usually the only way to uncover them.

Where time permits, it is recommended that the transaction rate be ramped up beyond the perceived peak load that has to be supported to understand just what can be supported on the platform and what component(s) break first. There are often supplementary "what if" questions that people wish to ask, such as, "If I use a bigger database server how much more throughput can I support." Modeling tools can help here although the application code may need to be instrumented to provide sufficiently detailed metrics to populate the model. Alternatively, approximate answers can be sometimes obtained through detailed analysis of the available metrics and the use of simple spreadsheets.

9.4 SOAK TESTING

The objective of soak testing is to ensure that the system can run for hours or days at a time without developing creeping faults that lead to significant performance degradation or, in the worst case, for the system to hang or crash. The length of a soak test will depend on the type of system and the business requirements. Safety-critical systems are the most important in this respect, where soak tests may last weeks or even months. Commercial systems are typically less stringent and despite what the client may prefer, it may be acceptable to reboot the system at a quiet period once a week or even once a day until a problem is resolved. I have seen one totally inappropriate ITT for a commercial system that did not appear to have any significant availability requirements but mandated soak testing of one week. If the system failed to last a week it had to resolve the problem and start the soak test again.

Ideally, the scripts and data that were used for stress testing can be used for soak testing but it is set up so that it simply cycles around the scripts for the desired length of time. One possible problem with this approach is that any database inserts, for example, new customer, may fail when they are attempted again. A solution is to remove transactions that perform database inserts or deletes from the scripts.

9.5 OPERATIONAL-READINESS TESTING

Time has to be made available to ensure that the system is ready to go into production, even if that ultimately means that any stress and soak testing running on the production environment have to be curtailed in order to meet an immovable launch date. The tasks that have to be undertaken will depend on the system but they may include:

- Backup/recovery procedures
- Cluster fail-over (within site)
- Fail-over to remote site
- Log shipping (database after images) to remote server
- Remote mirroring
- System management software
- Overnight management tasks

9.6 SUMMARY

The key points from this chapter are:

- Decide if stress testing is necessary; sometimes it is not.
- Be pragmatic about the scope of any stress testing, bearing in mind the time that may be available.
- The key to success is thorough planning.
- Do not underestimate the effort required to set up and run stress tests.
- Do not spend too much time debating the precise workload mix; there is a strong possibility that the actual mix will differ.
- Stress testing tools are usually mandatory. Tools that can assist in analyzing the results are particularly useful.

10

POST-PRODUCTION

10.1 ABSTRACT

Capacity management is a mature and well-understood activity that has been in existence for over 20 years. The main change over the last 10 years has been the large increase in the overall size of technical infrastructures, and in the number of hardware servers that have to be covered. The approach that is adopted by an organization depends on the human resources that are available. In all but the larger organizations, where dedicated resources may be available, it will be a subset of the comprehensive approach that is advocated in books and papers on the subject. This chapter summarizes the comprehensive approach and discusses a minimalist, exception-based approach.

10.2 INTRODUCTION

It is usual to keep a close watch on the performance of a new application during the first three to four months of live running. This period typically corresponds to the warranty period for those applications that have been provided by software vendors. At this point it will become a standard production system that will come under the auspices of the Capacity Management (CM) function. As CM is a mature area, discussion is limited to a brief summary and noteworthy observations.

The approach to CM will depend on the human resources that are available. Small-to-medium organizations are unlikely to be able to afford a full-time resource, and because of this they tend to react to problems rather than to proactively monitor performance. Large organizations that do have a full-time resource(s) have been finding it more difficult to cope in recent years. They have probably moved from the relative comfort of looking after a modest number of hardware servers, to the challenge of covering possibly scores of hardware servers. The general requirement

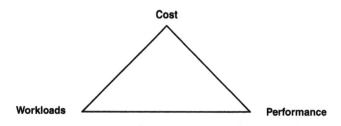

Figure 10.1 Capacity Management Factors

for all sizes of organizations is to minimize the effort required to monitor all the servers and at the same time to increase the effectiveness of that monitoring. This requires as much automation as possible and the adoption of an exception-based approach to performance monitoring and tuning. Let us start by summarizing the comprehensive approach to CM, and then look at approaches to minimizing the effort.

10.3 CLASSIC CAPACITY MANAGEMENT

The succinct objective of capacity management is to achieve and maintain satisfactory service levels in a timely manner, and at an affordable cost, as Figure 10.1 shows.

Figure 10.2 illustrates an example of a full-blown capacity management system. Application sizing has already been covered and it is omitted from this section.

10.3.1 Performance Monitoring/Reporting

The objective is to obtain early warning of actual or potential performance problems in the production system. Techniques vary but the preferred approach is to employ exception reporting to highlight individual instances where agreed-upon performance thresholds are exceeded, and to constrain any detailed reporting to (say) monthly. Thresholds typically include:

- Utilization of major hardware components,
- Availability of major hardware and software components, and
- Response times/batch turnaround times.

Automation is the key to handling large volumes of data from multiple servers. There are mature system management tools that will collect metrics from individual servers and store them on a central CM database, from where sophisticated reports can be produced. In addition, alerts can be raised when specified thresholds are exceeded.

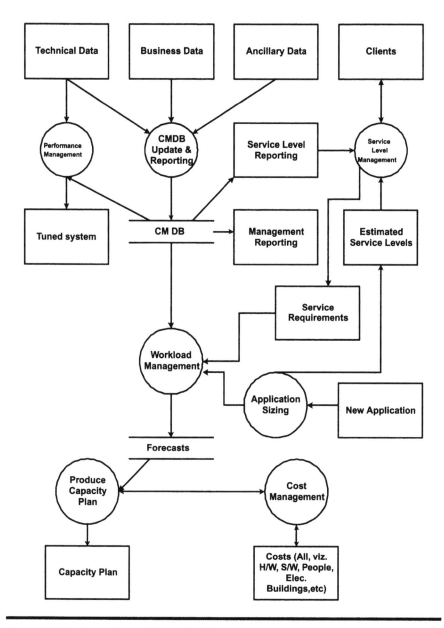

Figure 10.2 Overview of Capacity Management

The main issues that surround performance monitoring and reporting are the relative lack of granularity of the metrics. Although it is straightforward to obtain global-level information (e.g., total CPU usage on a server), it is frequently difficult to split that usage down to the transaction level. This is largely due to deficiencies in the monitoring tools. The problem was less pronounced in the 1970s and 1980s when software was largely bespoke; that is, it was easier to instrument the application, and the general monitoring facilities that were provided by mainframe and minicomputer vendors were generally superior to current offerings. The general move over the last ten to fifteen years towards the use of development toolsets and database management systems has made it significantly more difficult to provide any effective breakdown of resource usage. Useful detailed metrics can be provided by (say) a DBMS but they tend to be from the perspective of the DBMS, not from a transaction perspective. The capture of response times has always been problematic. Once again, some proprietary systems have the ability to capture response times within the host server, but not typically end-to-end. This particular problem can be addressed by software, often from a testing-tool vendor, submitting simulated transactions and capturing the response times. This approach is discussed later in the minimalist approach.

10.3.2   Workload Management

This subject is primarily concerned with breaking a system down into discrete workloads such as applications or business areas, and understanding the characteristics of these workloads with respect to their transaction load, including peaks, and the effects of working practices and particular events on the transaction load. Transaction loads are mapped onto key business drivers where it is sensible to do so (e.g., volume of new business or size of customer base), to aid the analysis of the overall application costs and to help justify any necessary hardware upgrades.

The total hardware resource usage that is attributable to a workload is broken down into its component parts to provide resource profiles, either at the application or transaction level. Resource profiles contain information on the amount of hardware capacity that is consumed, for example, CPU, disk, memory, and network bandwidth. See Section 5.4 for more detailed information. Once again, the problem of metric granularity can constrain this construction of resource profiles.

Finally, data volumes are broken down, where feasible, by workload.

The outputs from this process, viz. the transaction loads, resource profiles, and data volumes, provide the basic ingredients for forecasting exercises that may be carried out quarterly, biannually, or possibly annually. The inputs to these exercises are derived from business forecasts, and by discussions with IT and business people to understand the effect of changes and new applications that are due to be implemented during the forecast period. Spreadsheets, albeit potentially complex, can be used to forecast future usage and projected hardware utilizations.

10.3.3 Capacity Planning

The objective of capacity planning is to forecast the effect of changes in usage over the planning horizon on the existing hardware capacity, and on performance. The major deliverable is typically a list of costed recommendations for hardware upgrades.

There are several techniques that can be used. The simplest and quickest approach is to use trending. The obvious problem with this approach, if used blindly, is that it fails to take account of step changes in business volumes or radical changes in functionality. A better approach, where feasible, is to use the output from the latest forecasting exercise, as described above in Section 10.3.2, Workload Management.

During the 1980s and early 1990s analytic modeling tools were popular as capacity planning aids. The tools are used to construct a baseline model(s) of current usage. What-if questions on projected future usage can then be quickly and easily composed, and the model will calculate hardware utilizations and response times. These tools were popular, in part, because in the majority of cases the performance metrics were typically of the right granularity and the scope of a model was limited to a single server, which obviously simplified the whole process. Since the early 1990s this type of tool has gradually declined in popularity. The reasons for the decline are twofold: the unsatisfactory granularity of performance metrics, as previously explained, and the advent of multitier and distributed applications that can make modeling a much more complex task, which some of the original tools find difficult to support. Nevertheless there are some modeling tools that have moved with the times, and can be extremely useful.

10.3.4 Service Level Management

In many organizations this area is addressed as a separate subject, outside the scope of CM. The scope of service levels will vary depending on the requirements, but they will typically include system responsiveness (response times and batch turnaround times), meeting deadlines (e.g., the output of a daily billing run to be produced by 6 A.M.), help desk performance, system availability, and the time taken to repair software problems.

In my pedantic mind I view service levels as being either agreements (SLAs) or simply objectives (SLOs). I consider that agreements should be binding to be effective, and this means that there should be financial penalties to ensure that they have teeth. Where there are no financial penalties, typically when the provider and the recipient of service are part of the same organization, I prefer to call them objectives. Where there are financial penalties I would go one step further than many others, recommending that there should be financial penalties on both sides. Typically it is only the service provider who is liable, but in my view the client can be equally responsible for problems, for example, higher volumes or peaks than agreed upon, inadequate acceptance testing of new releases, and requests for additional online time without adequate notice that affects overnight processing and management tasks leading to online service being late starting the next day. The achieved service levels during such problem periods are normally simply excluded from any service-level calculations. As it is quite possible that the provider may suffer financially (e.g., there may be knock-on effects that affect the service that is provided to other clients), in an equitable system both sides should be liable.

Not surprisingly, the negotiation of SLAs is more difficult when financial penalties are involved, particularly when the provider and the client are not part of the same organization. In the majority of instances that I have witnessed, the client fights hard for unrealistic requirements, particularly on availability and response times, and the provider, if forced into a corner, will try to ensure that he is in a position to control the decisions on when he may be in breach of the agreed-upon service levels, and for how long. For example, with availability he may only start the clock when he is convinced that the system (or part thereof) is unavailable, which may be a number of minutes after the event has occurred. Similarly, he is likely to stop the clock as soon as possible, for example, when a reboot is underway. In addition, it is difficult to automate accurate service-level monitoring. This obviously provides some scope for latitude in the figures that are recorded. There is no ready solution to this problem other than the simplistic view that has been quoted previously, that technical and commercial matters should never be mixed. If price is the issue it should be negotiated separately.

10.3.5 Cost Management

Although it is included in the diagram it is debatable just how many organizations include the subject as part of capacity management. Cost covers many areas in addition to hardware and software. Examples include overall infrastructure, accommodation, staff, utilities (heating, lighting, water, rates, etc.), and external resources employed. Ideally, all cost overheads should be allocated to individual workloads, whether a client, an application, or a business area, on some acceptable pro rata basis so that the full cost that is attributable to a client or business can be derived. These costs can be broken down further to provide a cost per business transaction or per customer.

10.4 A MINIMALIST APPROACH TO CAPACITY MANAGEMENT

As indicated earlier, significant time can be saved through the adoption of a primarily exception-based approach to performance management. Use response times and batch turnaround times as the primary indicators of any problems. For online transactions, set up a facility to submit an agreed-upon set of simulated transactions periodically, and to capture the resultant response times. The set could be submitted every ten to fifteen minutes, hourly, twice a day at peak times, or whatever is considered appropriate. Use software to analyze the response times and to raise exceptions for poor performance. Some of the testing-tool vendors have products in this area, and indeed some of them can provide a monitoring service. As these simulated transactions are fixed they may not fully reflect the user's experience. It is advisable to supplement this system with active feedback from users.

Ideally, key global and where possible, process- or thread-level performance metrics should be monitored and periodically analyzed. Automation of monitoring and report production is the key to minimizing the human effort required, whether by the use of proprietary systems management tools, or by employing standard utilities using rudimentary job scheduling, possibly coupled with the use of spreadsheets. A default set of metrics for a server may include CPU utilization, soft and hard paging rates, disk IOs/sec average disk service time and utilization, packets in/out per sec, bytes in/out per sec, HTML requests, and ASP or JSP pages per sec. Supplement this information with any detailed metrics from individual products, such as the DBMS or other logs such as the Web. Always beware of the overheads that monitors incur, as they may affect the performance of the production system. System-level monitoring usually incurs a modest overhead, on the order of 1 to 2 percent of the CPU per monitor. Traces can be very onerous, using 15 to 20 percent of the CPU, or even more, depending on what is actually being traced. With respect to logs, beware of potential disk performance problems. It is preferable to put them on dedicated disks or arrays, where possible, to avoid contention with accesses to production files. Summary reports, ideally in graphic form, should be produced weekly or monthly, depending on the time that is available to look at them. Once again, proprietary tools are strong in this area. It is eminently possible for an experienced analyst to review a week's worth of reports for a system with (say) ten servers within an hour, sufficient to identify any problems or potential problems of note.

Regular disk usage monitoring is important, although its frequency may depend on how much spare disk space there is, and hence how much pressure there is to clean up and get rid of unwanted files. It can vary from daily, to monthly, to ad hoc.

Workload Management (WM) can seldom be justified as a separate topic. I was involved in a CM system where WM forecasting was done quarterly and the results were fed into six monthly capacity planning exercises. There are probably very few organizations that can manage to justify this level of commitment. A more normal approach is to limit forecasting to a single annual capacity planning exercise. Naturally, there may well be requirements for extraordinary capacity planning exercises, for example, company takeover or major new clients. Each application should be treated as a single workload unless there is good reason, and time, to break it down further. Forecasting input to the process should be limited to business growth or decline, plus major changes in usage such as the introduction of new applications. If a modeling tool is being used for capacity planning the data in the CMDB will be used to construct a baseline model of peak period, which can then be used as a basis for predicting the impact of increased volumes and transactions, plus other changes in the planning period. Note that it is extremely hard work to construct a baseline model manually. It can take several days. An automated software-driven approach is essential. If you are considering an analytic modeling tool a key criterion should be the availability of automated model construction software for each platform.

Service-level management tasks should be outside the scope of CM except for the provision of monitoring reports, for example, response time and availability analysis.

Finally, cost management should be strictly limited to the costs of hardware equipment and software. This information should be made available to somebody else whose job it is to address overall cost issues.

11

SOFTER ISSUES

11.1 ABSTRACT

The time that is available to deliver solutions is diminishing as the pressure from businesses increases. Techniques that allow us to focus more effectively on the core requirements will be beneficial. Such techniques are often nothing to do with technology-related skills, but they are frequently softer personal skills.

11.2 INTRODUCTION

One of my colleagues who reviewed the text doubted the relevance of this chapter, considering that it only had relevance to software development. It is my strongly held contention that performance and technology are not subjects that should be treated in isolation from the development processes. They should be an integral part of the project, frequently overlapping development and commercial elements, as shown in Figure 11.1.

The starting point for this chapter is the increasing pressure to deliver projects more quickly, coupled with the desire of the client to be actively involved and to change her mind as late as possible in the day. This approach is influenced by the seductive RAD (Rapid Application Development) methodology. I remain to be convinced that RAD in its pure form is appropriate on large systems where a large and complex infrastructure has to be built. However, the original Waterfall project model is becoming increasingly inappropriate. My personal observation is that a hybrid of Waterfall and RAD is emerging where the overall plan may follow the Waterfall approach but work on the ground more closely resembles RAD, as the time available for design and implementation is being relentlessly squeezed.

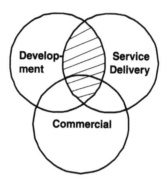

Figure 11.1   Positioning

This can be illustrated by a very large project. In contrast to my view that procurement cycles are shortening, this particular procurement lasted twelve months. It included time spent producing sophisticated prototypes. After the award of contract the development of a pilot system was to take ten months. It started with business workshops, followed by the first version of a Functional Specification (FS) after three months. There was significant feedback on the FS and a second version followed five months into the project. There was still some internal dissatisfaction within the project team, and an unofficial third release was quietly worked on to plug the remaining gaps, and to produce a more coherent document. Meanwhile, working back from the projected pilot date the various stages of testing were planned to take three months. Using a strict waterfall model this left an entire month in the middle to design and program a very large system. It goes without saying that tasks had to be tackled in parallel, wherever possible. Assumptions had to be made by designers and implementers. People and tasks that are most at risk in this scenario are those farthest down the solution chain, for example, integration testing, system testing, and performance testing. The plan had to be extremely fluid. On another large project, we ended up with a negative amount of time available for performance testing. The inevitable decision was to carry out this testing after the system went into production but before the user population was ramped up.

At certain stages in the project, work may have to be performed at a speed that may well be uncomfortable. Softer skills can greatly help here. The following sections cover some of the softer issues that you may well find in other books such as *PeopleWare* by Tom DeMarco and Timothy Lister, which specifically covers development, but I make no excuse for covering them here. They relate to all IT staff.

11.3 DEVIL'S ADVOCATE AND SEDUCTIVE TECHNOLOGY

The majority of IT people prefer to work with the latest technologies, as they perceive that experience with the latest and greatest products or development frameworks will make them more marketable, and will further their careers. Technologies are given the hard sell through magazines, Web sites, and arguably most importantly through the medium of books. A veritable plethora of books is available on any given technology. However, it is difficult to find balance in the majority of publications. I followed the writing of one particular author who related to us how wonderful a particular technology was, studiously avoiding any discussion of the pros and cons. However, when the technology moved on he wrote about the wonders of the new version that solved all those annoying problems that we were having with the previous version, which he had never previously mentioned.

Every organization needs at least one person who is prepared to play devil's advocate, questioning the claims of new technologies and looking for limitations. I am not necessarily promoting the idea of a supremo who can simply veto the use of a new technology, although that can sometimes be necessary. It is more a case of identifying those features that should be avoided or used in moderation until the technology has matured. On a large system it is infinitely preferable to be forewarned about significant problems rather than being faced with expensive reworking.

11.4 COMMUNICATION

Mistrust, apprehension, and fear tend to increase as you get farther away from home territory (Figure 11.2), with a resultant deterioration in the effectiveness of communication.

Figure 11.2 Communication

11.4.1 Meetings

Meetings are important vehicles for assessing progress and discussing issues. They should be highly focused and avoid falling between stools. For example, progress meetings are not occasions for individuals to catch up on information that they should already know. They are not really the place for in-depth discussions on some burning topic of the moment. Progress updates should be concise. I am sure that we have all seen wide variations in the length of time different individuals take to report roughly the same size of remit, ranging from two to thirty minutes.

Technical meetings frequently lack focus, having no agenda, and being prone to amble on until the attendees eventually tire. Every meeting, even impromptu meetings, should have an agenda and an agreed-upon finish time. For meetings with more than three attendees it is preferable to have a chairperson whose job it is to ensure that the meeting does not get becalmed.

11.4.2 Communication Within the Project Team

Areas for improvement typically include the following.

- *Effective dissemination of information.* The extremes are just filing findings without informing anybody, or clogging up people's e-mail inboxes by sending them to everybody on the project. It is preferable to find out who really needs to know, and to e-mail them. Anybody else who may possibly be interested should be encouraged to locate the information himself. For working papers and findings, a system where the author updates some form of index by topic, and where all team members can browse and locate the document if they are genuinely interested, is preferred.
- *Requesting feedback.* Although formal documents such as specifications are probably circulated with review forms, more informal documents on design and infrastructure tend to be viewed as merely for information, when the author may well be seeking views to corroborate or contradict her findings. It is incumbent on the author to request feedback, albeit informal. Establish a project standard for informal documents, for example, no response within an agreed-upon period of time means that there is no feedback.
- *Effective use of e-mail.* It is a wonderful invention but it is undoubtedly overused. The ratio of e-mail, telephone, and messaging often appears to be unbalanced. There is something wrong with spending hours catching up on e-mails when you have been out of the office for a day or two.

- *Geographically split project team.* Individuals who are used to traveling a great deal, who vary working at home with working in the office, or who are part-time on a project, are usually effective at communicating with their colleagues, by use of phone, e-mail, and video conferencing. For those team members who are more or less permanently based in one office there is sometimes the danger of "out of sight out of mind"; that is, communication is not as effective as it is with individuals in the same office. This can be a problem where discrete parts of a project are based in offices that are geographically split. On one project the client-facing team was in the center of the city, the technical and development teams were 20 miles away (1 to 1.5 hours travel), and the service delivery team was over 100 miles away. Notwithstanding the willingness of individuals to travel for the odd day or two per week, communication undoubtedly suffered, particularly at crucial stages of the project. There is no magic solution here; individuals simply have to work harder at effective communication.

11.4.3 Communication Across the Organization

To find satisfactory communication across an organization is an agreeable rarity. Ignorance of what is going on in the adjacent project is not uncommon, even when they may be tackling similar problems, and notwithstanding that they may both share the brightly colored, enticingly cozy coffee area that is supposed to encourage creative discussion. When I get involved with multiple projects/bids in an organization, it is not unusual for me to act as something of a facilitator by introducing colleagues with common problems to each other, which is somewhat bizarre when I am not a company employee.

An intranet where it is easy to find information (what is that!?) can help. At the very least it could hold a simple index of projects, the technologies being used, and the particular problems encountered; findings from investigations into various areas of technology; technical postmortems; and useful white papers. The ready availability of this type of information should help to stimulate productive communication between projects.

11.4.4 Communication Between Organizations

If communication within an organization can be difficult, it is a piece of cake when compared with communication across a consortium. In a primary/subcontractor relationship there are often problems on both sides of the divide.

Taking the subcontractor's side, the primary contractor has a tendency not to work with you, certainly not as a partner (the term much loved and used by sales and marketing), but to try to dictate how things should be done. Other subcontractors are loath to talk to you, as they view the primary contractor as their sole point of contact and in certain cases they may resent your presence, possibly because they thought that they were going to get part or all of your scope of work.

From the primary contractor's side, the subcontractor is difficult to deal with, particularly when you attempt to demonstrate that their software is not satisfactory and they simply become very protective and will not allow you to assist.

All sides tend to protect their wares as if they were state secrets and it would be a disaster if another organization got even the least sniff of them. Other difficulties include misplaced hubris and speaking different languages, that is, the use of different terminology and slightly different processes, which can lead to lots of misinterpretation.

If the parties are not co-located, and frequently they are not, problems are exacerbated.

There are no easy ways to resolve these difficulties. The first step is to get any necessary NDAs (NonDisclosure Agreements) in place as soon as possible. Much precious time is frequently wasted in the early stages of bids and projects by the seemingly interminable delays in getting over this initial hurdle. The next step has to be the establishment of common denominators by the lead technical persons. This is a tacit acceptance that different cultures may be at work but there is an agreed-upon set of core tasks with objectives and deliverables. The timely sharing of information is key. For example, as a subcontractor I require sufficient information to allow me to size the system and sign up to any performance guarantees. Failure to provide satisfactory information is only likely to lead to risks remaining with the prime contractor, rather than flowing down to the subcontractor. With respect to design questions, it is essential that any thought processes be shared, rather than the tendency to present solutions as *faits accomplis*. One company that I worked with had a propensity for calling meetings, announcing their solution, and expecting their partner(s) to agree or disagree with them instantly. Finally, on the subject of testing, the simple expedient of a subcontractor lobbing software over the wall for the primary contractor to perform integration testing in isolation seldom works. The inevitable delays in testing mean that reasonable performance testing is even more unlikely. Ultimately, cooperation can only result from a mutual understanding of the disparate approaches that each organization adopts; simply diving into technical detail on day one is a recipe for disaster.

11.5 AWARENESS OF COST

This is really tied in with awareness of time. Technicians tend to inhabit a cost-free zone when they come to work. All too often the project manager is the only person who is aware of the cost implications. Occasionally on larger projects, it may percolate down to team-leader level. I believe that people generally understand cost better than time. "We have so far spent 100 person days more than we budgeted on performance testing" is useful but slightly artificial without putting it in a monetary context. However, the danger of cost awareness is the natural attraction to cheaper and potentially inappropriate labor.

There is frequently little awareness of cost implications when considering performance requirements during a project. Functionality tends to be the main focus of attention until a system goes into production, with performance almost not even on the radar. After the system has gone into production, the situation changes dramatically when performance problems surface. Where significant remedial work is subsequently required there seems to be a subconscious view that this is absolutely normal, and that it is almost a right that the developers should be given additional time to make the system perform satisfactorily, notwithstanding the cost implications. Projects generally seem to be poor at collating information on the effort and cost required to rectify performance problems for the benefit of future projects. This is a shame as the figures might be quite illuminating and they might convince project managers of the cost benefits of addressing performance proactively.

Team members who are responsible for pricing hardware and software licenses should be given some idea of the cost parameters within which they have to work. It is dispiriting to spend time producing beautifully crafted and costed configurations, only to be then informed that the solution is too expensive.

11.6 AWARENESS OF TIME

It seems to be a human trait on projects to attempt to justify Parkinson's Law, starting a task slowly, and gradually increasing speed as the end date appears over the horizon. The problem with this approach is that there is seldom any allowance for contingency. People who work on short assignments (e.g., consultants) are much more likely to hit the ground running because they have no alternative. The secret (and I am not sure how you do it) is to encourage people to work at a constant pace with an extra gear held in reserve, to be used when called upon. I remember occasional visits to a team that was working on a functional specification to see how they were getting on with the collection of volumetrics and the detailing of the functional complexity. The usual answer was that they were still coming to grips with the requirements and that it was far too early for them to even comment. When I returned about two weeks before the FS document was due to be published, they were much too busy to talk to me. Did I not realize that they had a deadline to meet?

11.7 OVERENGINEERING

This is a tricky subject. Managers tend to criticize team members on the grounds that the solution is unnecessarily complex and sophisticated. Sometimes the criticism is valid. The cardinal rule is that a system needs to be fit for purpose. Many systems do not need to be fully scalable, and none need be aesthetically pleasing or especially elegant, notwithstanding the pride of the developers. Equally, there are occasions when the criticism is not warranted. This frequently occurs when scalability is required but the project estimates have not taken account of it. There is also the muddied middle ground when it is agreed that scalability is required, but not just yet! This is fine if the project can afford to throw the first system away and start again. However, attempting to bolt scalability onto an existing design can be a painful and expensive exercise. The pragmatic approach to engineering is a judgment call that needs to be made at the beginning of the project, after taking due account of the requirements, costs, and the risks.

11.8 SMOKE-FILLED ROOMS

Intense commercial negotiations will occur near the end of the bid/feasibility stage. Nobody from the bid or project team is usually involved in this process and it is extremely unlikely that the rationale behind the eventually agreed-upon deal will ever be satisfactorily revealed. Bargaining is a fact of life, and it just has to be accepted. What is frequently unacceptable is that little attempt is made to retrofit the agreed-upon deal price to the carefully crafted quotation, or to provide any rationale behind the deal. This is particularly the case with the hardware and overall technical solution. Usually the dealmakers have moved on and the unfortunate project team is lumbered with the resultant mess. I have witnessed one project with multimillion pound hardware requirements that had been slashed by the dealmakers. The project was forced to spend time, spread over a period of several months, trying to second-guess and unpick their surreptitious workings. As the project timescales were aggressive this was time that could be ill afforded. An attempt should be made to retrofit the price to the project estimates before the ink has dried, no matter how tenuous or precarious it may be. The project needs to know where it stands from the start, and it is up to the dealmakers to provide the rationale.

11.9 TEAM BALANCE

All teams need a balance of expertise and experience, albeit within the bounds of any cost constraints. Expertise and experience can be difficult to find; there is never enough to go around. When it can be located, it is frequently deemed to be too expensive for the project. Project managers have a natural and understandable tendency to hoard budgets, particularly if the budget was cut even before the project got started. This means that they are likely to use less experienced and consequently cheaper staff. This may be supplemented at various stages by the short and sharp use of senior staff for reviews, or to address a particular problem of the moment. In dire circumstances when the project is in serious trouble the cavalry (a hoard of senior technicians) might be summoned, but usually by then the budget has gone out the window anyway. It would be interesting to know how successful this hoarding approach is across the industry, taking into account overruns, reduced profit, or even loss, and the effect on credibility in the client's eyes in terms of the likelihood of repeat business. Ultimately, it is a judgment call. In the case of performance and related issues I have observed many projects where the hoarding of budget has been counterproductive. I am a keen fan of the judicious use of highly experienced staff in the early stages of a project to ensure that the architecture and design approaches are pragmatic, effective, and affordable. If a project gets off on the right foot there should be less of a requirement for subsequent reviews, reworking, or calling in the cavalry.

11.10 MULTI-TASKING

It is a well-established fact that there are not enough really experienced senior technicians to go around. If your project has one or more of them who are full time, you should thank your lucky stars. The more normal situation is that an organization has a small core of such technicians. The usual set-up is that these people are full time on a project that reluctantly lets them out for the odd one-day trips to help other projects. This approach obviously tends not to work very well at all. The preferable approach is that these valuable people are not full time on any one project, but that they are spread, part time, over several projects. This is not to everybody's taste. Many people are uncomfortable trying to balance the needs of several projects. They cannot countenance the idea of holding the details of several projects in their minds at one time. Inexperienced people, perhaps not surprisingly, seem more prone to find such an idea difficult, although there are many senior individuals who also find it troublesome.

To fulfill this role, the technician has to detach herself from the low-level detail, no matter how attractive it may be, and to work at a slightly higher level, concentrating on the big questions of product selection, the overall infrastructure and application design, and implementation issues. One possible approach is to use a senior person as part technician and part mentor. He has project responsibilities for decision making but he also makes full use of less experienced staff, guiding them, and judging when to let them loose to make their own decisions.

11.11 CLIENT RESPONSIBILITIES

Clients will quite rightly negotiate hard both during the procurement and the ongoing project to get the best possible price and the best possible solution. The problem is to understand just how far to push before the point is reached where the timeliness and the quality of the finished product will be affected.

Realistic requirements are a prerequisite. Unrealistic nonfunctional requirements, as discussed in Chapter 4, are only likely to waste time and divert precious effort away from the core requirements.

Active involvement in the project is laudable if it helps to shape a better solution, but not if the client is continually thinking on the fly, and changing his mind as many are wont to do. A client also has to judge the time to back off if deadlines are to be met, even though the supplier may not yet be vigorously objecting (although it is a sure bet that there is furious debate going on back at the supplier's camp).

Clients are often as keen as suppliers to use the latest technology, not least for the perceived kudos that may be attached to it. The use of new technology needs to be approached with care. It is as much the client's responsibility, as it is the supplier's responsibility, to decide whether to use a new technology, and if so, to what extent. A large project that I was involved with needed to support very high volumes. The client's technical staff was seduced by one of the hot technologies of the moment. The supplier was more than happy to go along with the client's wishes, being equally enthusiastic in the beginning. Unfortunately, it was agreed that the technology would be used in every part of the system, as it seemed to provide a "clean" and highly flexible solution. Protests within the supplier's organization that the technology was only suitable for certain low-volume parts of the system went unheeded until seven to eight months into the project when initial benchmarks started to support that view. At the management level, the supplier was loath to share the bad news, presumably hoping that the problem had been overstated. The project was running late (for this and other reasons) and the client started to get fidgety. When the supplier eventually came clean and suggested a major redesign, the client became extremely unhappy and the future of the project was endangered.

Unfortunately, there was no happy ending to this tale. This is a familiar but avoidable story. Who was to blame? Well, both parties. It is a well-worn phrase, although seldom acted upon, "To get the bad news out of the way as soon as possible." Equally, the client should have been frequently double-checking with the supplier, "Are you sure that this is going to fly," after forming their own view of the feasibility of the solution. Perhaps the client should have insisted on greater participation in the high-level design discussions. They were actively involved in the project generally, but not involved enough in this key area. However, I remain to be convinced that they would have been prepared to lower their technical expectations. It was too easy to blame the "inept" supplier. Opprobrium, general supplier bashing, and even financial penalties may be small crumbs of comfort when set against any deleterious effects on the business.

11.12 TECHNICAL POSTMORTEM

Project postmortems are usually mandated in standards and quality manuals, but they are seldom covered in any depth. Technical postmortems are usually mentioned as a section within the project postmortem. They are usually limited to useful phrases such as "We had problems with this technology" and "If we had our time over again we would not have started from this point," that were obviously written by the project manager. Technical managers frequently complain that they ran out of time before they were able to get around to writing the postmortem. I am a fan of the word "concise"; let me say that a useful technical postmortem document is precisely that, typically two to four pages. If the solution does not scale it is eminently possible to say that, along with some supporting information, without writing *War and Peace*. Anybody who wants to know the gory details can be pointed at the necessary project documents or at the relevant person. Good technical postmortems can be worth their weight in gold to an organization.

11.13 ALL-ROUNDERS

This may be a cry from a bygone age but individuals who have experienced different aspects of IT are more likely to produce better quality work. I limit myself to a single example about my own experience. I consider myself to be a better sizing and performance person because in the beginning I created a beautiful program, then I supported that rubbish, and finally when operating the server I saw how abysmally it performed. I consider that the ever-more aggressive project timescales and cost constraints demand more rounded technical staff. The move to ever-greater specialization brings with it the greater likelihood of items being missed (disappearing down the cracks). This is less likely to happen with individuals of wider experience. Almost by default a person who is involved in architectures and performance-related issues needs to be something of an all-rounder, having at least a good appreciation of a wide range of technologies.

12

SO WHAT?

An obvious reaction to a suggestion to alter the approach to any given subject is to question its value, particularly if it is considered that the existing methods are perfectly satisfactory. It is interesting in the IT world that new technologies are frequently welcomed without question, whereas new (or altered) processes are viewed with great skepticism. This concluding chapter is aimed at the skeptics, primarily management. It commences with a brief comparison of how functional and nonfunctional issues are tackled in the early stages of a project, discusses why performance is tackled as it is, and summarizes the recommended approach.

12.1 "MY WAY"

The Chaos Report by The Standish Group (1994) paints a gloomy picture when highlighting the numbers of project failures and the reasons for those failures. However, it is primarily concerned with the functional and development aspects. Well, if the functional side is generally in poor shape, the nonfunctional side is arguably in a worse state.

To take a single example, the majority of functional requirements are often overambitious, when compared to both the budget and the time that is available for development. Although a state of denial can exist for a considerable time, the sheer visibility of the problem (i.e., its potential impact) will eventually lead to unavoidable decisions surrounding relative priorities. Considerable thought will gradually go into de-scoping the functionality and producing a phased implementation plan. This will take into account lack of development time, any dangers to the business of too much change in too short a time, and any short-term lack of funds. In short, decisions, albeit imperfect and tardy, will be made on a relatively informed basis.

The problem with nonfunctional issues is that they tend to lack such visibility, particularly in the early stages of the project. As a result, they warrant limited discussion at the project level during the development stages. Indeed, in many cases, they do not become visible until the system is about to go into production, or frequently afterwards, and only then because performance problems begin to surface. Unfortunately, this lack of visibility can encourage a "nonapplied" approach to decision making; generalized decisions are based solely on previous experience (or worse still, somebody else's previous experience) that do not directly relate to the proposed system. Criteria for decision making frequently include:

- Value for money, the well-used mantra that tends to mean that cheap must be good;
- Technology seduction. Even management is prone to this disease; the latest and greatest technology must be the best and will bring kudos to the company and adorn the individuals' CVs (won't it?);
- A vendor who is prepared to underwrite performance. This is usually the hardware vendor who often has little involvement with the project and cannot possibly be in a position to do so. How does she do it? Simple — underwrite the performance of the system as specified at the time (early in the project), wait for the inevitable major changes to occur, and eventually state, when pressed, that the original guarantee is no longer valid;
- Occasionally, benchmarks from which inaccurate conclusions are often drawn;
- Quick hardware upgrades will be a sure panacea for all eventual performance problems. In my experience, the odds that hardware upgrades on their own will sufficiently cure the problems are evens for small systems, one in three for medium systems; and one in ten for large systems;
- "Just in Time" capacity to meet growth demands — a variation on quick upgrades. This is a reasonable requirement but to achieve it the underlying infrastructure and design principles need to be sound, for example, the design must be capable of exploiting the additional capacity. Unfortunately, the "nonapplied" approach is unlikely to result in sound principles being adopted.

Are there any potential saving graces when such an approach is adopted? There are in fact two possibilities that both revolve around reduced usage of the system in the early production stages: de-scoped functionality and wildly optimistic business projections. Even if this reduced usage is only a temporary state of affairs it can provide some valuable breathing space. The problem is always that if the original solution

Table 12.1 Correction of Nonfunctional Problems

Item	Small (%)	Medium (%)	Large (%)
First-pass tuning (up to 1 person-year) resolves problems	60	30	20
Significant rework and hardware upgrades required	30	45	40
Fundamental infrastructure and application redesign required	10	25	40

was inappropriate (e.g., poor design, lack of scalability, use of immature technologies, etc.), it may be extremely expensive to redress the balance, even with some breathing space. Table 12.1 is based on my personal experience; it indicates the probability of additional effort and significant cost being required to rectify nonfunctional problems. Note that the table does not include purely functional rework.

There can be a variety of reasons why the "nonapplied" approach is adopted. Obvious examples include:

■ The structure of the organization, where development and service delivery to all intents and purposes work in isolation from each other, militates against an applied approach. Unfortunately, performance and scalability issues straddle both areas;
■ Lack of faith in staff leads to an overreliance on the views of vendors; and
■ Technicians take too long to do anything, and even then they have a tendency to sit on the fence.

There are, of course, myriad other complex reasons for adopting a particular strategy, including competitive, time, commercial, and budgetary pressures. Whatever the approach, it is imperative that decisions are made on an informed basis. It is important to assess the risks of failing to meet the requirements, ranging from the effects on the business and on staff, to the speed with which problems can be rectified. Unfortunately, many decisions are relatively ill informed.

12.2 INFORMED APPROACH

The objective of this book has been to promote an approach that fits in with the current requirement to implement systems in ever-shortening timescales. In essence, the recommended approach is focused and fit for purpose, where decisions are made on an informed basis and in a timely manner. It does not have to be costly or particularly time consuming, although it does require the focused use of experienced staff at key points in the process. The fundamental principles include:

- Involving experienced people at key decision-making points in the bid/feasibility study and design stages;
- A coherent performance assurance process with the emphasis on pre-empting problems. This involves having the confidence to predict capacity needs during the early stages of the project;
- Understanding the issues surrounding the use of new technologies;
- Making product selection a more robust process;
- Using benchmarking techniques judiciously;
- Assessing the risks and associated costs at the bid or feasibility stage, and again in the early stages of design to ensure a pragmatic solution;
- Understanding the issues and costs that surround the ability to grow a system from modest affordable roots;
- Always having a realistic plan B in the back pocket;
- Early testing of key transactions and a pragmatic approach to stress testing; and
- Divorcing commercial and technical issues.

In the final analysis, a major objective for technicians is to provide management with sufficient information for them to make informed decisions. For those managers who still prefer to travel in hope, I finish with these points:

1. Remember Wirth's Law (software gets slower as the hardware gets faster).
2. Arguably more important, always remember that Murphy was a dangerous optimist.

PART 2

TECHNOLOGY
FOUNDATION

13

INTRODUCTION TO TECHNOLOGY TASTERS

The basic foundation that underpins effective performance and technical architecture work is a solid understanding of the major hardware and software technologies that are used in server-based systems. The simple objective of these tasters is to provide a brief introduction to a range of technologies. In my experience, there are a small number of key aspects, typically no more than six, that heavily influence the performance and scalability capabilities of any particular technology. The tasters attempt to convey these key pointers. There is, quite deliberately, no attempt to compare products or technologies; the objective is to provide sufficient grounding that the reader can confidently perform his or her own reviews. Although the tasters contain useful information that can assist performance analysts and technical architects, they are no substitute for a comprehensive understanding that can only come from more in-depth study. My background is in commercial IT systems and it is therefore inevitable that the material is heavily biased in that direction.

Although it is intended that an individual taster may be read in isolation, it is inevitable that some prior knowledge may be required on another topic. Figure 13.1 shows the basic hierarchy of the tasters, which serves as a guide to the order of reading.

Each taster follows this format:

- *Basic Terminology* — a glossary of basic terms
- *Technology Outline* — a brief introduction to the subject, including any key architectural aspects
- *Performance* — key factors that influence the performance of the technology, plus the identification of potential problems

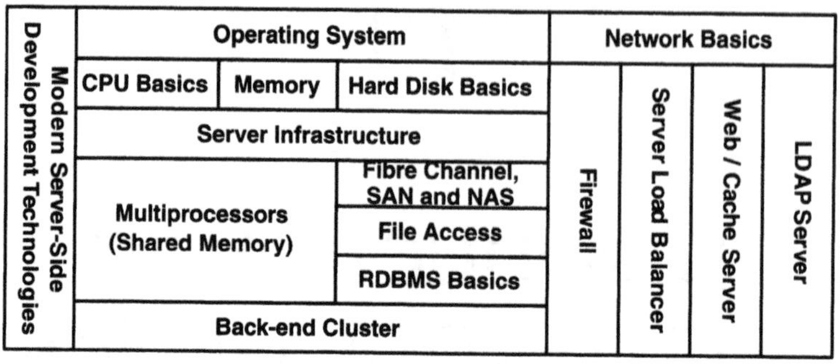

Modern Server-Side Development Technologies	Operating System			Network Basics				
	CPU Basics	Memory	Hard Disk Basics	Firewall	Server Load Balancer	Web / Cache Server	LDAP Server	
	Server Infrastructure							
	Multiprocessors (Shared Memory)		Fibre Channel, SAN and NAS					
			File Access					
			RDBMS Basics					
	Back-end Cluster							

Figure 13.1   Taster Hierarchy

- *General Observations* — relevant remarks on vendors, maturity of the technology, and specific issues
- *Further Reading* — this is limited to the most useful material that I have found. I have deliberately refrained from quoting specific URLs for material that can be found on the Web, as they seem to have a limited shelf life; addresses are often changed when sites are revamped, frequently with no link to the new address.

On the general subject of further reading I particularly recommend the following.

Tannenbaum, A.S., *Modern Operating Systems,* 2nd ed., Prentice-Hall, Englewood Cliffs, NJ, 2001. This is my favorite book. It contains much useful information on hardware and low-level software.

Cockcroft, A. and Pettit, R., *Sun Performance and Tuning,* 2nd ed., Sun Microsystems Press, Mountain View, CA, 1998 is an example of a vendor-specific publication. This is an excellent work on hardware and low-level software for technicians that mainly focuses on tuning existing systems.

Dooley K., *Designing Large-Scale LANs*, O'Reilly, Sebastopol, CA, 2002. An excellent and practical book on LAN technologies.

IBM System Journals. IBM is to be applauded for publishing detailed papers on a wide variety of topics. Many vendors tend to smother what could otherwise be very useful technical documents in so much spin that they are of limited use. The articles that I have read in the *IBM System Journals* seem much less prone to marketing spin.

Finally, CiteSeer is an extremely useful Web site where it is possible to find valuable technical papers on a wide variety of topics.

14

OPERATING SYSTEMS

This is arguably the most complex area with which IT professionals deal; Operating Systems (OS) are usually one step removed from the intricacies of hardware. This taster does not attempt to describe the features or the many problems that are associated with operating systems, rather it limits itself to brief observations on key performance areas. Tannenbaum's *Modern Operating Systems (second edition)* is highly recommended to any reader who is interested in the detail of operating systems.

14.1 BASIC TERMINOLOGY

- *Blocked* indicates that a process or thread is waiting on an event before it can continue. This can be a hardware event such as an IO that the process or thread had previously issued, or a software event, possibly waiting for a procedure that it had invoked to return control.
- *Dispatching* effectively causes a process or thread to start executing on a specified CPU.
- *Interrupts* are used to signal that an event has occurred; this may be the completion, successful or otherwise, of an IO request. The system clock produces an interrupt every timer tick. The rate of timer ticks is related to the speed of the system clock. This particular interrupt provides the operating system with the opportunity to decide what to do next.

14.2 TECHNOLOGY OUTLINE

From a performance perspective the main message has to be that support for multiprocessors makes operating systems significantly more complex, and that this complexity can greatly affect performance.

14.2.1 Processes and Threads

Work running under an operating system is usually parceled up into processes. Each process contains a group of related resources, for example, program code, data, registers, open files, and so on. Associated with each process is its address space, an area of memory that the process can read and write. This memory space contains the program code, data, and related areas. Simplistically, an operating system will support multiple concurrent processes, running a program in each one.

On a system with a single CPU, it can only execute one program at a time. This means that when a process is suspended (e.g., it has issued an IO and is waiting for it to complete), the operating system has to save all the current information from that process so that it can be restarted later, to be able to execute a program in another process. This method of saving the current process's information and restoring the information of the next process to be executed is termed context switching. Context switching, along with creating processes and getting rid of them, uses significant resources.

A process is split into two elements, user space and kernel space. User space typically contains application code, whereas kernel space is normally part of the operating system or associated system code, containing low-level system routines that the application code may call. All processes share the kernel space. It should be noted that not only does moving from process to process result in a context switch but moving from user space to kernel space within a process also causes a context switch.

A process also has the concept of a thread of execution. A traditional process typically has one thread of execution. However, it is possible to have multiple threads of execution within a single process. Each thread has its own registers, stack, and program counter, but it shares process items such as the address space and open files. For this reason, a thread is sometimes called a lightweight process, as switching from one thread to another within a process is significantly less expensive than switching from one process to another. See Figure 14.1 for an illustration of how address spaces, processes, and threads interact.

Threads can be implemented in two ways. It may simply be the user space that contains the threads. The operating system is unaware of these user threads. It simply sees and controls processes. Special software is required to control and switch between user space threads, usually termed a user-level threads package, just as the operating system controls processes. The other way to implement threads is to use an operating system that is aware of threads and can dispatch them rather than processes. For example, on a dual CPU system, the operating system may be able to dispatch two threads at the same time from the same process, one on each CPU.

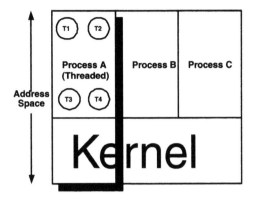

Figure 14.1   Process, Thread, and Address Space

14.2.2   Memory Management

In the 1970s systems were severely constrained by the moderate amounts of memory that it was possible to configure. This led to the implementation of Virtual Memory Management systems (VMMs). The idea was to allow the system to think that it had significantly more memory than was actually the case. This was achieved by using fast backing storage (e.g., disk or drum) as auxiliary memory. The VMM was responsible for moving items between real and auxiliary memory, either at the address-space level (swapping) or at the memory-page level, typically a modest number of kilobytes (paging). Memory management systems are mature and sophisticated. The main performance objective is to minimize the delays to the applications that may be caused by managing memory. Techniques include:

■ Avoiding swapping for nonbatch or nontimesharing work, as it is a significant overhead
■ Locking down performance-critical areas in real memory so that they are not paged
■ Minimizing paging IO overheads by moving multiple pages per IO
■ Only physically removing pages from real memory when necessary, thus allowing the possibility of recently invalidated pages to be reclaimed before they are physically removed
■ Using any spare memory to increase the size of the file system buffer cache, and thereby improve file system performance. The amount of memory that is available for this caching is dynamically adjusted depending on the pressures on memory
■ Performing management and housekeeping activities asynchronously

14.2.3 Scheduling

In general, this is a mature area although the range of facilities that is offered may vary among operating systems. The objectives of all operating systems should include giving each process a reasonable share of the CPU and keeping all parts of the system as busy as possible. Different workload types will have different requirements:

■ For batch, throughput is important.
■ For interactive work, the ability to achieve and maintain satisfactory response times is essential.
■ For real-time systems it is usually imperative that no data is lost.

There are two broad types of scheduling algorithm, nonpre-emptive and pre-emptive. In the nonpre-emptive case a process runs until it becomes blocked, waiting on an IO or another process, or until it voluntarily surrenders the CPU. In the pre-emptive case, a process runs for a maximum amount of time (usually a modest number of timer ticks). If it is still running when the maximum time is reached, the scheduler will regain control, usually via a clock interrupt, and schedule another (usually higher-priority) process.

14.2.4 Device Management

The main objectives are to optimize the speed of device IOs, while ensuring that the CPU does not waste too much time looking after them. Normally, IOs are performed asynchronously from the perspective of the operating system. An IO is issued and the process that issued it may become blocked until the IO is completed. The operating system can schedule other processes to execute until an interrupt is raised to indicate that the IO has finished. Techniques such as DMA (Direct Memory Access) are used to offload the detailed "hand-holding" of the IO from the CPU so that it can get on with other work.

14.3 PERFORMANCE

Operating systems that are innately thread-aware (i.e., they can dispatch threads) will perform better than user-level thread packages.

However, the performance of modern thread-based commercial applications may depend more on the design and the constraints of the development toolset than on the operating system. For example, the seeming advantage of threads over processes may be totally offset by the volume and resource costs of the interthread communication and thread synchronization that is required within the application.

A common technique for improving the performance of blackbox software is to implement it in the kernel space to avoid context switching between user and kernel space.

Good memory performance is achieved where the majority of pages that are required, although they may not be currently valid pages, are in fact recently used pages that are still in memory, albeit flagged as invalid, and they can be reclaimed before they are physically overwritten. This is sometimes referred to as a soft page fault. A hard page fault requires physical IO to bring the required page into memory.

Notwithstanding the advantages of soft faults, the excessive generation of such faults through the gratuitous use of memory should be avoided. I have seen some systems with thousands of soft faults per second when supporting only modest transaction rates.

Where it is sensible to do so, shared code (where this is an option) should be used rather than multiple instances of local code, to avoid needless memory usage.

As indicated earlier, an operating system that supports multiple CPUs is significantly more complex than one that only has to support a single CPU. Performance issues are much more pronounced. In particular:

■ Process to CPU affinity can be very important. Process A that was running on CPU 1, enters a wait state for whatever reason, and then it is eventually redispatched to run again. If the interval from the end of the first-run state to the beginning of the second-run state is short, it will be advantageous if the operating system can dispatch it on CPU 1 again, as the processor's level-2 cache may still contain relevant items from the first-run state, thus minimizing the need to access them again from slower main memory;

■ In NUMA systems (see Chapter 19) if the same CPU cannot be used when the process is redispatched, it should at least be dispatched on a CPU on the same board (or SMP node) to avoid the overhead of transferring memory between nodes;

■ Locks have to be taken out on parts of the operating system kernel to maintain data integrity and avoid processes that are running simultaneously on separate CPUs from trying to modify the same area. The length of time that these locks are in existence will affect multiprocessor performance. Mature operating systems will, over time, minimize the length of these locks; and

■ Any IO restrictions may have an impact on performance. Examples include: IOs can only be issued by a specified CPU(s), or the same CPU that issued the IO has to handle the interrupts that are generated on behalf of that IO.

14.4 GENERAL OBSERVATIONS

It is inevitable that operating systems evolve gradually; a new operating system cannot become an overnight success, despite what the marketing people might wish you to believe. In particular, effective support for multiprocessor systems takes time.

The more noncore features that are added to an operating system, the slower its maturity is likely to be.

14.5 FURTHER READING

Tannenbaum, A.S., *Modern Operating Systems,* 2nd ed., Prentice-Hall, Englewood Cliffs, NJ, 2001. This is essential reading.

There are useful books to be found on any given operating system. Here are two examples of operating systems that run on Intel platforms, and hence on multiple vendor platforms:

Solomon, D. and Russinovich, M., *Inside Microsoft Windows 2000,* Microsoft, Redmond, WA, 2000. Presumably, a version on Windows 2003 will appear shortly.

Bovet, D.P. and Cesati, M., *Understanding The Linux Kernel*, O'Reilly, Sebastopol, CA, 2001. A useful book, although it predates Linux 2.4, which provides full multiprocessor support.

15

CPU BASICS

CPU (Computer Processing Unit) implementations vary by vendor. This topic provides a generalized introduction to the features and performance characteristics of a single CPU. It provides the foundation for the subsequent discussion of multi-CPU systems, which are more complex. See Chapter 19.

15.1 BASIC TERMINOLOGY

- *Address* is the location in memory that is accessed by a given instruction.
- *Register* is a general-purpose working area that is required for the execution of many instructions.
- *Clock cycle* is the smallest unit of time at which a CPU operates. A 700-MHz CPU will have 700 million cycles per second. A CPU starts and completes individual tasks (or parts of a task) within a clock cycle.
- *Integer unit* is typically used to handle simple numbers. As a generalization, commercial software will mostly use the integer unit.
- *Floating point unit* is used to handle complex numbers. It is mostly used in scientific calculations.
- *Nanosecond* is one thousand-millionth of a second. It can be abbreviated to ns.

15.2 TECHNOLOGY OUTLINE

In its very simplest form a CPU executes computer program instructions. The instructions themselves, and the data on which they operate, are usually obtained from the main memory system. However, the CPU and main memory are physically separate components and they communicate over a link that is commonly called the system bus (Figure 15.1).

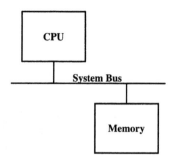

Figure 15.1   CPU and Memory Components

If a memory access takes 100 nanoseconds then a 700-MHz CPU can be idle for 70 clock cycles while it waits for the access to complete. In fact, it could spend most of its time in an idle state while it waits for memory accesses to complete. This is just one, albeit striking, example of problems that can affect CPU performance. Significant delays are unacceptable, as CPU chips are relatively expensive components. Therefore, a great deal of work in CPU design focuses on minimizing delays in efforts to keep the CPU busy.

Figure 15.2 shows a high-level functional view of a CPU. The main techniques that are used to maximize performance include the following.

15.2.1   Data and Instruction Caching

This is arguably the area where most benefits are seen. The objective is to hold data and instructions in fast access memory that resides either on the CPU chip, or close to it, thus minimizing the number of accesses to main memory over the system bus. The caches are memory components that can hold recently used data or contiguous data that was fetched along with the required data. There are typically up to two levels of processor cache although some implementations have three. The level-1 data cache resides on the CPU chip and is usually fairly modest in size, up to 64 KB. There is also a level-1 instruction cache. The level-2 cache normally resides off the CPU chip, although in some implementations it is on the chip. It is larger, typically up to 8 MB in size.

The claims of one vendor illustrate the relative data access performance: a 600-MHz CPU will take two cycles (3.3 ns) to access data from the level-1 cache, 20 ns from the level-2 cache, and 100 ns from main memory.

15.2.2   Bit Width

The more bits that can be moved or manipulated at one time, the better performance is likely to be. Systems are frequently described as being

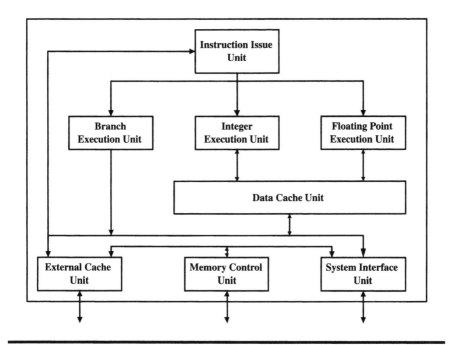

Figure 15.2   Functional View of CPU

Fetch	Decode	Dependencies	Register Read	Execute	Exceptions	Register Write

Figure 15.3   High-Level View of Pipeline

architectures of a specific bit size, for example, 16, 32, or 64 bits. There are in fact different types of bit widths: register widths, address bus widths, and data bus widths. It is possible to have a mixture of widths. For example, many systems that are described as 32-bit architectures have 64-bit floating point registers, and some have 36-bit addressing. Architectures have been gradually increasing in size and will continue to do so. For example, 128-bit buses are fairly common.

15.2.3   Pipelining Instructions

The basic idea is to split up the entire process for handling an instruction into its constituent parts. These parts form the pipeline. Instructions are fetched from memory in chunks and they are fed into the pipeline (the left of Figure 15.3) and execution proceeds along the pipeline. At any one point in time there will be multiple instructions in the pipeline, each at a different stage of completion. A modern pipeline typically consists of 8 to 14 stages, although the diagram is limited to a high-level view.

15.2.4 Branch Prediction

A problem with pipelining is that it assumes that program execution is purely sequential, which of course it is not. Frequently a branch will be made to another part of the program, based on the data content. A simple example is

```
IF A > B THEN DO Y OTHERWISE DO Z
```

Here, the contents of A and B will decide whether the program avoids DO Y and jumps to DO Z. As the name implies, branch prediction is about speculating ahead of time what the result of the comparison might be so that the correct piece of code can be pre-fetched and fed into the top of the pipeline before the result is known and thus avoid delays. Types of prediction can include: a guess (e.g., always assume that the comparison is true), maintain a recent history of results and base the prediction on it, or the compiler provides hints (possibly based on pro-filing). The downside of branch prediction is that if it is found to be incorrect the incorrectly fetched instruction(s) have to be cleared out of the pipeline and replaced with the correct ones. One alternative approach is to execute both strands, dispensing with the erroneous strand when the result is known.

15.2.5 Parallelism

The actual execution of an instruction is performed in an instruction unit. There are different types of units: integer, floating point, branch, and load/stores. There can be multiple instances of each type of unit. It follows that there is the capability of performing multiple instructions in parallel. For example, if there are two integer units it is possible for each to execute a separate integer instruction concurrently. This assumes that there are two integer instructions that are ready to be executed, and that the result of the first instruction is not a prerequisite for the second instruction. Techniques have been developed to allow instructions to be executed out of order to improve parallelism, as long as it is valid to do so, that is, where there are no dependencies. The register that is used in an instruction can even be altered temporarily to avoid a clash, purely for the purposes of the execution, if there are no dependencies.

Intel has recently introduced the concept of hyperthreading on Xeon processors where the objective is to make better use of the CPU, in particular to increase the use of the multiple instruction execution units. The initial implementation allows the CPU to be split into two logical processors. From the perspective of an operating system there is no difference between a physical and a logical processor, and it can dispatch threads on each logical processor. Each logical processor maintains a copy of the architectural state, including general purpose and various other registers. Items such as the caches and instruction execution units are shared between the logical processors. Claims of ~20 percent improvement in performance using this technique have been made.

15.3 PERFORMANCE

CPU performance is dictated by the chip design, the clock speed that the CPU runs at, plus the size and effectiveness of the processor caches.

The most commonly used industry benchmark for measuring performance of a CPU (and memory) is SPEC's CPU suite, the latest version being CPU2000. It produces two benchmark ratings for single CPU systems: SPECint2000 (integer-based) and SPECfp2000 (floating point). I generally find that these results are relatively reliable when comparing products. This is not to say that application code will achieve the same performance; the benchmark exploits the use of the processor memory caches to a degree that real-world software is unlikely to match. It pays to check that the hardware specification in a benchmark matches your proposed specification, and also that all features can be exploited by your proposed software. In the latter case it is possible to find new CPU chips that existing software cannot make use of unless it is modified to exploit the new facilities.

Inevitably, vendors adapt compilers over time so that they produce code that is optimized for this benchmark and thus obtain better ratings. SPEC addresses this issue by periodically changing the benchmark in an attempt to restore a level playing field.

On the subject of compilers, it should be noted that improvements in compilers frequently lag behind the introduction of new chips, and in turn alteration of application code to make use of performance features frequently lags behind the compilers.

15.4 GENERAL OBSERVATIONS

The key point is that CPU power has been increasing rapidly, year after year, and looks likely to continue to do so. However, this is not a signal for complacency; advances in software development techniques will attempt to use more power than is available for the foreseeable future (Wirth's Law)!

Vendors naturally make great claims for their latest CPU designs. However, I have never seen a vendor who has been way ahead of the competition for any significant period of time. The 64-bit Alpha chip undoubtedly stole a march when it was first introduced in 1992 and it subsequently managed to stay ahead of the pack for most of its life. However, vendors tend to keep something up their sleeves for emergencies, and the competition usually managed not to fall too far behind by increasing the clock speed, increasing the size of the processor caches, releasing compilers that produced more optimized code, or by putting more CPUs on a single server to improve throughput.

SPEC's CPU2000 benchmark provides a reasonable method of comparing the power of different uniprocessors, as long as the fine print of the submitted results is read carefully, for example, the amounts of processor cache that were configured and the versions of operating system, compiler, and compiler options that were used. Remember that every vendor is striving for the highest rating, irrespective of the cost of the configuration and the fact that the settings may not necessarily be employed in a typical application. It is possible to use the uniprocessor ratings in hardware sizing calculations but only through the close monitoring and analysis of the performance of application code, such that the typical resource costs of key functions can be derived by converting CPU time into the equivalent SPEC rating. CPU2000 will also produce ratings for multiprocessor systems; I do not use them, as I consider that the benchmark does not reflect the system overheads that will limit multiprocessor performance in a real-world application.

Vendors are gradually building chips with two CPUs on a single die (square of silicon). On the surface this is a good move, as twice the number of CPUs can be housed in a given server model. The success of this approach will depend on the overall system design, for example, processor cache performance and sufficient bus bandwidth to cater for the additional traffic.

CPU performance forms only one part of overall system hardware performance, albeit it is invariably the main driver. Ultimately, the CPU will rely on effective implementations of other key components such as the system bus(es), the main memory system, and IO subsystem to exploit its performance potential.

15.5 FURTHER READING

A sound understanding of CPU technology can be gained by investigating the current offerings from the major vendors. The available Web sites typically provide useful overviews of chip designs. I would suggest that any review should include IBM's Power4, Intel's Itanium, HP (alias Compaq)'s Alpha EV6 chip, and Sun's UltraSPARC III.

16

MEMORY

Memory can be thought of as being arranged in a hierarchy, which consists of various cache levels and the main memory. As discussed in Chapter 15, the level-1 caches are situated on the CPU chip; the level-2 cache is either on the CPU chip or very close by; and level-3 caches, where they are used in multiprocessor systems, are usually connected to the system bus. The objective of these caches, particularly level-1 and level-2, is to keep the CPU busy and thus improve performance by minimizing the dependency on the relatively slower accesses to main memory, usually called RAM. This topic describes recent memory technologies used in these caches and in main memory.

16.1 BASIC TERMINOLOGY

- *DRAM* (Dynamic Random Access Memory) is the popular type of memory chip that is currently used in main memory.
- *Level-1 Caches* are small memory caches that reside on the CPU chip. There is an instruction cache and a data cache; both are small in size.
- *Level-2 Caches* are larger than level 1. In some implementations, they are on the CPU chip; in others they are off-chip.
- *Level-3 Cache* implementations vary. One approach is to have one cache per board, where a board may contain up to four CPU chips.
- *RAM* (Random Access Memory) is a generic term that is synonymous with main memory.
- *SRAM* (Static Random Access Memory) is fast but relatively expensive memory that is used for processor caches.

16.2 TECHNOLOGY OUTLINE

The basic memory technology for servers utilizes SRAM and DRAM. They can both be described as volatile memory; that is, without power they

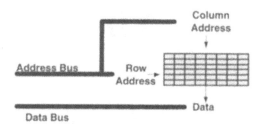

Figure 16.1 Memory Grid Access

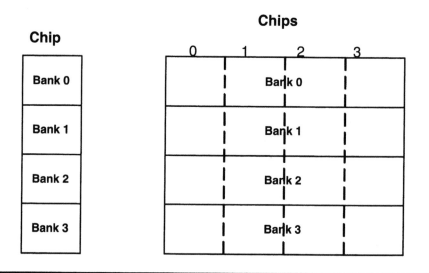

Figure 16.2 Memory Banks

will lose the information that is stored on them. Individual memory cells which each represent a single bit are set to 0 or 1. Memory on a chip is organized as a grid with rows and columns of cells, as shown in Figure 16.1. A cell is read by supplying row and column coordinates on the address bus, with the resultant contents being pushed onto the data bus.

Standard methods of improving access performance include page-mode and parallel accessing. Page-mode grabs subsequent cells in the same row, thus reducing the row access overhead. Parallel accessing can occur across multiple memory chips, memory modules, or across banks. Banks are a method of partitioning memory. A chip can be subdivided into multiple banks (Figure 16.2, left). A refinement is to stripe a bank across multiple chips or modules, as shown on the right of Figure 16.2.

16.2.1 SRAM (Static Random Access Memory)

The main feature of SRAM is that each memory cell can hold its current charge and thereby preserve its current state. It requires four to six transistors to achieve this. In general, SRAM is fast and power efficient. Simplistically, it works by accepting an address (row and column coordinates), locating the required data, and either outputting the content onto the data bus when reading, or taking the data from the data bus and storing it in the specified location. SRAMs either work asynchronously or synchronously. In this context, an asynchronous mode of operation means that it is event-based; for example, a request is detected and it is acted upon. Synchronous operation is time-based; that is, it shares the clock with the CPU and chipset and operations are performed within clock cycles. Two of the main modes of synchronous working are flowthrough and pipelined. Flowthrough provides a faster response, whereas pipelining gives better overall throughput. There are other types of SRAM such as DDR (Double Data Rate) and QDR (Quad Data Rate) that are typically used in networking devices. They are not discussed here. The speed of SRAM makes it suitable for use in level-1 and level-2 processor caches.

The term "set associative" is frequently used in relation to processor caches. A fully associative cache means that any main memory block can be stored anywhere in the cache. Checking if a given block is present in a cache can be time consuming, particularly as caches increase in size. A method of ensuring satisfactory performance at reasonable cost is to partition the cache into areas or sets. Each set is restricted to handling only certain blocks of main memory. This means that only one set needs to be searched to find a given block. The term "n way set associative" means that each set is n blocks or slots in size.

16.2.2 DRAM (Dynamic Random Access Memory)

The negligible size of level-1 caches, usually a modest number of KB, and the modest size of level-2 caches, a small number of MB, make them ideal candidates for SRAM. However, main memory sizes are much larger and the use of SRAM would be both bulky and expensive.

DRAM uses only one transistor per cell, giving it pronounced size and cost advantages. The disadvantage is that the charge leaks quite quickly unless it is refreshed every few milliseconds. This refresh is achieved by touching on each row. It is for this reason that memory grids are rectangular, having less rows than columns to minimize the refresh overhead. Nevertheless, pre-charging, as it is called, is still a significant performance overhead. There have been a number of technology improvements over recent years to improve DRAM performance, as briefly summarized here.

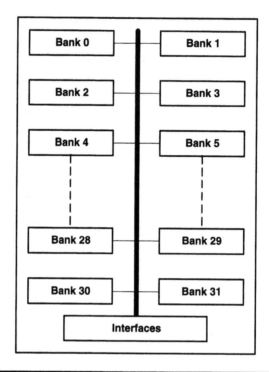

Figure 16.3 RDRAM 2 x 16*d* Bank Architecture

■ *FPM* (Fast Page Mode) performs four accesses at a time by keeping the row active after the initial access and issuing three more column addresses to get the subsequent data. This method saves on pre-charging and reduces the number of row activations. It is ~30 percent faster than conventional DRAM.

■ *EDO* (Extended Data Out) is a refinement of FPM. It can overlap reads. It is ~20 to 30 percent faster than FPM.

■ *SDRAM* (Synchronous DRAM), as the name implies, works from a clock. Previous techniques were asynchronous. SDRAM attempts to minimize the overhead of pre-charging by using banks, and having one bank pre-charging while another bank is being accessed. It is ~30 percent faster than EDO.

■ *DDR SDRAM* (Double Data Rate) can transfer data on both the rising and falling edges of a clock cycle, thus doubling the amount of data that can be transferred per clock cycle.

■ *RAMBUS* technology is a significant departure from the other techniques. In early generations RDRAM (RAMBUS DRAM) subdivided a chip into a number of banks, as shown in Figure 16.3. Each

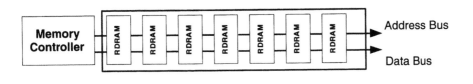

Figure 16.4 RAMBUS Channel

bank was a DRAM array, which could read/write 16 bytes at a time. Multiple banks could be concurrently accessed (although not adjacent banks). The internal data buses on the chip were in total 16-bytes wide. Cost pressures have led recently to a variant where there are four totally independent banks, which results in a slight loss of performance.

Individual chips are connected to the RAMBUS channel, which is 16 bits wide. Multiplexing and demultiplexing techniques are required to convert from the wider core buses to the thinner channel bus, and vice versa. It should be noted that the RAMBUS channel is unidirectional, as shown in Figure 16.4.

The advantages of RAMBUS are that (a) it can get a lot of data from the banks onto the channel, and (b) the channel itself can work at high speed, for example, 400 MHz plus.

16.3 PERFORMANCE

The performance of SRAMs, when used as CPU caches, has largely managed to keep pace with the significant increases in CPU performance. This is partly due to the fact that CPU designers have direct control over precisely how the caches are incorporated into their solutions.

Level-2 caches are likely to be less successful for applications that handle large amounts of randomly accessed data such as modern commercial database-based systems.

Although DRAM performance has been improving over time, it has been gradual, as opposed to the relatively meteoric advances in CPU performance.

Vendors frequently quote memory bandwidth (x GB/sec), as if it somehow constituted memory performance. More bandwidth is good, of course, but it is only one element of overall performance. The important metric is the number of clock cycles it takes from a CPU making a request to main memory to the receipt of the initial response. There are techniques that can help to hide delays, for example, intelligent pre-fetching of data by the CPU and out of order processing (as described in Chapter 15).

16.4   GENERAL OBSERVATIONS

Many server vendors now appear loath to disclose details of the memory technologies that they employ. They might argue that this allows them to change technology or possibly memory vendor when it is advantageous to do so, either from a performance or cost perspective, and that the client should not be concerned as long as overall performance is not impeded.

Currently, DRAM technology seems to be a battle between DDR SDRAM and DRDRAM. RAMBUS is a proprietary technology, owned by RAMBUS Inc. and there is much vitriolic debate on the relative merits of the various technologies.

16.5   FURTHER READING

There is an excellent series of articles on memory technologies by Jon Stokes on the arstechnica.com Web site.

Fernando, S. and Kanakaratna, G., *RDRAM* on the www.rambus.com Web site is a useful introduction to RAMBUS technology.

DRAM Memory Trends in 2002 on the www.simmtester.com Web site is very useful.

Cuppu, V., Jacob, B., Davis, B., and Mudge, T., *A Performance Comparison of Contemporary DRAM Architectures, Proceedings of the 26th Annual International Symposium on Computer Architecture,* IEEE, Piscataway, NJ, 1999. It can be found at www.citeseer.com and is well worth reading.

17

HARD DISK BASICS

This taster describes the fundamentals of hard disk technology, commencing with some background on its evolution. It goes on to cover popular RAID techniques. More advanced information can be found in Chapter 20.

17.1 BASIC TERMINOLOGY

- *Access Time* is normally defined as the sum of the seek (moving to the required track) and latency (rotational delay) times.
- *Platter* is a circular magnetic plate on which data can be recorded. A hard disk is composed of multiple platters.
- *RAID* (Redundant Array of Inexpensive Disks) is a generic term that provides disk resilience in a number of defined ways.
- *SCSI* (Small Computer System Interface) is a parallel access standard for peripheral devices.

17.2 TECHNOLOGY OUTLINE

A hard disk is composed of a number of platters where information can usually be stored on each side of each platter, with the exception of the top- and bottommost surfaces. Each recording surface is split into tracks (concentric circles); tracks are subdivided into sectors.

A set of movable read/write heads (one per recording surface) moves in unison across the disk to allow individual tracks to be accessed. If the heads move to (say) track 100, data can be accessed from that track on each surface without further movement of the heads. The sum of all tracks on all surfaces that are under the read/write heads at a given time (track 100 in our example) is called a cylinder. Sequential recording can be achieved by filling up all the sectors in a track on one surface, then filling

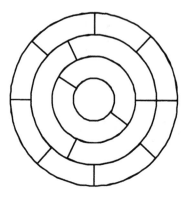

Figure 17.1 Disk Surface Showing Tracks, Sectors, and Zones

up the same track on the next surface, and so on until the last surface has been filled. The heads then move to the next cylinder, and so on.

It is obvious from Figure 17.1 that the tracks get smaller as they get closer to the inside of the disk. Originally, each track had the same number of sectors and hence the same capacity. This meant that the outer tracks were greatly underutilized. Modern disks overcome this problem by using zoned bit recording (ZBR). Here, ranges of contiguous tracks are split into zones, where each zone is assigned a number of sectors per track, the outermost zone having more sectors per track than the inner zones.

17.2.1 Basic Disk Accessing

At the disk device level, an access has three major components: seek, latency, and data transfer. Seek is the movement of the heads to the required track. When a vendor quotes average seek time, it should reflect the time taken to move the heads across one third of all the tracks on the disk. Beware that some vendors' figures may not reflect this "standard." Some vendors may say "less than x ms," whatever that means! Having reached the desired track, there is typically a delay until the required sector comes around under the heads. This is latency (or rotational delay) and it is defined as 50 percent of the time taken for a single disk revolution. The final step is to actually read or write the required data ($dxfr$). Figure 17.2 shows the number of milliseconds taken for each step for a single 8-KB block, excluding any queueing due to contention for the device. Figure 17.2(a) shows a disk from the middle to late 1980s, and 17.2(b) shows a more contemporary example (2002).

As an aside, the figures show that although disk performance has improved over the last 15 to 20 years it is very modest when compared to CPU speed improvements. The examples also demonstrate that seek time, and to a less extent latency, dwarfs the data transfer time ($dxfr$).

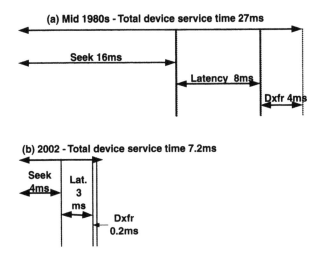

Figure 17.2   Comparison of Disk Service Times

It follows that efforts to reduce the seek time by minimizing the movement of the heads, through careful placement of files or file systems, are likely to produce the best improvements in device performance. It should be noted that these disk service time figures are not the same as the response times to disk requests that the server will see. Additional delays must be added to the service time, for example, any queueing for the disk plus disk controller, channel, and other infrastructure overheads. These delays are typically a function of how busy the individual disk or the disk subsystem is.

Up until the early 1990s, disks were fairly dumb devices, the intelligence being in the disk controller, which was responsible for communicating with the host system and for controlling how the disks worked (see Figure 17.3). From the server's perspective it would frequently only issue one IO to a device at a time, waiting until that IO completed before issuing another IO to the same device. A typical controller might look after four to eight disks, sometimes more. However, the controller could impose some noticeable delay, particularly if it was handling concurrent IOs. I remember coming across one extremely rudimentary implementation ten years ago where the controller was tied up for the entire IO and hence it quickly became a bottleneck under any significant disk load. A standard technique to reduce the overhead was that the controller would support parallel seeks across the disks under its control so that it only had to "single thread" the latency and data transfer components. A further refinement came with the introduction of Rotational Positional Sensing (RPS). This was the ability to know where the required sector was in relation

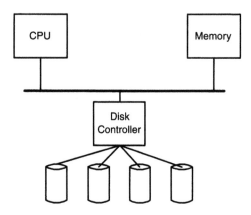

Figure 17.3 Simple Disk Set-Up

to the heads. This meant that the controller was not tied up during latency. It could do other things while waiting for a signal that the sector was about to come under the heads.

Another major improvement in controller performance was the introduction of memory caches to reduce the amount of physical accesses that were required. Readahead techniques were used to grab the next n sectors during a read and store them in the cache on the basis that they might shortly be required, particularly if sequential accessing had been detected. A read access that was satisfied by the cache was significantly quicker (a typical service time of less than 1 ms) than one where a physical read was required. Early caches were limited to reads. Cache writes (sometimes called fast writes) require nonvolatile memory, possibly implemented via battery backup, as the server will have been informed that the write was successful once it was in the cache. In reality, it will be written later (asynchronously) at some convenient point and there is the obvious danger that the power could fail between the two points.

Disks gradually became more intelligent and they were able to handle seeks, latency, and data transfer themselves. SCSI technology exploited this intelligence.

An early SCSI implementation is shown in Figure 17.4 with a host adapter (a sort of controller) and a number of disk devices that are daisy-chained together.

The potential performance constraints with SCSI were that communication between the host adapter and the disks were via a bus (in fact, the daisy-chained cables that connected one device to the next), only one device could use the bus at a time, plus the fairly limited speed of the bus (~5 MB/sec in early implementations), and they could result in poor performance for IO-intensive applications. On the plus side, disks started

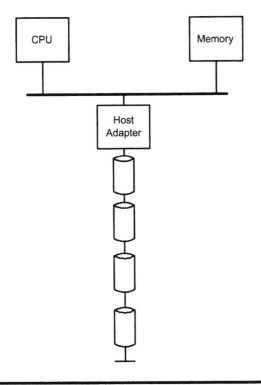

Figure 17.4 Single SCSI Channel

to have their own on-board caches, albeit limited in size, ranging from 128 to 256 kilobytes up to a small number of megabytes.

The main improvements to SCSI over time were:

- Periodic increases in SCSI bus bandwidth. For example, Ultra3 SCSI has a maximum bandwidth of 160 MB/sec; and
- The introduction of tagged queues and command re-ordering. With respect to tagged queues, in essence, a server can issue multiple IOs to a device, rather than one at a time. The host adapter or the disk can queue them, rather than the server. In addition, the disk can re-order multiple requests to improve performance. For example, it can use the information on the current position of the heads and the sectors (using RPS) to decide which request it can do quickest, for example, perform the request on the nearest track first (seek optimization).

Fibre channel technology has been challenging SCSI over the last four to five years. It is discussed in Chapter 20.

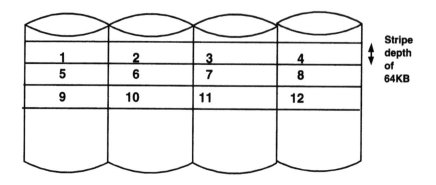

Figure 17.5   Disk Striping

17.2.2   Logical Volumes

A file system could be limited in size by the constraints of a single physical disk. This led to the introduction of logical volumes, a layer of abstraction that sits above the physical disk. A logical volume can be a subset of a single physical disk or, more usually, it can span multiple physical disks. This latter feature allows larger file systems or databases to be created, overcoming the single disk limitations.

17.2.3   RAID

RAID appeared in the late 1980s although one of the concepts, mirroring (sometimes called shadowing), had already been around for some time.

The primary purpose of RAID is arguably to provide data protection. Historically, disks have tended to be one of the more troublesome components, in terms of reliability. There are various levels of RAID, each of which has potential performance and cost implications. Discussion is limited to the more popular levels, RAID 0, RAID 1, and RAID 5.

With the exception of RAID 1 (mirroring), all RAID levels employ striping. As shown in Figure 17.5, striping spreads the blocks across multiple physical disks to form a virtual disk.

There are two terms of note: stripe width and stripe unit. Stripe width is the number of physical disks that are used to form the stripe: four disks in Figure 17.5. Stripe unit (also called "chunk size," "stripe depth," or "logical block") is the amount of space on each disk for a stripe instance. The stripe unit can be synonymous with the size of an IO. It can vary in size, depending on the system; 16 KB to 256 KB is typical. In Figure 17.5 a single stripe instance (items 1 to 4, 5 to 8, or 9 to 12) can be accessed concurrently by issuing four parallel IOs, each of 64 KB. A striped volume consists of multiple stripe instances.

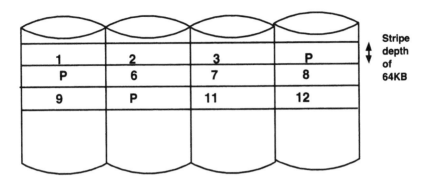

Figure 17.6 RAID 5 Example

The advantages of striping are (a) increased capacity of a volume (multiple physical disks can present a single virtual disk to the software), and (b) improved performance through the ability to perform IOs in parallel across the stripe.

RAID 0 is a slight anachronism in that it provides no resilience; it simply provides a striping capability.

RAID 1 (mirroring) provides resilience by simply replicating all writes to a specified disk onto a separate disk (its mirror pair). This is the most expensive RAID solution, as double the number of disks is required. RAID 1 on its own does not support striping. However, there are variants of RAID 1, RAID 0+1 and RAID 1+0, which do incorporate striping. RAID 0+1 provides striped mirrors. Using the simple example of a four-disk stripe in Figure 17.5, in RAID 0+1 there would be separate primary and secondary four-disk stripes. A possible problem with this configuration is that if one disk fails (in, say, the primary four-disk stripe) the entire primary stripe is out of action, leaving just the secondary mirror stripe. If a failure were to subsequently occur on one of the disks in the secondary stripe before the primary was repaired the stripe would be totally unavailable. Using RAID 1+0 in the example, there would be a single stripe set consisting of four mirror pairs of disks. This provides a more resilient solution than RAID 0+1, as both disks in a single mirrored pair would have to fail for the stripe to become unusable.

Other RAID levels, including RAID 5, provide data protection by the use of parity. One disk in each stripe instance contains parity information that will allow the contents of any single failed disk in the stripe to be re-created.

Figure 17.6 shows RAID 5 where the parity is rotated among the disks in the stripe. This is done to prevent the possibility of a single dedicated parity disk becoming a performance problem. A RAID 5 solution requires fewer disks than an equivalent RAID1 system. In the four-disk array example, there are effectively three data disks and a single parity disk. Note that the size of a RAID array can vary, depending on the implementation; that is, it is possible to have larger arrays.

17.3 PERFORMANCE

Vendor claims on IOPS (IOs per second) and throughput are so stratospherically unrealistic that I frequently tend to simply ignore them. Benchmarks that use unrealistic cache hit rates, purely sequential accessing, huge IO sizes, and so on, often belong in file 13 (i.e., the bin!).

SCSI protocols have evolved to produce performance improvements, although the benefits of individual refinements are sometimes overstated. For example, simply moving a queue for a disk from a device driver within the operating system to the controller or the disk itself is of no benefit *per se*. Seek optimization may bring some improvement, but I am not convinced that it is significant in a typical commercial system. It is noticeable that some device drivers sensibly constrain the number of outstanding requests to a controller or device to avoid significant performance degradation in the disk subsystem.

The advantages of disk controller caches may not be as pronounced on RAID systems as they used to be. The increased number of IOs that can be necessary to support striping may reduce the cache hit rate for reads, particularly where random access predominates, as the cache is used to store possibly extraneous reads. In addition, part of the cache may be required to handle parity, where it is used.

A balanced disk subsystem is a key aspect of overall system performance. I have encountered innumerable systems where the majority of IOs is performed on one small part of the subsystem, rather than being spread evenly, leading to poor overall performance. Disks are significantly slower than either CPU or memory, and therefore failing to take even simple precautions to avoid degraded disk performance is simply shooting oneself in the foot. It is easiest to start with file or file system placement. Before the advent of RAID this was usually a manual task. RAID striping has brought the benefits of spreading data across spindles without the manual effort. However, some thought is still required on the likely accessing patterns to decide how many stripe sets are needed and what data should be placed on which stripe set. I notice that the latest tendency is to suggest that the entire system be configured as a single RAID array. I would not recommend such an approach, except for low-volume systems. It is not just the disks that need to be balanced; multiple SCSI channels, disk controllers, and IO buses may be required to ensure that these items do not become bottlenecks. See Figure 17.7.

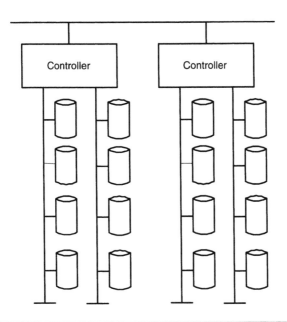

Figure 17.7   Simple Balanced Disk Subsystem

As discussed in Chapter 5, the use of sensible utilization thresholds can help to ensure that satisfactory performance can be achieved. For example, in a system where random access predominates the following might be used: 40 percent for a disk device, 30 to 40 percent for SCSI channel, or 20 to 30 percent for a controller. Ask the vendor for advice.

RAID 1 can fulfill read requests from either the primary or mirror disk, thus improving read performance. A write is done in parallel to both disks. The slight downside is that the time taken to complete the write is the time taken by the slower of the two writes.

RAID 5 provides good read performance due to the striping. Write performance is relatively poor due to the overheads of calculating and writing parity in addition to the data. Where part of a stripe is being modified, the old data and parity have to be read so that the parity can be adjusted to exclude it, and then it must be recalculated to incorporate the new data. Simplistically, this may involve at least four IOs (read old data and parity plus write new data and parity), although techniques such as staging and parallel IOs can reduce the overhead. Beware that vendors have a tendency to claim that RAID 5 performance is excellent, "as good as RAID 1" except for "small writes." Small writes are what I have just described above. What they do not say is that the majority of commercial systems, particularly those using databases, invariably use these "small writes." Overall, RAID 5 is satisfactory for read-intensive applications, while RAID 1 is preferable for write-intensive applications.

RAID functionality can be implemented in software (part of the server operating system) or in hardware (RAID controllers). From a performance perspective, hardware-based RAID is preferable. With respect to software-based solutions, RAID 1 functionality has a modest software overhead and it is often used to mirror the internal systems disk. RAID 5 has a significant software overhead and it is not recommended, particularly where there is any significant write traffic.

17.4 GENERAL OBSERVATIONS

Many system implementations start with promising disk subsystem performance, frequently because there is little data on the system and everything is neat and tidy. Gradually, the amount of data will increase, IO activity will grow, and untidiness will creep in, although it can be three months or more before it becomes apparent. Problems can include fragmentation of data over the disk, leading to longer seeks, and poor file placement, leading to bottlenecks. Rectifying problems after implementation can be extremely time consuming, particularly reorganizing databases or file systems or moving them. Therefore, sensible planning before implementation is invariably fruitful.

RAID implementations can vary and where disk IO performance is crucial it will pay to investigate proposed systems in detail. There is a general tendency to generate more IO and use more bandwidth than may be necessary to obtain possible performance improvements. For example, in random access mode how likely is it that a full stripe needs to be read; is the majority of data likely to be dispensed with. This is a trade-off, more IO and bandwidth used in return for some performance improvements.

The RAID 1 versus RAID 5 debate is often heated. It should be noted that it is possible to mix them, for example, RAID 1 for volatile data and RAID 5 for nonvolatile data. My personal preference is for RAID 1+0 unless there are significant budgetary constraints.

17.5 FURTHER READING

Massiglia, P., ed., *The RAIDbook: A Handbook of Storage Systems Technology*, 6th ed., Peer to Peer Communications, 1997.
There is a variety of Web sites that include useful background material on hard disks and RAID. I would particularly recommend www.storagesearch.com, but www.pcguide.com and tomshardware.com are among others that are also useful.

18

SERVER INFRASTRUCTURE

This taster describes the "glue" that joins the major components of CPU, memory, and IO to form a server. It outlines contemporary approaches to the design of SMP-based servers. It is recommended that the tasters in Chapters 14 through 17 be read prior to this topic.

18.1 BASIC TERMINOLOGY

- *Cache coherence.* In this context, a memory location may be resident in one or more processor caches. If one CPU alters its contents, the versions in the other caches must be invalidated and replaced by the new contents.
- *Infiniband* is an emerging faster technology for IO and interconnects that uses serial IO.
- *PCI* (Peripheral Component Interconnect) is an established bus architecture using parallel IO that was originally developed by Intel.
- *SMP* (Symmetric MultiProcessor) is a generic term for a server with multiple CPUs.

18.2 TECHNOLOGY OUTLINE

Simplistically, as shown in Figure 18.1, a server can be viewed as consisting of three main components: CPUs to execute instructions, memory to store code and data during program execution, and IO to allow data to be read from/written to other devices such as disks and network.

18.2.1 System Bus

These elements have to communicate with each other, which is done via the "system bus." This is a logical and, perhaps, a misleading term. It

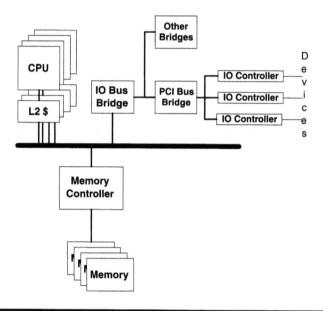

Figure 18.1 Simple Server Infrastructure

makes high-level diagrams easier to draw but it does not reflect the physical implementation. PC architectures typically use the terms North Bridge (processor/memory connection) and South Bridge (IO connection). The terms North and South correspond to their position relative to the PCI bus. Minimally, a single logical shared bus will be split into address and data components. Typically in modern server systems, there will be multiple buses. For example, each CPU/level-2 cache may have its own dedicated bus to write to while listening to traffic from other processors on separate buses. Another approach is to connect the components via a switch interconnect. Whatever the topology, each CPU/level-2 cache is connected to our logical bus, along with a memory controller and IO bridge. ■ Chipsets provide the necessary physical glue to connect CPU, memory, and IO components.

18.2.2 CPUs

The CPU is the fastest component and techniques are required to keep it busy, minimizing the time that it needs to spend waiting for responses from memory or IO devices. One of the key techniques is to keep instructions and data close to the CPU to avoid lengthy waits when main memory accesses are required. Level-1 and level-2 processor caches (implemented in SRAM) are used for this purpose. Level-1 data and instruction caches are typically modest in size (kilobytes) and they reside on the CPU chip. The level-2 cache is bigger, a modest number of megabytes. It may be on or off the CPU chip, depending on the implementation.

18.2.3   Memory Controller

Main memory is implemented with DRAM, which is significantly cheaper but also slower than processor cache memory (SRAM). Communication between the memory controller and the memory chips can be asynchronous (event-based) or synchronous (clock-based). Synchronous communication is the more usual on current systems. The controller will decide what memory location will be stored where on the available memory. It will also dictate items such as interleaving (parallel access across memory chips/modules to improve performance).

18.2.4   IO Bus Bridge

The IO bus bridge allows various bus technologies to be connected to the system. The most popular IO bus in contemporary systems is PCI, although InfiniBand may replace it. In the case of PCI, the IO bus bridge is connected to a PCI bus bridge. In turn, it is connected to a number of IO controllers that can support 32- and 64-bit buses running at 33 and 66 MHz. The CPU sends requests to the IO controller. The controller implements DMA (Direct Memory Access) to transfer requested data directly to main memory, that is, not troubling the CPU.

18.2.5   SMP Implementation

Workgroup server implementations will vary with anywhere between one and four CPUs plus associated memory on a single board. For midrange and enterprise servers the typical approach is to configure a single board along the lines illustrated in Figure 18.1. It includes four CPU slots, up to four memory slots, and optionally an IO bus bridge. Other PCI elements will be housed on separate board(s). Note that each CPU slot may contain one or two CPUs, depending on the number of CPUs on a single die. There is a general move towards having two CPUS on a chip. Thus, up to four or eight CPUs and 32 GB of memory can be accommodated on a single board.

Larger, modern SMP systems are typically produced by using multiple boards that are interconnected (Figure 18.2). The methods of interconnection can vary; rings and crossbar switches (Figure 18.3) are common.

The interconnection logic that is required on each board will typically support internode cache coherence and IO requests. Depending on the

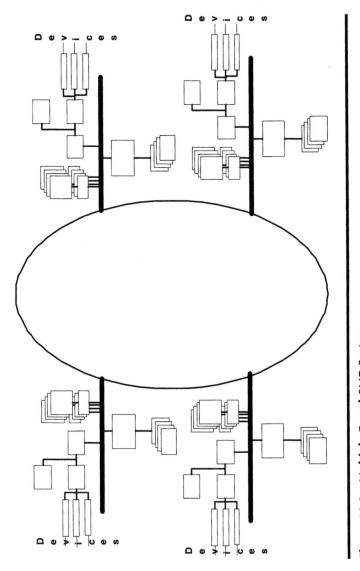

Figure 18.2 Multiple-Board SMP System

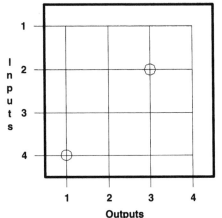

Outputs
Crossbar Switch. Each node can connect directly
to another node. The example shows node 2
connecting to node 3 and node 4 connecting to
node 1.

Figure 18.3   Crossbar Switch

implementation it may include a cache (See Chapter 19 for further information). Some systems will have separate interboard connectivity for IO.

18.3   PERFORMANCE

Vendors tend to quote the available bandwidth for each discrete bus. This is calculated as the width of the bus multiplied by its speed. For example, a 128-bit-wide bus running at 400 MHz has an available bandwidth of 6.4 GB/sec. However, available bandwidth is not the same as achievable performance. Contention for the bus, the nature of the bus protocol itself, and bus protocol overheads will all affect the achievable performance. More bandwidth is obviously better but it is only a small part of the story. Just because one vendor supplies more bandwidth than another it does not necessarily follow that performance will be better, the devil being in the implementation detail. There is a recent disagreeable tendency for some vendors to take a system that consists of multiple "nodes" and to simply aggregate the bandwidth on each node. For example, Figure 18.2 shows a server with four "nodes." If each node has 6.4 GB/sec of system bus bandwidth the stated claim is 25.6 GB/sec (4 × 6.4 GB). This might be a reasonable claim if each node were working in parallel with, but in total isolation from, the other nodes. In reality, there will be communication between the nodes. For example, in a shared memory SMP system there will be cache coherence-related traffic across the nodes to maintain integrity. Node 1 which requires accessing memory that is currently stored on node 4 may involve accesses to the buses on both nodes, each running at 6.4 GB/sec plus traversal of the ring or switch interconnect, which may well be running at a lower speed. Notwithstanding that there may be techniques to improve such remote access, at no point are we running above the speed of a single bus.

Different components run at different speeds, which can cause unnecessary delays. The key objective is to try to achieve a balanced system where no component delays the others. The CPU will invariably be the fastest component. It can access the level-1 processor cache within a single clock cycle. Access to the level-2 cache is slightly slower, typically two clock cycles. Access to main memory is significantly slower; it can take 50 to 100 times longer than a level-2 cache access. It follows that vendors have to work hard to minimize the effect on performance due to this disparity. Techniques such as pre-fetch (grabbing subsequent memory locations on the grounds that they may well be required) and the CPU performing other work (e.g., out-of-order execution) can help to mitigate the problem. IO is also slow, relatively speaking. However, it is usually performed asynchronously; that is, the CPU can issue an IO and go off to execute another task while the IO is in progress. When the IO has completed the system is informed (raising an interrupt) and a CPU can then continue with the task that issued the IO.

18.4   GENERAL OBSERVATIONS

It is important to read scalability claims carefully. Increases in CPU speed and in the size of the processor caches will inevitably generate more memory accesses and hence they will put more pressure on the system bus, with the increased volume of cache coherence traffic, and also on main memory. As stated above, the idea that additional boards result in greater bandwidth should be viewed skeptically. Achievable scalability depends on the types of workload and on the software design. Standard commercial workloads using a DBMS running on a multiboard server are potentially the most prone to scalability problems, due to remote access overheads.

18.5   FURTHER READING

Charlesworth, A., The Sun Fireplane Interconnect, *Proceedings of Supercomputing 2001,* 2001. A Useful background to Sun's Enterprise server range based on UltraSPARC III. Paper available on Citeseer.

IBM's Web site (www.ibm.com) contains a technical overview of the Power4 chip that includes information on the use of the chip to build P-range servers with up to 32 CPUs.

A technical overview of HP (alias Compaq)'s GS320 Alpha server with up to 32 CPUs can be accessed via www.hp.com.

Intel's Web site (www.intel.com) contains a paper on the use of the E8870 chipset to build multiple CPU Itanium-based servers.

19

MULTIPROCESSORS (SHARED MEMORY)

The majority of multiprocessor systems in the commercial world are based on a single image implementation, that is, one instance of the operating system controlling all the CPUs, the configured memory, and the IO subsystem. As the name "shared memory" implies, all CPUs can access any part of the total physical memory. There are other types of multiprocessor system; multiple nodes each with their own operating system instance, CPUs, memory, and devices that communicate with each other by message passing. These "loosely coupled" systems are not discussed in this taster.

19.1 BASIC TERMINOLOGY

- *DRAM* (Dynamic Random Access Memory) chips are used in main memory modules.
- *Snooping* is a technique whereby a CPU monitors the traffic from other CPUs on the bus, looking for messages that indicate that another CPU has modified any of the memory locations that it currently holds in its cache.
- *SRAM* (Static Random Access Memory) chips are faster but more expensive than DRAM. They are typically used in processor level-1 and level-2 caches.

19.2 TECHNOLOGY OUTLINE

It is significantly more complex for an operating system to handle multiple CPUs, as opposed to a single CPU. In some early multiprocessor implementations, many low-level tasks (e.g., handling IOs and their related

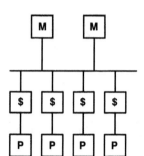

Figure 19.1 UMA Example

interrupts) were assigned to a master CPU, as it kept the complexity of the necessary operating system changes down to an acceptable level. As a consequence, overall performance could be poor, as the master CPU could quite easily become a bottleneck because it had to do significantly more work than a slave CPU. For example, a dual CPU system might only have provided 1.3 to 1.4 times the performance of a single CPU system. As operating systems became more sophisticated, the reliance on a master CPU gradually diminished, as the other CPUs were able to perform more of the low-level tasks. The term SMP (Symmetric MultiProcessor) was coined to differentiate the improved operating systems from the master–slave implementations, which were then belatedly given the acronym AMP (Asymmetric MultiProcessor)!

19.2.1 SMP (or UMA)

Until the middle to late 1990s SMP systems were typically implemented using a shared memory bus, as shown in Figure 19.1 where there are four CPUs (P), each with their own caches ($), and two memory modules (M).

This approach is also known as UMA (Uniform Memory Access). The fundamental challenge is cache coherence. The individual CPUs will be holding data in their own processor caches, as described in Chapter 15. Where memory is being shared, each CPU may have a copy of a specific memory location in its cache. If one of the CPUs then modifies this item, it follows that all the other cache copies are now out of date, and they have to be invalidated. A mechanism is required to ensure the coherence of the caches. The MESI (Modified, Exclusive, Shared, Invalid) protocol provides one solution. It is an example of a broadcast protocol that employs "snoopy" techniques.

The example in Table 19.1 shows the steps that are required when just two processors (P1 and P2) have cached copies of a memory location x that P1 subsequently modifies.

Table 19.1 Handling Modifications Using MESI

P1	P2
Modifies x	
Broadcasts "x is invalid" message	Invalidates copy of x
	Issues read x from main memory
Tells P2 to wait	
Writes modified x to main memory	
	Retries and reads x from main memory

As processor speeds have increased and main memory sizes have risen, there is increased pressure on the bus to support higher levels of protocol traffic. Above a modest number of processors (say eight) performance may start to suffer due to the sheer volume of traffic. There are techniques to mitigate the problem: a single bus supports (say) four processors plus associated main memory, and it is connected via a repeater to another bus that similarly supports CPUs and memory. This increases the cost but it will increase the number of processors that can be supported. Introducing another element such as a repeater will obviously have some impact on performance. In summary, UMA is fine for workgroup and low-end midrange servers, but it does not provide a scalable solution at the higher end.

19.2.2 ccNUMA

The idea behind NUMA (NonUniform Memory Access) is for a system to have multiple nodes, each with a small number of processors, main memory, and bus. All the components of a node may fit onto a single board. The individual nodes are then linked together by some form of interconnect, as shown in Figure 19.2.

Snoopy techniques for cache coherence work satisfactorily within the confines of a single node. However, if a processor needs to access a memory location that is on another node it obviously needs to go over the interconnect. Each node will have a remote access device or controller (shown as D in Figure 19.2) for this internode communication. Notwithstanding the speed of the interconnect, access to a remote memory location will be significantly slower than a local access, on the order of seven- to tenfold.

To minimize the delay the controller will cache remotely accessed items so that, in theory, any subsequent accesses to these items can be retrieved from this cache, thus obviating the need for another remote access. This is fine if the data exhibits low volatility; that is, it is largely

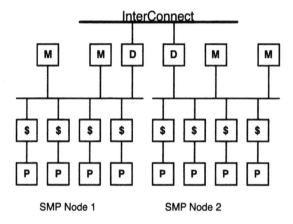

Figure 19.2 Two-Node NUMA System

read-only. If not, and this applies to the majority of commercial applications, there is still the problem of ensuring cache coherence (the cc in ccNUMA) across the nodes. To facilitate this, each remote access device or controller maintains a directory of the items in its cache. The process of invalidating copies of an item that has been modified and retrieving a new copy still apply. The protocol that is used to ensure cache coherence across the nodes is usually point-to-point rather than the broadcast mechanism that is used in UMA. Refinements to ccNUMA to minimize the effect on performance of this cross-node coherency traffic include the replication or migration of items to the node that is most heavily accessing them.

19.2.3 S-COMA

S-COMA (Simple Cache Only Memory Access), as shown in Figure 19.3, is broadly similar in concept to ccNUMA, but whereas the latter typically works at the cache-line level, usually a small number of bytes (say 32 to 64), S-COMA works at the page level, replicating and migrating pages to the node where they appear to be most needed.

This approach demands much larger caches than are found in the remote access devices that ccNUMA uses. SRAM, which is typically used in processor caches, is expensive and therefore DRAM, which is used in main memory, tends to be employed in S-COMA. A portion of DRAM-based memory is set aside for this cache, which is sometimes called a level-3 cache or attraction memory (AM). It is usually under the control of the operating system's memory manager, along with the rest of main memory.

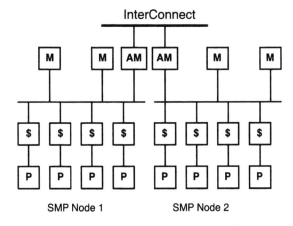

Figure 19.3   Two-Node S-COMA System

19.2.4   R-NUMA

The cost of replicating or migrating a large amount of cache-line traffic can impair ccNUMA performance. Although S-COMA is preferable in this respect, moving a smaller number of larger lumps, its performance can be affected by operating system overheads in setting up the local translation plus potential page thrashing, particularly for large sparse datasets.

R-NUMA (Reactive NUMA) is a hybrid of ccNUMA and S-COMA that attempts to provide the best elements of both approaches. It dynamically decides on the fly whether the fine-grained cache line of ccNUMA or the coarser page-level replication and migration of S-COMA is preferable.

19.2.5   Vendor Implementations

The previous sections have outlined a number of approaches for building large multiprocessor systems. However, individual hardware vendors are likely to develop their own designs, which may well be a hybrid of these and other techniques. For any large-scale server that you are interested in, with in excess of (say) eight CPUs, it is important to understand just how it has been designed.

19.3   PERFORMANCE

Notwithstanding the approach that has been adopted in constructing a multiprocessor server, the behavior of the operating system in supporting multiple processors is important in ensuring good performance. Simple examples include: rescheduling a process or thread on the same processor that it last ran on to make best use of any processor caching that has already been done; and minimizing the length of time that locks exist on kernel data structures.

UMA configurations need to be balanced to be effective. There should be no one element that will impair the performance of the other parts: the bus bandwidth needs to be sufficient to support the processors and memory, the processors need adequately sized caches, and main memory accesses should be fast enough to keep up with the CPUs and the bus. Multiprocessor performance does not scale linearly. This is attributable to items such as bus contention, operating system overheads, and locks. Reasonable hardware/operating system performance scalability targets for UMA implementations are: 1.9 to 1.95 for a dual processor system, 3 to 3.4 for a quad system, and 6 to 6.2 for an eight-way system.

ccNUMA and S-COMA performance will be influenced by the speed of the interconnect and the effectiveness of the internode protocol. Interconnects are typically implemented as a unidirectional ring (or multiple rings) running at 1 Gbps with fiber or 1 GBps (parallel copper) or as a switch running at up to 10 Gbps currently (higher speeds are likely in the next two to three years). The secret of good performance is to minimize the need for remote accesses. The operating system can help by ensuring node affinity, that is, keeping a process or thread on its original node. The need to support large volatile, shared memory areas that may span several nodes (e.g., database caches) is still a problem.

The sizing of S-COMA caches is important. As it is under the control of the operating system's memory manager it may be subject to page thrashing, and hence poor performance, if it is undersized.

19.4 GENERAL OBSERVATIONS

Ultimately, the success of any multiprocessor, shared-memory system must be judged on its ability to support a company's workloads. It is eminently possible to have successful implementations of UMA, NUMA, S-COMA, or hybrids with tens of CPUs when there is either little need to share memory, or where the data is mostly static; that is, mostly read-only access is required. The killer question for large shared memory systems is just how well can they perform when the data is volatile, such as in commercial database systems. From the perspective of scalability, standard UMA is usually satisfactory for up to eight CPUs on UNIX systems, possibly more depending on the implementation, possibly less on 32-bit Intel-based systems; again it depends on the implementation and the operating system. Systems that are based on NUMA, S-COMA, and so on kick in from eight CPUs upwards.

The general message is to be wary of any multiprocessor performance claims. In the first instance they are only likely to reflect hardware and operating system performance. The behavior of any required middleware, DBMS, and the application need to be factored into the equation. TPC-C, the OLTP benchmark, can provide a clearer picture of likely scalability. DBMSs are mature products that scale better than most other software so that it is possible to drive the CPUs almost flat out. In addition, vendors are able to configure large memory and IO subsystems such that disk IO performance does not really come into the equation. These factors allow us to focus on the scalability question. Workload types other than DBMS may exhibit different scalability, and therefore different benchmarks may be employed. Beware that benchmark figures can be boosted in a number of ways:

- Configuring large L2/L3 caches
- Minimizing remote accesses, possibly by adopting some form of data partitioning so that the majority of accesses are local
- Predominantly read-only memory access to minimize internode traffic
- Quoting remote memory access times from the internode cache on the local node, as opposed to the time taken to access the remote node (ideally both items should be quoted)
- Comparing the performance of an optimized NUMA system against a poorly underconfigured UMA system

As with all benchmarks, ensure that the figures are meaningful to your circumstances.

Notwithstanding how well a multiprocessor system scales at the hardware and operating system level, the various layers of software that sit above may significantly affect the achievable level of scalability. Some Web server and application server products have innate scalability limitations, and of course your application design can quite easily constrain the scalable potential of a system.

Finally, be wary of impressive sounding bus bandwidth figures where there are multiple buses. Some vendors simply add up the bandwidth of each bus and quote the aggregate figure to make it appear as if they can support much more work than they actually can (of course, they do not say this — they simply leave you to draw the wrong conclusion).

19.5 FURTHER READING

Tannenbaum, A.S., *Modern Operating Systems,* 2nd ed., Prentice-Hall, Englewood Cliffs, NJ, 2001, Ch. 8.
SGI, Data General, and Sequent (subsequently bought out by IBM) were early implementers of NUMA technology. The SGI Web site

(www.sgi.com) provides reasonable background information on NUMA-based servers.

Dolphin (www.Dolphinics.com) provides products to link NUMA nodes using SCI (Scalable Coherent Interface).

Charlesworth, A., The Sun Fireplane Interconnect, *Proceedings of Supercomputing 2001*, 2001. A useful background to Sun's Enterprise server range based on UltraSPARC III. Paper available on Citeseer.

Falsafi, B. and Wood, D.A., Reactive NUMA: A Design for Unifying S-COMA and CC-NUMA, *Proceedings of the 24th Annual International Symposium on Computer Architecture*, ACM/IEEE, New York, 1997. Paper available on Citeseer.

Hagersten, E., *Wildfire:* A Scalable Path for SMPs, *Proceedings of the Fifth IEEE Symposium on High Performance Computer Architecture*, 1999. A Variation of S-COMA and R-NUMA techniques. Paper available on Citeseer.

Liberty, D.A., Simple Coma Shared Memory and the RS/6000 SP, white paper (IBM).

IBM's Web site (www.ibm.com) contains a technical overview of the Power4 chip that includes information on the use of the chip to build P range servers with up to 32 CPUs.

A technical overview of the HP (alias Compaq) GS320 Alpha server with up to 32 CPUs can be accessed via www.hp.com.

Unisys Cellular Multi Processing and Uniform Memory Access paper discusses the use of level-3 caches on a multiprocessor system. It can be found at www.unisys.com.

Intel's Web site (www.intel.com) contains a paper on the use of the E8870 chipset to build multiple CPU Itanium-based servers.

20

HARD DISK:
FIBRE CHANNEL, SAN,
AND NAS

This taster follows on from Chapter 17, Hard Disk Basics. It covers fibre channel, which is arguably the technology of choice for SANs, and it provides an introduction to SAN infrastructures. The features of NAS, which is frequently compared to SAN, are summarized. The main focus is on the hardware aspects of these technologies. Discussion of software issues commences in Chapter 21 and continues in Chapter 23.

20.1 BASIC TERMINOLOGY

- *NAS* (Network Attached Storage) is a self-contained disk subsystem that includes a server that runs a network file system (e.g., NFS or CIFS). It is accessed over a LAN.
- *Network File Systems* provide a common data store that can be accessed by multiple clients. Client/server communication is via an RPC-based protocol.
- *SAN* (Storage Area Network) provides the capability to pool storage and to allow multiple hosts to access allocated part(s) of this storage.
- *SCSI* (Small Computer System Interface) is a parallel access standard for peripheral devices.

20.2 TECHNOLOGY OUTLINE

20.2.1 Fibre Channel

Fibre Channel (FC) technology appeared in the late 1990s. In essence, it works in serial bit mode; that is, it transfers one bit at a time, rather than

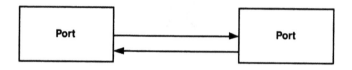

Figure 20.1 FC Point-to-Point

the parallel 8- or 16-bit mode that is used by SCSI. As the name implies, it was originally designed to use fibre optics, but support for copper cables was added. The original claims for FC, when compared to SCSI, included:

- Faster transfer rates of 100 MB/sec (200 MB/sec in full duplex). The waters have since become muddied here as SCSI speeds have improved (320 MB/sec on Ultra320 SCSI) and faster FC speeds are promised.
- The ability to work over longer distances, theoretically up to 10 km (although only with expensive long wave multiplexers), more typically up to 500 m. SCSI has limited distance support, up to 25 m.
- More scalable. Up to 126 devices on a fibre loop (equivalent to a SCSI bus) although I personally would not dream of putting 126 devices on a single loop. Up to more than 16 million targets. Once again, a nice high but totally theoretical number if performance is important.
- Easier to share devices between hosts. This is arguably the key differentiator for the majority of installations.
- Hot spares are easier to introduce without bringing the subsystem down.
- Supports multiple protocols. It is important to note that SCSI functions at two levels; the lower levels of its protocol are hardware specific and the upper levels are software-based. FC has its own corresponding hardware-specific lower levels but it can support the software layers of other protocols, particularly SCSI and IP.

For FC-based disk subsystems SCSI was the software protocol of choice for the obvious reasons that it was mature, and because it provided an evolutionary path for both vendors and users. In addition, initial FC implementations were able to support existing SCSI disk drives, via a bridge, until affordable FC drives became available.

FC supports various topologies to connect the disparate elements of a disk subsystem: point-to-point, arbitrated loop, hub, and switch.

Point-to-point (Figure 20.1) can be used on its own, or as a subset of a fabric or arbitrated loop. A simple example may be a link between a host and an external disk controller.

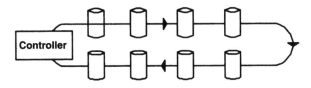

Figure 20.2 FC Arbitrated Loop

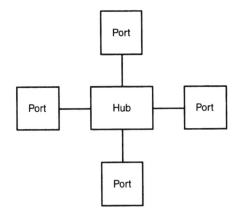

Figure 20.3 FC Hub

The arbitrated loop was developed with peripheral connectivity in mind. Figure 20.2 shows a controller with a single loop containing eight disk drives. It should be noted that all the devices share the loop's bandwidth, and that therefore it becomes a possible queueing point, similar to the SCSI bus.

The problem with a simple loop is that a failure will make all the devices that are connected to it unavailable. A cure for this problem is the use of a loop hub. As shown in Figure 20.3, a failure in one part of the loop will leave the other parts working. Once again, all elements that are connected to the hub share the bandwidth.

Alternatively, a loop switch (Figure 20.4) can be used. The devices or ports that are connected to a loop switch assume that they are on a loop. The loop switch intercepts the loop traffic and then acts as a standard point-to-point switch; that is, it emulates a loop but acts as a switch. As usual on the subject of hubs and switches, a switch provides better performance. Multiple source-to-destination transfers can be in operation concurrently, thus providing multiple sets of bandwidth.

Loop switches are relatively low priced and they can be used to construct small- to medium-sized disk subsystems.

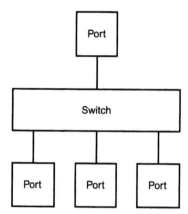

Figure 20.4   FC Switch

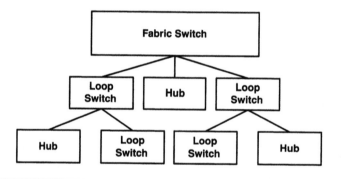

Figure 20.5   Fabric Switch

Fabric switches, sometimes called backbone switches, are more sophisticated, and hence expensive, switches that are used in the top layer(s) of a multitier SAN (See Figure 20.5). For example, they can connect several loops.

20.2.2   SAN

The above-mentioned topologies can be used as some of the basic building blocks in the construction of a SAN. SAN is a somewhat vague term that has different meanings to different people. Let me attempt to add my own definition to the pot. A SAN consists of a pool of storage devices that can, through a fibre-based infrastructure, be accessed by multiple hosts. This is a simple definition that quite deliberately avoids using the word "sharing" that seems to plague many definitions.

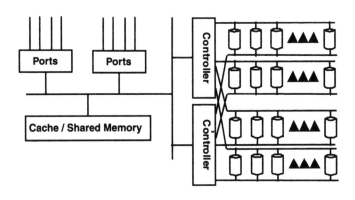

Figure 20.6   Top-End Disk Subsystem

Many people assume, not helped by some of the marketing literature, that a SAN provides the ability to share devices, file systems, and even files within file systems among hosts. Hosts may access the same physical device, albeit separate parts of the same physical device. They cannot access, and hence share, the same file system or files within that file system without additional underlying software. Such software does exist, although it is some distance from the nirvana that customers seek, and it is discussed in Chapter 23. It follows that my definition is primarily limited to physical hardware connectivity.

The primary attraction of SANs is the ability to consolidate and centralize the storage requirements of disparate systems. This can result in better overall use of the available disk capacity, potentially more scalability depending on the architecture, and easier management of backups and other housekeeping tasks.

20.2.3   Top-of-the-Range Disk Subsystems

This is the point to mention top-of-the-range, state-of-the-art disk subsystems (Figure 20.6). They are the Rolls Royces of disk subsystems that naturally come with an appropriate price tag. They may be directly attached to a mainframe server or form part or all of a SAN.

The features will typically include:

- Extremely high levels of resilience
- 32 or more fibre channel ports for host connectivity
- Large cache/shared memory (32 GB+)
- Eight or more controllers
- Dual-port fibre channel disks, each connected to two loops for resilience (each loop in turn connected to a separate controller)

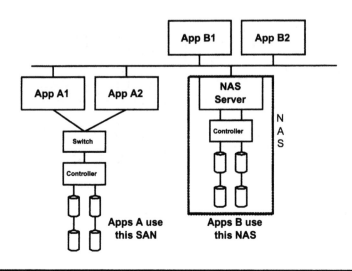

Figure 20.7 SAN and NAS Connectivity

- Support for hundreds (possibly thousands) of disks
- Software to support controller-based copying and remote mirroring to another disk subsystem, plus other management tasks

20.2.4 NAS (Network Attached Storage)

The term "appliance" has become a trendy phrase that is meant to imply the ease with which a pre-configured device can be quickly added to a configuration, usually by attaching it to the server LAN. Arguably, the term was first used for disk subsystems that were so packaged.

In essence, a NAS appliance is a self-contained file server. It is a server with its own disk subsystem that provides a file-sharing capability to disparate servers via a network file system protocol such as NFS or CIFS.

Figure 20.7 shows App. Servers A1 and A2 that use a SAN to share devices, whereas App. Servers B1 and B2 share files over a server LAN to the NAS. The terms file IO and block IO are frequently used to differentiate NAS from SAN or from directly attached storage. NAS uses file-level IO via RPC-based protocols. A process running on a server (B1 or B2 in the diagram) issues file-level commands (e.g., open, read, write, and close) over the LAN to the NAS. Directly attached storage and SAN are said to use block IO, that is, low-level commands from the servers A1 and A2 to access specific sectors on a disk directly. This is a slightly contrived method of differentiating the technologies. Both sets of technologies in fact use both file-level and block-level commands. The difference is that NAS has an additional layer, an appropriate RPC-based network protocol between the two levels, as shown in Figure 20.8.

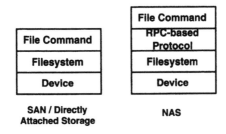

Figure 20.8 Outline Process for Disk Access

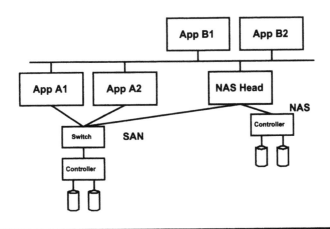

Figure 20.9 NAS–SAN Hybrid

File system support can be specific, for example, either UNIX or NT, or in some implementations support may be offered for both types. Dual support may be via some form of emulation or it may be built on top of a proprietary file system.

Initial NAS implementations used general-purpose operating systems. However, some vendors have since developed proprietary operating systems that focus on the provision of high-performance IO. Other changes include the advent of a NAS appliance with two servers to provide resilience and multiple node solutions to provide scalability, in terms of both disk capacity and processor power.

So-called NAS–SAN hybrids have also appeared. The initial implementations employed what is termed a NAS Head. It is connected to a self-contained file server (as usual) but it also includes SAN connectivity, as shown in Figure 20.9.

20.3 PERFORMANCE

An element of a fibre infrastructure (e.g., a loop or a hub) works at 100 MB/sec in single duplex mode, but remember that all the devices within that element share the bandwidth; that is, it is a potential queueing point.

Also on the transfer speed theme, be aware that a fibre-based design will invariably involve multiple hops to get from disk to host, for example, arbitrated loop to controller, controller to switch, possibly to another switch where there is a switch hierarchy (currently cost-effective switches typically have a modest number of ports which may result in several levels of switch), and finally switch to host port. From a disk response time perspective, each hop will introduce some delay, although it should be negligible.

NAS is eminently suitable for systems where the volume of disk IO is not huge. On systems where there is significant IO, NAS has potential performance limitations. In particular, the LAN bandwidth that connects it to the application server(s) may well become a bottleneck. For a general-purpose server LAN, any significant disk traffic may affect the performance of not only the disk requests themselves, but also the performance of other servers on the same LAN. Even on a dedicated LAN, disk performance may still be affected by a lack of bandwidth unless it is possible to configure and use multiple LANs. SANs typically have significantly more bandwidth to/from the servers, as there can be multiple connections from each server, all running at up to 100 MB/sec.

Although a 1-gigabit Ethernet LAN supporting a NAS may be considered to be equivalent to a 100 MB/sec fibre channel in terms of pure bandwidth, the overheads of Ethernet, TCP/IP, and the RPC protocol are greater than the software overheads of SAN/directly attached storage access. Throughput may well be less than half the fibre figure.

As previously mentioned, any disk subsystem, whether it is a directly attached SAN or NAS should be a balanced configuration, where no component is an obvious bottleneck. For example, a SAN needs a balance of fibre channel bandwidth, controller to cache to controller port bandwidth, and controller port to host bandwidth.

20.4 GENERAL OBSERVATIONS

In the fibre channel versus SCSI debate, SCSI has not stood still. A steady evolution has included increases in bandwidth and improvements to the protocol. SCSI still has a place in small- to medium-sized configurations, or possibly as a subset of a fibre-based solution, for example, the continued use of SCSI disk drives. However, for larger installations, particularly those where storage area networks are germane, a fibre channel is a prerequisite.

It is inappropriate to compare NAS and SAN, as many people insist on doing. They are solutions to different problems, each having their place. NAS may be appropriate for systems with a need to share files, but with an unexceptional amount of disk traffic. SANs are particularly appropriate for systems with significant IO.

Sharing file systems or files within file systems on SANs requires additional software. See Chapter 21 for a discussion of this topic.

20.5 FURTHER READING

The following books are all well worth reading:

Field, G., Ridge, P., Lohmeyer, J., Islinger, G., and Groll, S., *The Book of SCSI*, 2nd ed., No Starch Press, San Francisco, 2000.

Clark, T., *Designing Storage Area Networks,* Addison-Wesley, Reading, MA, 1999.

Toigo, J.W., *The Holy Grail of Data Storage Management*, Prentice-Hall, Englewood Cliffs, NJ, 2000.

A very useful set of articles on storage by Henry Newman and Alan Benway can be found at www.swexpert.com.

21

FILE ACCESS BASICS

This taster commences with a description of a rudimentary UNIX file system and subsequent refinements, including the appearance of NTFS. It moves on to network file systems such as NFS and CIFS and subsequent attempts to improve their performance. Finally, it covers the use of both LAN-based and direct connection to improve file system throughput and performance. Multiserver-controlled file systems (typically called cluster or even SAN file systems) and database management systems that can support a database that spans multiple server nodes are covered in Chapter 23.

21.1 BASIC TERMINOLOGY

- *Cache Coherence* in this context signifies that where multiple clients access a file system, each client can see an up-to-date copy of the data.
- *Network File Systems* provide a common data store that can be accessed by multiple clients. Client/server communication is via an RPC-based protocol.
- *SAN* (Storage Area Network) provides the capability to pool storage and allow multiple hosts to access allocated part(s) of it.

21.2 TECHNOLOGY OUTLINE

21.2.1 UNIX File System Basics

There are many approaches to file system structure and access techniques, the majority pre-dating the appearance of UNIX. However, this taster focuses primarily on the original UNIX file system concept and its subsequent variants, as they are the most frequently used on large server-based systems.

i-node

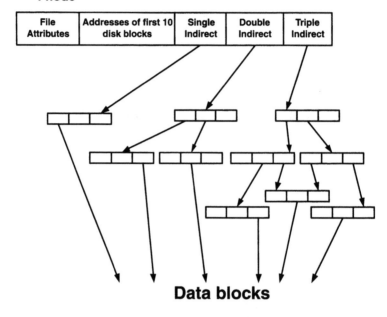

Figure 21.1   UNIX File System i-Node

A file system consists of two main elements: a directory that contains information about the files that are held in the file system (sometimes called metadata) and the file data itself. From a performance perspective, arguably the most important aspect of the metadata is the information that indicates where the data can be located. This is the index-node (more usually termed i-node). The basic concept is that the data is stored in blocks and that each i-node entry contains the address of a single disk data block. For small files a small, single-level i-node is sufficient. Large files require a hierarchy of index levels. In this case, an entry at the top level may contain the address of a block of addresses. This technique of indirection, as it is known, can go down to three levels, as shown in Figure 21.1. It follows that random accessing of a large file may involve additional accesses to locate the required index block. Performance is also affected by the size of a block; a smaller block size means more address block entries and more data blocks, which potentially means more disk IO.

The file system has a host, memory-resident buffer cache that can aid performance for many systems, particularly for read-intensive applications and storing frequently used files (or parts of) and thus minimizing the amount of physical disk IO that is required. Operating systems can make use of any spare memory to increase the size of this buffer cache. In fact there are often kernel parameters that allow the size of the buffer cache to grow and shrink between specified minimum and maximum sizes, depending on the pressures on memory. For this reason it usually pays to err on the generous side when sizing server memory, as any spare space can be used for the buffer cache to improve performance.

As discussed in Chapter 17, the service time for a physical IO is dominated by seeking and rotational delay; the data transfer time is extremely modest in comparison. It therefore pays to read as much data as possible, within reason, to reduce the need for additional IOs with the attendant seek and rotational delays; that is, larger IO sizes are generally preferable. The file system can further improve application performance by performing some IO asynchronously; if it detects sequential accessing it can read ahead (this can also reduce the overall seek time if the data is contiguous); it can also write behind although this can affect data integrity if a system failure occurs. On the subject of data integrity, many implementations provide journaling; this is a feature that logs proposed changes to metadata, and helps to ensure that the file system does not become corrupted in the case of a failure. Needless to say, journaling imposes an overhead.

Standard file system techniques do not necessarily suit all types of application software. Multiplatform software such as DBMSs will frequently have their own file structures and access mechanisms. Fortunately, raw partitions are provided to meet this need. In essence, they allow the application software to circumvent file system structures, buffer cache, and so on, and handle file accessing in their own way. Another feature, Direct IO, is a halfway house; it makes use of the file system structures, but it bypasses the buffer cache, making it suitable for software that has its own caching techniques (see Figure 21.2).

21.2.2 UNIX File System Refinements

Modifications have been made by various vendors to improve the basic UNIX file system implementation. It is probably obvious, especially to people who knew life before UNIX and Windows, that the allocation of space, one block at a time, is not particularly clever from a performance viewpoint. One refinement has been to allocate blocks in chunks, usually known as contiguous extents. In essence, the larger the chunk is, the less i-node overheads. The possible disadvantage of larger chunks is that they are inevitably more prone to fragmentation problems, that is, the appearance over time of unused parts of an extent.

The requirement for an IO request to access both metadata and data can lead to excessive disk head movement thus increasing average seek times. This problem can be tackled in a number of different ways. One approach is to separate the metadata and data by keeping them on separate

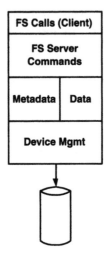

Figure 21.2   Simple File System Call Structure

physical disks. An alternative approach is to bring them closer together; here a disk is partitioned into contiguous areas, sometimes called cylinder groups, where the concept is to have both i-node and file data in the same or adjacent cylinder groups, thus minimizing the disk head movement. A third refinement is to store the first n bytes of data in the i-node itself. Depending on the implementation, it may be possible to store small files entirely within the i-node.

With respect to journaling, disk performance can be improved by housing the intent log on a separate device from the file system.

21.2.3   NTFS

The NT File System (NTFS) was created for use with Windows NT. It was developed in the early 1990s. It postdates initial UNIX file system software and therefore it naturally contains some of the features that can be found in UNIX file system refinements. It includes features that are not discussed here, including data compression and fault-tolerant volumes.

NTFS uses a relational database table, called the master file table (MFT) to keep track of the contents of a volume. The size of an MFT record can be 1, 2, or 4 KB; it is determined when the volume is formatted. One objective of the relational approach is to speed up directory browsing and accessing. As shown in Figure 21.3, a small file can be wholly contained within the MFT record itself, thus minimizing the number of accesses required. For larger files, the MFT data attribute will contain an index to the clusters that hold the data. A cluster is the unit of allocation on the disk; its size, an integral number of disk sectors, which is decided

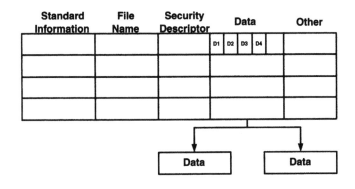

Figure 21.3 MFT Records (Files)

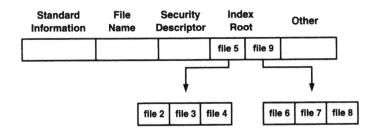

Figure 21.4 MFT Record (Directory Entry)

when the volume is formatted, can vary. Larger clusters can provide better performance and reduced fragmentation, at the cost of wasted disk space.

An MFT record can also contain a reference to a directory. In this case the MFT record contains the index of files, or the index root for a large directory that cannot be contained within a single MFT record (see Figure 21.4).

Finally, similar to certain UNIX file system implementations, NTFS provides a recoverable file system via the use of a log file to record changes.

21.2.4 Network File System

An early requirement in the early 1980s was the ability to make the data in a file system available to multiple clients. The easiest way to provide such a facility was simplistically to take the simple software structure (see Figure 21.2) and tease out the minimum amount of software from the top-level calls to file access routines, place them at the other end of a network, and create a protocol to allow the two parts to communicate,

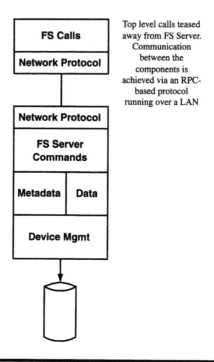

Figure 21.5   NFS Call Structure

as shown in Figure 21.5. The concept was aimed at file-level sharing rather than record sharing, and locking techniques were extremely rudimentary. NFS, the original UNIX-based network file system was (and still is) referred to as "stateless."

Although NFS provided a welcome functional solution, there were performance implications:

- The overheads of the protocol, and the network bandwidth that is available, can have a significant impact on IO performance.
- Early implementations of the protocol were very rudimentary with often a one-to-one mapping between a call by the client and a low-level routine on the server. This could result in the requirement for many round-trips to perform certain actions. Directory processing was a particularly poor area in this respect. Browsing a directory or even a hierarchy of directories using the lookup call can result in many round-trips just to find a file.
- Only small IOs were supported.
- Client-side caching was typically weak and possibly nonexistent and could therefore result in additional IO traffic.
- Writes were synchronous (i.e., write behind was not allowed).

Gradually, some improvements to performance were incorporated, including:

- Attempts to reduce the number of round-trips per function;
- General protocol refinements such as piggy-backing (i.e., sending multiple requests together in a batch);
- Asynchronous writes, albeit with the attendant dangers of loss of data integrity in the case of failure, although NFS V3 introduced a commit command to check that data has been written to disk; and
- Larger IO.

I have concentrated on NFS. The equivalent software for Windows is CIFS. As it postdates NFS, it learned from some of the problems experienced with early implementations of NFS. From a performance perspective, the key differences in CIFS are:

- It is stateful. The use of locks allows client-side caching of data;
- There is less one-to-one mapping of client calls to server routines, particularly in the area of directory processing;
- There are products available that provide Windows and UNIX interoperability. SAMBA is the most noteworthy, allowing Windows-based clients to access a UNIX-based file system using CIFS protocols.

21.2.5 Cache-Coherent Shared File System

Arguably the next logical step for a single-server, shared file system was to introduce full cache coherence. This means that the client can be sure that it is always using the latest version of a file, and not a stale version. The provision of cache coherence is potentially a costly overhead, as clients have to obtain locks or tokens on the files that they wish to access, and they have to handle messages that inform them that their currently cached copy of the file is no longer valid. Although the possible impact on performance will depend on the volatility of the data, this type of system will require a reasonably fast interconnect between client(s) and server to minimize the latency.

21.2.6 Shared File System — Direct Connections via SAN

The LAN invariably has an impact on the performance of a network file system. One approach to improving performance is to use direct SAN connections from the client nodes to the disks rather than the LAN to provide significantly more IO bandwidth.

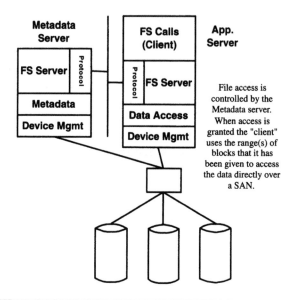

Figure 21.6   SAN Direct Connection to Data

A typical solution is to separate the metadata and data software components. The metadata element is housed on a separate server and it manages all aspects of, and access to, the file system. See Figure 21.6.

A client node request to open a file will go to the metadata server over the LAN as usual. Assuming that no other client node is using the file, the metadata server will grant access and return a range of physical disk blocks that contain the file data (to read) or a range of blocks to which it can write. Reads/writes can now be performed directly by the client node over its SAN connections to the data. The metadata server itself carries out any changes to metadata. Some implementations allow the use of multiple metadata servers to provide a degree of scalability, each managing its own pool of files.

21.3   PERFORMANCE

In general, there are many parameters that can be used to tune IO subsystems. Notwithstanding the amount of system tweaking that can be carried out, the primary responsibility lies with the developers to avoid copious disk IO traffic wherever possible, through sensible design, effective indexing and accessing techniques, and caching, where appropriate. This section is limited to general comments on performance.

Note that general improvements were covered above in Section 21.2.2.

It is difficult to obtain information on file system bottlenecks that are caused by low-level locks within the file system itself. This is most likely to be a problem on heavy write/update applications. In-house bench-marking may be the only satisfactory method of establishing the point at which it becomes an issue.

Synchronize file system block size with the IO size and the stripe unit size where appropriate to minimize the likelihood of extraneous IO traffic. Check the recommendations for the products that you are using.

Due to the protocol and network latency, vanilla-flavored, LAN-based single-server network file systems are not usually suitable for systems that need to provide good responsiveness under high volumes of disk traffic.

The addition of direct SAN connections will increase performance, although the level of improvement will depend on the amount of metadata access activity, which still involves client/server LAN traffic.

21.4 GENERAL OBSERVATIONS

Any high-activity file system needs careful design consideration. Vanilla-flavored variants are unlikely to fit the bill. One solution may be to partition the data across multiple file systems to overcome any bottlenecks. How-ever, it may be necessary, ultimately, to consider the use of improved products that provide increased throughput and performance.

High write rates can still be a problem, even with improved products. Consider partitioning as a possible solution.

This is a further reminder that discussion in these topics centers primarily on performance, but other factors need to be considered when evaluating file system solutions, particularly the resilience of multiple server solutions and the cost implications.

21.5 FURTHER READING

Tannenbaum, A.S., *Modern Operating Systems,* 2nd ed., Prentice-Hall, Englewood Cliffs, NJ, 2001, Ch. 6.

Eckstein, R., Collier-Brown, D., and Kelly, P., *Using SAMBA*, O'Reilly, Sebastopol, CA, 1999.

Various vendors provide improved file system products. For example, check out the Veritas and Tivoli Web sites although I have to say that the material that is generally available is lacking in detail.

22

RELATIONAL
DATABASE BASICS

The introduction of relational DBMSs in the 1980s was arguably one of the most important events in the history of IT, particularly in the commercial world. Unlike many other fads in the development arena that disappear almost as quickly as they arrive, the products have persisted, gradually evolving into the mature offerings that are currently available. This is not to say that they are perfect, far from it, but they do stand head and shoulders above most other development products. Books on tuning individual RDBMS products run to many hundreds of pages. Therefore, it is challenging to attempt a taster on the subject. I have limited the topic to what I consider to be the fundamentals, particularly avoiding areas where products have strayed from their roots. As shown in Figure 22.1, it covers network communication, SQL processing, disk storage, transactions, and parallel processing. Multinode databases are covered in Chapter 23.

22.1   BASIC TERMINOLOGY

- *JDBC* (Java Database Connectivity) is the equivalent of ODBC in the Java world.
- *ODBC* (Open Database Connectivity) provides a mechanism to access multiple DBMSs from different vendors, potentially from a single client.
- *OLTP* (Online Transaction Processing).
- *RDBMS* (Relational Database Management System).
- *SQL* (Structured Query Language) is a standardized query language for accessing a database.

22.2   TECHNOLOGY OUTLINE

Figure 22.2 provides a simple overview of a typical RDBMS.

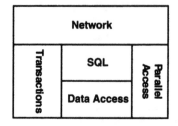

Figure 22.1   RDBMS Topics

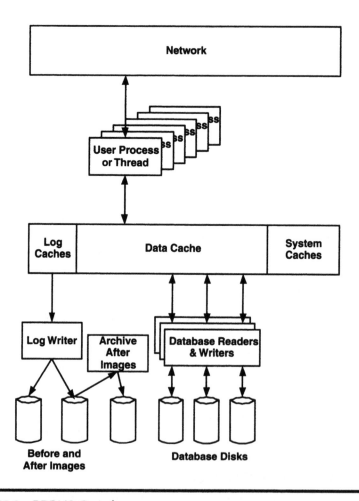

Figure 22.2   RDBMS Overview

22.2.1 Network Communication

In the early versions of RDBMSs support was primarily limited to dumb terminals. Each user had a process on the DB server, or shared a process or address space, and all processing took place on this server. Communication between the user and the server was limited to screen handling.

The advent of client/server systems, where a significant proportion of the application software resided on the client, introduced the need to provide network protocols that would allow the client to submit SQL statements to the DB server, and to receive the responses. Similar to NFS, the initial versions of these protocols tended to concentrate on providing functionality, and they simply teased away the existing database calls and allowed them to be sent from the client.

This could result in many round-trips (sometimes running into the hundreds) between client and server to execute relatively straightforward SQL statements. The number of round-trips could lead to poor performance, particularly where communication was over a WAN. One of the primary objectives of succeeding versions of these protocols was to reduce the number of round-trips that are required. One of the improvements in this area is the ability in some products to specify the size of network packets when query results are returned to the client; this is particularly useful when any reasonable volume of data has to be retrieved from the server, as it can limit the number of packets that have to be sent.

Other simple recommendations for reducing network traffic include:

■ Using stored procedures, where appropriate, to minimize the traffic that relates to parsing, binding, and any other pre-execution tasks
■ Only retrieving necessary data, for example, avoiding unused columns
■ Avoiding any unnecessary post-processing on the extracted data — let the DBMS do all the work.

A key change in the early 1990s was the introduction of ODBC (Open Database Connectivity) that attempts to provide the flexibility for a client-based application to access multiple databases, potentially from different vendors. Figure 22.3 illustrates some basic approaches to ODBC implementation; the right-hand side shows the encapsulation of a database vendor's proprietary network protocol.

Although ODBC (and subsequently JDBC for Java-based applications) provide flexibility, they can also introduce a number of potential performance issues, including:

■ *DB Connections.* Database connection and disconnection are expensive in resource terms, and therefore a mechanism in the

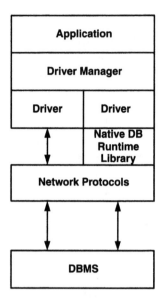

Figure 22.3 ODBC Outline Call Structure

ODBC driver that can allow established connections to be reused is a prerequisite for reasonable performance. This is usually called connection pooling.

■ *Hidden SQL.* The mapping of ODBC functions to a given DBMS can result in the need for the driver to generate and execute additional SQL behind the scenes. One example is support for scrolling a result set in the client application. Scrolling either up or down may lead to the need to execute additional SQL.

■ *Other Driver-DBMS Mapping Issues.* Discrepancies in the support for specified data types or particular SQL features can result in additional processing.

■ *Two-Phase Commit.* This is used when a transaction is updating multiple databases in parallel. This is a more complex, and hence more resource intensive process, than a single database update. Some drivers may only support two-phase commits, which is an unnecessary overhead if there is only one database involved.

22.2.2 SQL Processing

A significant amount of processing is required before an SQL statement can actually be executed. "Preparing" a statement, as it is sometimes called, can often use significantly more processing power than is actually required in executing the SQL. There are two types of SQL, static and dynamic.

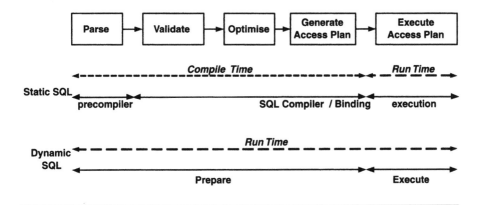

Figure 22.4 Comparison of Static and Dynamic SQL

Static SQL is typically embedded within a program and does not change, whereas dynamic SQL is either generated on the fly (e.g., ad hoc queries), or it is assembled by a program building an SQL string. The approach to handling both types is illustrated in Figure 22.4.

Some products perform the preparatory work for static SQL as part of the overall program compilation process, using a pre-compiler to extract and parse embedded SQL statements and a binding utility to validate the statement, optimize it where necessary, and generate an access plan.

The approach for dynamic SQL, and indeed an alternative approach for static SQL, is to perform the preparatory work when the DBMS first encounters the statement. The output from this preparatory stage is cached in memory so that the overhead can be avoided when the statement is next processed. Naturally, this SQL cache needs to be large enough to store sufficient items of SQL to avoid the possibility of frequently used SQL being dropped from the cache to make way for other SQL, and hence having to go through the Prepare stage again.

The caching feature is supported in different ways by vendors. Some split the SQL processing into discrete Prepare and Execute calls. Typically a Prepare is executed once and the accompanying Execute many times. Another method is simply to compare the SQL statement character by character with those in the cache to see if it has already been prepared. In this latter case, it is incumbent on the developer to aid the effective use of the SQL cache. For example, the use of different literals in what is otherwise the same SQL statement can fox the system into thinking that they are in fact different statements. A way around this problem is to put the values into variables that are subsequently used in the SQL statement rather than literals.

A key objective during the preparation, whatever method is employed, is for the system to decide how best to access the data that is referred to in the SQL. Most products have one or more "optimizers" to perform this task. It is way beyond the scope of this book to attempt to go into the intricacies of optimizers. However, vendors typically make great, albeit often overhyped, claims for their optimizers. Some products use collected statistics to help them to decide on the best access paths. A common problem here is either the absence of statistics or out-of-date statistics. Many projects still seem to spend a significant amount of time trying to understand why the optimizer is doing what it is; for example, why it is totally ignoring their important index, and then trying to cajole the optimizer into doing what they desire. Any product should provide detailed traces or logs to allow inspection of the chosen access paths. Facilities that allow the optimizer to be influenced (e.g., hints) can be very useful in taming a seemingly idiosyncratic optimizer. The ability to cache or store access paths can help to minimize the work that the optimizer has to perform when the statement is next executed.

The judicious use of *indexes* is a key aspect of performance. I use the word judicious because indexes are not always a panacea. First, there is a processing and storage cost for each index entry. In a write-intensive application, the overheads of creating/updating an index may be greater than the benefits that accrue, particularly if only a small number of queries actually use the index.

Accessing a single row from a very small table (of say four or five pages) may be quicker using a full table scan rather than going through the index(es). Similarly, if a large percentage of rows in a table have to be extracted, a full table or range scan can be quicker than indexed access. Finally, the cardinality of an index can be important. For example, an index that has only two values (e.g., yes and no) may use excessive disk space and may not perform well if it is a major index as it will retrieve many rows.

Joins (the ability to merge data items from disparate tables in the response to a query) is one of the most powerful features. However, this power can also result in performance problems. A common problem in OLTP systems is to use overly complex joins. I have seen instances of SQL with 12 or more joins. Whereas large joins can be very useful for decision support or batch reporting functions it is usually counterproductive on OLTP systems. It will obviously vary from product to product, and from vendor to vendor, but four- to five-way joins are more than enough.

Sorts (induced by the presence of ORDER BY or GROUP BY clauses in an SQL statement) require space. If possible, there should be sufficient memory available to allow in-memory sorts. Where there is insufficient memory disk space will be used. Naturally, disk sorts are slower and are not really suitable for OLTP systems although again, they may be acceptable for decision support.

Some products support the concept of *array* or *batch processing*. Here, a single SQL statement can be applied to multiple data instances. An example is the bulk insertion of rows into a specified table. A single SQL INSERT is followed by the values for (say) 100 rows. The DBMS treats it as a single statement and thereby saves on many of the overheads that would be incurred if there were 100 discrete INSERT statements.

Stored Procedures typically contain a mixture of SQL statements and procedural code. From a performance perspective they have a number of advantages. They help to minimize network traffic between client and server. It is particularly useful if stored procedures can be "compiled" to minimize the amount of interpretation that is necessary during execution, and even better if the compiled versions can be cached in memory for future use.

Locking is the key means of ensuring the integrity of a database in a multi-user system. From a performance perspective, the longer that locks remain in existence, the more impact they will have on response times, and potentially on throughput. High granularity locks (e.g., at the table level) can have a greater impact than lower granularity row-level locks, as they are likely to affect a wider range of transactions. It is possible, although not necessarily desirable, to allow one transaction to read data that another transaction is amending in an effort to improve throughput. Examples include:

- *Dirty read* — read amended data that has not yet been committed.
- *Nonrepeatable read* — a transaction rereads data that has subsequently been changed (and committed) since the first read.
- *Phantom read* — a transaction re-executes a query and finds that there are more hits because another transaction has added more rows.

The ability to provide a consistent view of data to transactions is possible using the before image logs. This is a performance trade-off: is it better to incur the overheads involved in providing the consistent view; or is it better to wait until the lock is released.

Views seem to be particular favorites of designers and developers. A view is a virtual table that is made up of components from one or more physical tables. They are used for a variety of reasons: security (to hide data in a table), data complexity hidden, and presentation of data in a different format. However, views should be used judiciously, as they are produced on the fly by the DBMS, executing the necessary SQL behind the scenes. Frequently used, complex views can be a drain on resources.

Recently, *materialized views* have been introduced. As the name implies, they are physical, as opposed to virtual. Their main purpose is to provide summaries of data, and as such, they are more suited to data warehouse and decision support systems rather than OLTP. Naturally, there are storage implications to hold the summaries and performance implications, as the summaries have to be re-created when the master data changes.

Triggers provide a mechanism to invoke additional processing when an event occurs, for example, before/after an insert to a table. They can be used for many purposes; arguably, the main ones are maintaining referential integrity and enforcing complex business rules. Vendors typically recommend that triggers should be used in moderation. However, this does not appear to be heeded by many implementations. Triggers are frequently complex, and a careful check is required on their usage, as they can surreptitiously (not directly invoked by a transaction) consume significant resources.

22.2.3 Data Access

One of the key methods of ensuring good performance is to make effective use of the various memory caching techniques that mature RDBMS products provide. Before discussing application data caches there are various system caches whose use should be optimized. They include the SQL cache (as mentioned above), data dictionary cache, and buffers for before and after images. The most visible cache to a developer is the area set aside for database table and index blocks. Cache hit rates should be in excess of 95 percent for data and indexes, and 98 to more than 99 percent for system caches. It is important to note that caching data and indexes is not always good. Long-running jobs (e.g., billing runs) may have to process large volumes of data where caching can sometimes actually be something of a hindrance.

Where a standard file system is being used for database files beware that the file system will typically try to cache blocks as well. If the database prefers to do the caching, the direct IO facility that is supported by some operating systems will allow the file system buffer cache to be bypassed. Some products allow specified tables to be pinned in memory to improve performance, rather than being subject to being removed by an LRU (Least Recently Used) or similar algorithm. RDBMS products can typically be run across a range of hardware and software platforms, and they frequently have their own file formats. Support for RAW devices on Open Systems allows a DBMS to use its own formats, in preference to using the file system structure. Avoiding file system overheads can improve disk performance by 15 to 20 percent, possibly more (ask the vendor to provide figures). The usual downside of using RAW is that customized data management utilities are required, as it is not possible to use the standard file system variants.

The main objective of table and index file placement is to ensure that accesses are spread as evenly as possible over the available disks. A common problem is to find that one or two disks are supporting the majority of accesses and they become bottlenecks. As a rough rule of thumb try to keep the utilization of a disk below 50 percent for OLTP; 60 to 70 percent may be reasonable for batch or decision support. A first-pass method to balance accesses is to use software- or hardware-based striping facilities to spread files over multiple physical disks. This requires minimal effort and usually provides a reasonable return. Subsequent monitoring of actual access patterns can usually provide sufficient information to allow any necessary manual refinement.

Some books recommend the separation of index and data, presumably to reduce seek activity on the disks. I have never quite understood this advice. From the perspective of a single transaction, it may be a reasonable idea but in a system where multiple transactions are being processed concurrently I fail to see the benefits, as the accesses of multiple transactions will invariably lead to head movement.

Another method of minimizing seek activity that is proffered by some vendors is the use of clustered indexes. This approach attempts to keep data physically close to its index on the disk. This is likely to be more beneficial in low activity systems.

22.2.4 Transactions

Arguably, the foundation for database integrity is provided by transactions. Begin and commit define the scope of a transaction. In essence, any changes to the database are not physically made until the transaction has successfully completed when the commit has executed. During the transaction the original contents (before images) and the proposed changes (after images) are logged. If a transaction is completed successfully, the relevant changes can be written to the database. If a transaction fails, any effects can be undone by accessing the before images.

Some implementations keep before and after images in one log, and others keep them in separate logs. After image information is frequently archived, as it can be used in recovery situations where the database has become corrupted. Here, the most recent backup is restored, and then the after images are applied to bring the database back to the latest consistent point. For installations that do not perform full backups every day, there may be several days worth of after images to apply.

Before and after images can generate a significant amount of disk IO, and care needs to be taken to ensure that they do not become performance bottlenecks. Some of the methods of optimizing performance, subject to product implementation, include:

- Keeping them on separate disks or arrays, away from the database itself
- Keeping archive logs on a different disk/array from the active log to stop high disk activity when copying from active to archive log takes place
- Using RAW devices for the logs rather than file system devices
- Minimizing disk IOs where possible; for example, implementations that can write information relating to multiple transactions in a single IO are useful
- Using multiple log IO writers
- Having separate log buffers for each active transaction can avoid any log buffer contention, until the end of a transaction when they are transferred to the common buffer(s)

22.2.5 Parallel SQL Processing

Parallel processing is a generally available facility in many RDBMSs. However, the constraints (e.g., what type of statements can be parallelized and what subsidiary limitations there may be) will vary from product to product. It pays to read the small print very closely before deciding to use parallel processing, particularly when database updates are involved.

There are two discrete objectives in parallel processing; improving the response time of a transaction and increasing overall throughput.

Assuming that an SQL statement can be parallelized, a master or coordinator will split the work into a number of subtasks, as shown in Figure 22.5. On a query it may be that the data is physically partitioned across a number of tables, and that a subtask can be assigned to one or more partitions. If the data is not partitioned it may be possible to assign a subtask to a range of data within the table.

The relative success of parallel SQL will depend on precisely how much of the work can be devolved to sub-tasks. If the master task has to perform any appreciable work to collate the results from the subtasks (e.g., joins and sorts) the improvement in response times may not be as great as was thought. For parallel SQL to be beneficial, there must be sufficient resources available for the subtasks to use. To take a simple example, on a uniprocessor system, if an SQL statement spends 50 percent of its time using the CPU and 50 percent performing disk IO, there is little point in having more than two parallel tasks, even if there is no other work running on the system, because the CPU will become over-subscribed and the subtasks will just end up queueing for it, thus negating the benefits. Similarly, it is necessary to have sufficient IO bandwidth to cater for the required number of subtasks; if they are all competing for the use of a single disk then queues will occur.

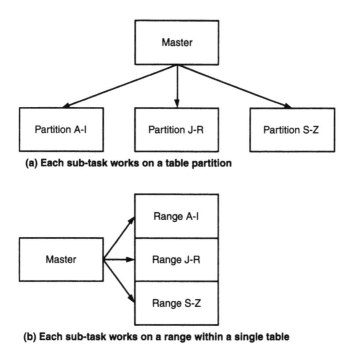

(a) Each sub-task works on a table partition

(b) Each sub-task works on a range within a single table

Figure 22.5   Parallel Query Approaches

Parallel SQL is particularly germane in multinode database systems. Products defined as "Share Nothing" work on the basis of partitioning data across the available server nodes. Each node is responsible for performing SQL on its own partition. Such systems therefore require the concepts of parallel SQL to access all partitions. Products defined as "Share Disk" also use parallel SQL in multinode solutions; it is just that the concepts are not so ingrained. Some of the issues relating to the performance of multinode databases are discussed in Chapter 23.

22.3   PERFORMANCE

A brief summary of key performance issues includes:

- Pragmatic database design. Fully normalized designs are likely to produce a number of performance issues. As the pressure to produce solutions in ever-shorter timescales increases, there is less scope to spend time denormalizing the design post-implementation.
- Lack of understanding of how the ODBC/JDBC driver interacts with the database, sloppy SQL, and the nature of any underlying

database networking protocol can all result in large amounts of network traffic between the client and DB server.

- It is extremely easy to write adventurous, poorly performing SQL. For a project of any reasonable size it is always recommended that a compact set of SQL guidelines be produced for developers.
- It is important to maximize use of all available system and data caches.
- Accesses need to be optimized, usually through the judicious use of indexes. However, remember that indexes are not always a panacea.
- The physical implementation of indexes, particularly on large tables, can be important to minimize the number of accesses that are required to locate them. Useful features include balanced tree structures, composite indexes, and bitmap indexes for decision support and low cardinality columns.
- Balancing IOs across an adequately configured disk subsystem is an important, but frequently forgotten, aspect of performance. Ideally, isolate before and after image logs from the database itself.
- Consider carefully the need for parallel SQL in a single node database. Although it is attractive and can bring improved performance, it can equally degrade overall performance in a high-activity system.
- The use of multinode database systems requires careful thought and design to ensure reasonable performance. Vendor claims that their products can obviate the need for careful design should be treated with a healthy degree of skepticism.

22.4 GENERAL OBSERVATIONS

Many people hold the view that relational databases are inherently IO bound. In my experience, this is not necessarily true. In cases where large volumes of data are being trawled through (e.g., decision support or large batch processes), the database may be well be IO bound. However, many OLTP systems that I have come across tend to be more CPU bound, mainly due to effective use of the various caching mechanisms, plus use of techniques such as multiblock reads and readahead.

Relational databases provide a rich set of functionality that comes at a price. They typically require significantly more processing power and memory than earlier database management systems, for example, hierarchical and network databases. The general maturity of the software plus the increases in hardware speeds has resulted in developers making ever-greater use of the features. It is therefore important to ensure that adequate hardware resources are available, particularly CPU and memory.

Relational databases are much more mature than application server software. When assessing where to place business processing, if there is a lack of confidence in the applications server it may be preferable to place some of the processing in the database layer, on the simple grounds that it is likely to be more reliable and better performing. If this approach is adopted on large-scale systems beware that there may be more pressure to make the database server scalable than the application servers.

As with any software, it pays to have a healthy cynicism towards the more recent features. In particular, be wary of the scalability of multinode databases and the overheads of XML database systems. Ideally, custom-built benchmarks should be run and evaluated before making a decision to use them on any large-scale systems.

Finally, there is a tendency for products to expand into other application areas. Although there may be cost incentives to use the DBMS for multiple purposes it is unlikely that it will perform as well as a native product.

22.5 FURTHER READING

I have no specific recommendations on general background reading. The majority of vendors provide sufficient background material that is freely available under the titles of "concepts" or "architecture," although it is sometimes necessary to read between the lines to understand how a particular feature is implemented. In addition, there are many comprehensive books available on the tuning of specific database products; I do not mention any specific titles.

Geiger, K., *Inside ODBC*, Microsoft, Redmond, WA, 1995. This book provides extremely useful background material on ODBC.

23

BACK-END SERVER CLUSTERS

A server cluster consists of multiple processor nodes that frequently act as a single logical system. Features vary from product to product, and can include high availability, load balancing, resource sharing, and parallel processing. There are two main categories of server clusters: primarily stateless specialist servers, such as firewalls and Web servers, and more general-purpose commercial servers that tend to be stateful, such as database and file servers. Stateless servers are discussed in Chapter 26. This taster concentrates on clustering software that is mainly aimed at general-purpose commercial servers. It commences with some background to server cluster technology, and discusses resilience features; the ability to share hardware and software resources; and parallel processing. Scientific high-performance clusters are not addressed.

23.1 BASIC TERMINOLOGY

- *Cache coherence* in this context signifies that, where multiple clients access a file system, each client can see an up-to-date copy of the data.
- *Fail-over* is the migration of a service (application and related resources) from a failed node to another node.
- *Network file systems* provide a common data store that can be accessed by multiple clients. Client/server communication is via an RPC-based protocol.
- *SAN* (Storage Area Network) provides the capability to pool storage and allow multiple hosts to access allocated part(s) of it.

23.2 TECHNOLOGY OUTLINE

23.2.1 Background

Digital introduced the VMS cluster in the mid-1980s. The main objective was to allow a number of servers to be linked together in a loosely coupled manner so that hardware and software resources could be shared. Arguably, the most widely used facility was the ability to specify shareable clusterwide devices such as disks, tapes, and printers. Even devices that were physically connected to a single server could be made available to other server nodes, via an interconnect. Distributed Lock Manager was the key to this technology.

UNIX vendors started to introduce their own "cluster" technology in the early 1990s. However, these products were significantly different from VMS clusters, mainly being limited to the provision of a high availability capability. If a server that was running an application failed, it was possible to automatically transfer the application, plus related disks, host IP address, and other resources, to another server; perform any necessary recovery tasks; and restart the application. This type of product was sometimes called "fail-over clustering," but it was frequently shortened to clustering, much to the annoyance of VMS devotees. The products have slowly evolved, mainly concentrating on extending and improving the high-availability features. Using their VMS experience, Digital led the way in introducing the concepts of global devices and resource sharing into its TruCluster product, and other vendors have since followed. The introduction of SANs and multinode file systems/databases have muddied the waters of device sharing and data sharing, as there are alternative approaches to achieving the same ends.

23.2.2 High Availability

The aspiration to run applications 24/7 has led to resilience features becoming the cornerstone of clustering technology for most businesses. The unit of fail-over is typically termed a service, resource group, or package (the term "service" is used in this taster). It consists of an application and the hardware and software resources that it uses, for example, disks, network cards, host IP address, and database. Each service will have a home server node where it normally runs. Simple clusters, as shown in Figure 23.1, may just consist of two server nodes with a shared set of disks. The second server node may simply be a standby that the service will be transferred to (failed over to) if the primary node fails. This is sometimes called "active-passive."

This can be a waste of resource. An alternative approach is to run two services, one on each node, which fail-over to each other, as shown in

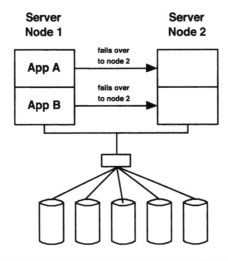

Figure 23.1   Simple Two-Node Fail-Over Cluster

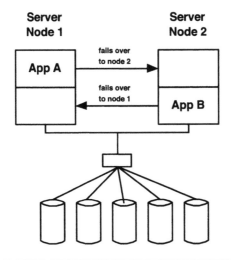

Figure 23.2   Active-Active Cluster

the diagram, sometimes called "active-active" (see Figure 23.2). The disadvantage of this approach is that in a failure situation one node will be running both services with a possible degradation in performance unless the servers have been sized to handle both services, but once again this increases the cost.

Larger and more sophisticated clusters may be configured as N, N+1, or N+n: that is, there may be zero, one, or more standby server nodes.

In the N case where there are no spare nodes, there will need to be additional processing capacity on one or more server nodes to allow fail-over to take place. More typically, one, or occasionally two, spare server nodes will be configured, not least so that maintenance can take place on a server node without necessarily having to take services down.

Products will vary on the options that can be used to decide to which node a service should fail-over. This may simply be a list consisting of first choice, second choice, and so on. Other options can include the server running the least number of services or the lightest loaded server.

The majority of products will provide a fail-back capability. When a failed server is working again the service is moved back to the home node. This can be desirable if performance on the fail-over node is unsatisfactory; for example, it is a less powerful server than the primary node (to keep costs down), or it is now running multiple services and it does not have sufficient power to support all of them satisfactorily. However, fail-back needs to be controlled. The service may have been unavailable for ten to fifteen minutes when the original fail-over took place, including time for any necessary application recovery. The last thing that is required, particularly if the failure was quickly fixed, is for another outage while the service is failed back. Even worse, a transient fault can result in the service being continually moved from primary to standby and back again!

Detecting service failures can be far from straightforward. The normal mechanism is heartbeat checking, where the server nodes check on each other by sending frequent "are you there" messages. The lack of a response within a configurable amount of time is taken as an indication that there is some sort of problem. If a server node has indeed failed due to a hardware or software failure, then fail-over processing can legitimately commence. However, there can be other reasons for the lack of a response. Some part of the network between the server nodes, either hardware or software, may have failed, and the server node may still in fact be running the service(s). If this was the case another node will attempt to start the service with data corruption highly likely, as both instances of the service will be accessing the same disks. One approach in this particular case is to have two network links between the servers to reduce the likelihood of a network failure. However, failure is still a possibility.

Most products have a mechanism for handling this type of problem. It is based around the concept of a quorum. Each part of the cluster works out how many nodes with which it can communicate. If at least 50 percent of the original nodes are present it continues to operate. If there are less than 50 percent then that part of the cluster will shut itself down. The problem here is what happens if each part of the cluster has 50 percent, for example, in a simple two-node cluster. This is called the

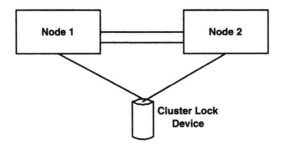

Figure 23.3 Cluster Lock Disk

split-brain syndrome. A mechanism is required to break this deadlock. A common approach is to have a disk to which both parts of the cluster have access. Each part attempts to reserve this disk; one will succeed and the other will fail. The part that fails will shut itself down and the successful part will continue. This disk is typically called a cluster lock disk (see Figure 23.3). Implementation issues concerning the number of server nodes that can theoretically access a cluster lock disk (typically using the SCSI disk reservation feature) will limit the number of nodes that this approach can support; it may be as little as two in some implementations. In addition, it is necessary to prevent any failed node from accessing shared disks to avoid data corruption; a mechanism called IO fencing is used for this purpose.

The discussion so far has assumed that a cluster resides in a single data center, and that there are therefore no distance issues. However, a cluster may span two data centers; this is sometimes referred to as a campus or extended cluster. The server nodes are split across two data centers, whereas the storage is mirrored from data center to data center. The idea is that in the case of a problem that knocks out one data center, the other data center will have enough server nodes plus a copy of the storage to carry on working. In this situation, a single cluster lock disk in one of the data centers would be insufficient; two disks will be required, one in each data center, that all nodes have access to — this is sometimes called a dual cluster lock.

Multiple site systems may require other approaches to the split-brain syndrome. An arbitration node, as shown in Figure 23.4, ideally in a third location with a separate power supply, rather than a cluster lock disk, is a possible approach for the extended cluster.

An alternative approach to multi-site clustering is to have a separate cluster in each data center with its own local fail-over capability and mirrored storage, as shown in Figure 23.5. Data is replicated between the two sites to keep them in sync. Individual server node failures are handled locally in the normal way. However, in the case of a site failure, all services

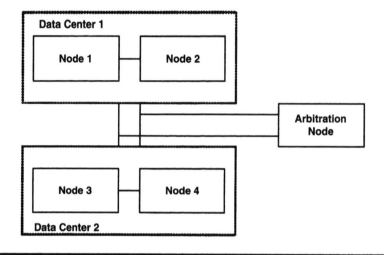

Figure 23.4 Arbitration Node

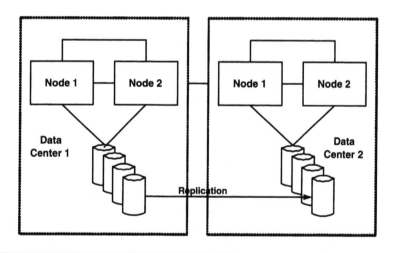

Figure 23.5 Multiple Clusters

are migrated to the other site. The decision to fail everything over to the other site is usually a manual decision ultimately, as it is a big step to take, not least because the storage on the primary site will get out of step and will ultimately require being resynchronized before it can be used again. The actual fail-over may be scripted to speed it up.

23.2.3 Shared Resources

Clusterwide devices such as disks, tapes, and printers are capable of being shared by the individual processor nodes. The most interesting aspect is arguably the sharing of disks, and more specifically the sharing of data on those disks. This subject is covered in the next section.

23.2.4 Scalability

Vendors frequently claim that their cluster products provide scalability. One claim from some vendors relates to "scaling out the network." This is, in the main, a mechanism to cater for multiple stateless servers, for example, Web servers. In essence, the software load-balancing technique described in Chapter 26 is used. Other areas where scalability is claimed are cluster file systems and multinode database systems.

23.2.4.1 *Multiple Server Shared File System*

This is the logical progression of a file system in order to make it more scalable. This type of system is sometimes referred to as a SAN file system or a cluster file system. In essence, pools of disks can be controlled as a single entity and accessed by multiple servers.

The typical approach (see Figure 23.6) is that one server node acts as the master for a file system; that is, it is the only one that is allowed to access metadata and to control locks. Other server nodes can read, and possibly write data directly but any metadata changes must be passed to the master for it to perform. This type of system will typically provide cache coherence across the servers via the use of locks or tokens. All communication between the server nodes is performed via some form of fast interconnect.

This type of system has to be made resilient by catering for server node failures, particularly of the master node. It is apparent that much internode network traffic can be generated in large-scale systems, and that therefore the performance of the interconnect that is used is important.

23.2.4.2 *Multiple Node Database*

Databases also need the ability to grow beyond the confines of a single server node. They have more complex problems to cope with, particularly locking, which is frequently done at a lower level of granularity, for example, at row rather than file level.

There are two main approaches that go under the titles of Share Disk and Share Nothing. As the name implies, in Share Nothing (see Figure 23.7) each node is solely responsible for accessing the tables in the disk devices that are connected to it.

This typically involves the physical partitioning of the data across the available nodes. Some form of function shipping (whole or subquery) is required to process the SQL on the appropriate node. Parallel queries are

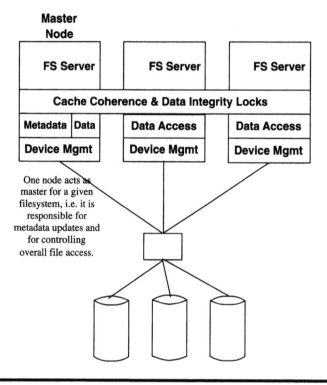

Figure 23.6   Multiple Server File System

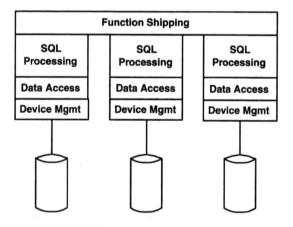

Figure 23.7   Share Nothing Database

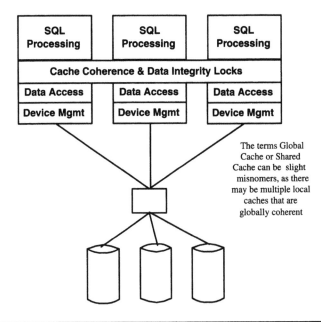

The terms Global
Cache or Shared
Cache can be slight
misnomers, as there
may be multiple local
caches that are
globally coherent

Figure 23.8 Share Disk Database

possible although this requires that the node that is charged with executing the original SQL must be able to distribute subqueries to the relevant nodes, and then collect and collate the responses.

Share Disk (see Figure 23.8) supports a database that is managed and accessed as a single image. Each node will have its own local cache. A global view of the cache is possible so that one node can have access to items that are currently in another node's cache. Note that the node that first accessed a block owns it. Ownership can be changed if it is detected that the majority of accesses are subsequently initiated by another node. Communication between nodes is achieved via the use of low-level protocols running over an interconnect that are used to maintain cache coherence and data integrity across the nodes.

The effectiveness of either Share Disk or Share Nothing systems is even more dependent on the speed and efficacy of the interconnect, given the greater volume of traffic that is required for record-level rather than file-level coherence.

23.3 PERFORMANCE

23.3.1 Heartbeat Checking

Connections between server nodes for heartbeat checking should be on dedicated links and network interfaces. If heartbeat messages use the same link as other traffic there is the danger of bottlenecks, and the subsequent failure of "I'm·alive" responses to be received within the acceptable time limits.

23.3.2 Speed of Service Fail-Over

This can be quicker if the processes have already been started prior to the failure and they are therefore capable of starting processing as soon as possible. The ability to do this depends on the cluster software and the application software. The major element of fail-over time is the part that is attributable to performing any necessary application recovery, for example, DB recovery. For this reason the users may not be able to access the system for ten to fifteen minutes, the actual time depending on the amount of recovery work that is required.

The use of remote mirroring to keep two data centers in sync needs careful design and implementation. Satisfactory synchronous mirroring requires low latency between sites to avoid performance problems. Asynchronous mirroring has overheads in both the hosts and the disk subsystems, whether they are software-based or hardware-based. Any significant distance between the sites, say in excess of 500 meters, may require the use of expensive fiber and long-wave multiplexers to support large volumes of replication.

23.3.3 Full Site Fail-Over

Because the decision to fail-over a complete site is manual, fail-over is not something that can be done as quickly as a simple local server node fail-over. Apart from the time that is necessary to fail-over multiple services, there is always the danger of data corruption if the primary disk subsystem fails suddenly or the link fails. This can lead to time being spent in identifying and rectifying the corruption, or at least in developing a temporary workaround. There may be other issues (e.g., network fail-over and staff-related issues) if there are other factors involved in the failure, apart from just a data center failure. Achieving a full site fail-over in two to three hours may be extremely good going. Figures that are quoted in some ITTs of full site fail-over in a matter of minutes are in most cases totally unrealistic.

23.3.4 Clusterwide Disk Sharing

Care needs to be taken with the placement of devices that need to support high volumes of shared access. In particular, a device that is locally attached to a single node may provide unsatisfactory performance if the majority of accesses is from other nodes via some form of cluster inter-connect.

A multiple server, shared file system should provide some degree of scalability. Write-intensive file systems will be less scalable than read-intensive file systems due to metadata updates being handled by a single master node. Overall performance will depend on the efficacy of the communication protocols between nodes, and crucially on the performance of the underlying interconnect.

The subject of multiple server node databases generates much debate. The Share Nothing approach is arguably better for decision support, whereas Share Disk may just have the edge only on OLTP. However, the nature of the application implementation can easily reverse this view. The potential bottlenecks are the volume of internode traffic on Share Nothing and data contention on Share Disk. However, this is slightly superficial — it depends on the individual implementation. Share Disk is arguably more flexible (e.g., the ability to re-master resources) and it is easier to cluster for resilience. In the final analysis, whatever approach is adopted, it is important in large systems not to rely totally on the underlying software to provide satisfactory performance and scalability. Data should ideally be partitioned, logically or physically, so that in the majority of cases internode traffic is either not required or it is at least minimized. Interconnect performance is absolutely crucial on these systems.

23.4 GENERAL OBSERVATIONS

The importance of interconnect performance has been mentioned several times, in this taster and elsewhere. Interconnect technology is evolving and performance varies greatly from vendor to vendor. Simple interconnects, for example, Ethernet (100 Mb or gigabit), may be satisfactory for systems with low to medium traffic. However, as the traffic increases and the protocols become more complex, low-latency interconnects are vital. For high-volume multiple node databases, latency should be measured in microseconds, not in milliseconds, to support the resultant internode traffic. Superior interconnects, sometimes called memory interconnects, naturally tend to have a higher price tag than commodity equivalents.

Clusters can be complex to install and to manage. Some vendors try to insist on installing the system and training a specified number of staff. This can be quite expensive, particularly if the cost is tied to the size of the server nodes. Ease of cluster management is an important criterion when evaluating products, more especially when multiple clusters in separate geographic locations need to be managed.

Software needs to be "cluster-aware." In many instances, the software is limited to a DBMS or a network file system, which is already cluster-aware, and hence is not a problem. Any other software, particularly bespoke software, may need to be modified to make it suitable for a cluster.

Be wary of software product vendors who claim scalability, as they may simply be relying on the facilities within a DBMS or file system or third-party load-balancing product when the product design may not be able to exploit these "built-in" facilities; that is, check that the product does in fact scale.

Do not assume that satisfactory database partitioning can always be achieved through the features that are supported by the RDBMS. Partitioning facilities within RDBMSs are evolving but they still have a long way to go. There is still no substitute for careful design.

Clustered or SAN file systems are relatively new and hence they are generally somewhat immature. Be wary of limitations, particularly on write-intensive applications, when evaluating products.

23.5 FURTHER READING

I have not come across any general reading material on back-end server clusters. Architecture, concepts, and system administrator manuals (if you can get access to them) relating to individual products are the best starting point. Products include TruCluster Compaq), Sun Cluster 3, ServiceGuard (HP), HACMP (IBM), Microsoft Cluster Server, and Veritas Cluster Server.

Similarly, vendor material is the best place to find information on cluster file systems and multiple node databases.

24

NETWORK BASICS

Network technologies, both hardware and software, form a huge area, making it somewhat challenging to distill the basics into a taster. From a hardware perspective, the emphasis is biased towards LAN rather than WAN technologies. Similarly, comments on software are limited to IP-based networks.

24.1 BASIC TERMINOLOGY

- *ASIC* (Application Specific Integrated Circuit) chips are purpose-built for a specified task.
- *IP* (Internet Protocol) is the most popular network protocol for communication between devices.
- *IP Datagram* is the basic unit of information that is passed across the network.
- *MAC* (Media Access Control) *Address* is a hardware address that identifies each node of a network.
- *TCP* (Transmission Control Protocol) provides a reliable transmission service that sits on top of IP.
- *UDP* (User Datagram Protocol) also sits on top of IP. It is thinner and faster than TCP but it lacks TCP's inbuilt reliability of transmission.

24.2 TECHNOLOGY OUTLINE

24.2.1 The Seven Layers

Before discussing technologies it is useful to introduce the frequently quoted OSI model. Its seven layers, shown in Table 24.1, break the various components of networking up into meaningful elements: the higher layers

Table 24.1 OSI Layers

Layer	Name/Typical Use
7	Application (e.g., FTP)
6	Presentation (data formatting, encryption)
5	Session (negotiate connections including passwords)
4	Transport (e.g., TCP, UDP)
3	Network (e.g., IP)
2	Data Link (e.g., Ethernet packets)
1	Physical (e.g., cabling and signals)

reflect why the network is there in the first place, to support applications that need to transfer data over network links, and the lower layers gradually move towards more technical and hardware-oriented matters. Although the OSI model provides a useful reference point, it should be noted that actual implementations will vary; some layers may not be used, and some functions may overlap layers.

24.2.2 IP

Internet Protocol has gained hugely in popularity since the early 1990s. It sits at layer 3 in the OSI model and it provides the foundation for IP datagrams, the basic unit of information that is passed across the network. The use of IP is now being extended into areas other than simply communication networks, for example, in the storage arena (SCSI over IP).

TCP and UDP are transport-level software components (layer 4) that sit on top of IP. TCP provides a reliable transport service, handling issues such as nonarrival, packets arriving out of sequence (because they went over different network paths), throughput, and performance. As it was originally developed for use over relatively unreliable WANs, it is regarded as a fat (i.e., complex) protocol. It is used by most applications, arguably because of its in-built reliability. UDP is a much thinner protocol, and hence it is a better performer. However, the penalty is that it does not provide reliable transport, as TCP does. Reliability has to be built in by the software developer. It follows that UDP is less popular than TCP.

The protocol suite, usually referred to as TCP/IP, is implemented as a stack, the term referring to the network layers. Many stacks are implemented in the operating system kernel.

Application-level protocols sit on top of TCP or UDP. Examples include FTP and HTTP. HTTP 1.0 is stateless; each HTTP request having to establish its own connection with a server. It is this lack of persistence that allows Web servers to support many thousands of users without needing to keep

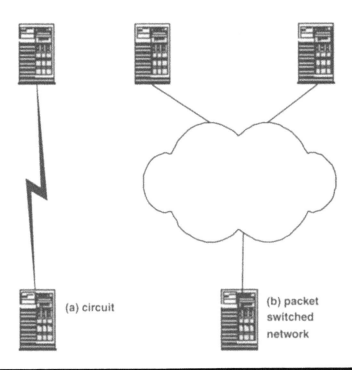

Figure 24.1   Point-to-Point and Packet-Switched

track of whether they are still connected. The disadvantage is the overhead of establishing connections every time. HTTP v1.1 does provide the capability to keep sessions alive but it is little used.

24.2.3   Brief Overview of WAN Technologies

As companies tend to purchase network services from a provider, and are thus not exposed to the low-level detail, this section is deliberately brief.

WANs were traditionally implemented using circuit switching or packet switching (Figure 24.1). In a circuit switching network a dedicated communications path is established between two endpoints through the nodes of the network. A telephone network is an example of circuit switching. In packet switching, dedicated paths are not used. Packets (small amounts of data) progress from node to node in a store-and-forward fashion along some path from source to destination. Packet-switched networks are used for computer-to-computer communications. Diagrams usually show a packet-switched network in the form of a cloud, as the precise path is not known.

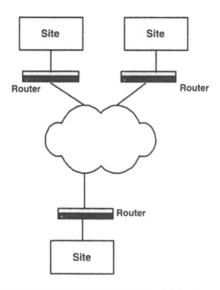

Figure 24.2   Routers

Early packet-switched networks had relatively high error rates, and therefore a significant amount of overhead was built into packet-switched systems to deal with error handling. The advent of faster and more reliable networks led to the introduction of Frame Relay, which was able to run at higher speeds, up to 2 Mbps initially, by removing much of the overhead involved in error handling.

ATM (Asynchronous Transmission Mode) evolved from Frame Relay. It uses small fixed-length cells of 53 bytes, as opposed to the variable length frames in Frame Relay, thus reducing the processing overhead, and resulting in small latency. It was originally designed to run at up to 622 Mbps, typically over optical fiber. Note that Frame Relay can run over the top of ATM.

ISDN (Integrated Services Digital Network) was originally intended to be a worldwide public telecommunications network, providing a wide variety of services. The initial implementation used a 64-Kbps channel as the basic unit of switching, and it has a circuit-switching orientation. ISDN is frequently used to provide resilience if the main network link is out of action.

Routers are used to forward packets along the network. They are connected to at least two parts of the network, for example, site LAN to ISP network (see Figure 24.2). They operate at layer 3 of the OSI model, for example, IP. They are used to aid network performance through the use of routing protocols that can find the best path between two points, and they can dynamically change the route when part of the network is

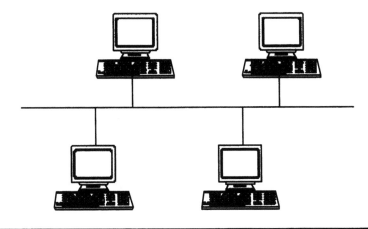

Figure 24.3   Bus

unavailable. There are two forms of routing, static and dynamic. A network person enters static routing information, whereas with dynamic routing the software works out the paths in conjunction with other routers. Dynamic routing naturally involves more overhead than static routing.

24.2.4   Basic LAN Topologies

There are four principal topologies that are used to connect devices on a LAN:

- *Bus* (Figure 24.3). Devices are connected to a single cable (the bus). Early Ethernet implementations using coaxial cable are a typical example, each device being connected to the cable via a "tap." Only one device can use the bus at any one time and a method of arbitration is required to resolve clashes where two devices both want the bus at the same time. In Ethernet, this process is termed CSMA/CD (Carrier Sense Multiple Access/Collision Detection).
- *Ring* (Figure 24.4). Devices are connected to a closed ring; Token Ring and FDDI are examples of rings. In Token Ring, frames (as they are termed) pass around the ring from source to target device and eventually back to the source, it is hoped with an acknowledgment that the message was successfully received.
- *Star* (Figure 24.5). All devices are connected to a central device such as a hub or a switch. Most technologies now use this approach, including Ethernet and Token Ring, although they still adhere to their rules; for example, an Ethernet hub will broadcast a message from a device to all other devices.

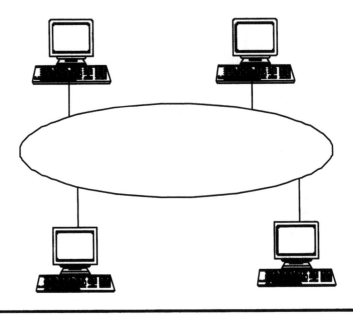

Figure 24.4   Ring

- *Mesh*. Every device is directly connected to every other device (full mesh), as shown in Figure 24.6, or to several devices (partial mesh). This is potentially expensive except in small networks.

24.2.5   Hubs and Switches

Devices are typically connected within a single LAN by plugging them into a hub or a switch. A hub effectively acts as a bus, simultaneously transmitting frames to all devices. A switch allows a 1:1 relationship between any input and output port; it can effectively be viewed as point-to-point communication. A hub is cheaper than a switch but it suffers from collisions, which, as indicated in the bus topology, can affect performance. A switch is more expensive but it suffers from minimal collisions (they only occur when an inbound and an outbound frame meet at a port), and hence it provides better performance.

24.2.6   Inter-Ethernet LAN Connectivity

The options for connecting LANs include the use of bridges, routers, and switches.

Bridges work at layer 2 in the OSI model. In the first instance they can be considered as a means of joining two or more LANs into a single larger LAN, as shown in Figure 24.7. However, only traffic that is destined

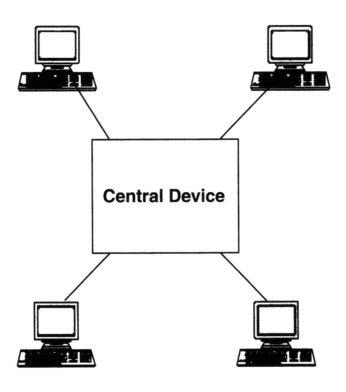

Figure 24.5   Star

for a device on another LAN should traverse the bridge; purely local traffic should be contained within the local LAN. Adaptive bridges learn which devices are on a LAN and they can therefore prevent traffic frames destined for local devices from needlessly crossing the bridge. However, any broadcast traffic is forwarded across the bridge. This is a potential disadvantage for IP-based systems, as they tend to perform a lot of broadcasting, not least for lower-level functions such as ARP (Address Resolution Protocol) that is used to map an IP address onto a MAC address.

Routers work at layer 3, the network protocol layer. They are more expensive than bridges, being more powerful and sophisticated devices, as they have to perform more work; for example, they have to look at the contents of the frame. They do, however, prevent broadcast traffic from spreading. Routers are normally used when any noticeable distance is involved, such as connection over a WAN. Note that bridges should not be used over WAN links because of the broadcast overheads. Routers provide other important network functionality, for example, load balancing of traffic, choice of best path, and reconfiguring in case of a failure.

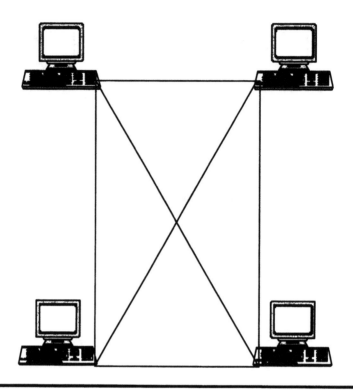

Figure 24.6 Mesh

Layer-2 switches (Figure 24.8) have become very popular in the construction of LAN architectures. LAN segments that are connected via a switch form separate collision domains, thus reducing overheads and providing better performance, although they remain part of the same broadcast domain.

The concept of Virtual LANs (VLANs) provides a mechanism to control the extent of a broadcast domain. The simplest method is to group two or more ports on the switch to form a single VLAN. Other possible groupings, depending on the product, are by MAC address, by layer-3 information (e.g., protocol type or network layer address), or by IP multicast group.

The switching fabric typically takes one of two forms: a multiplexed bus or a crossbar. The multiplexed bus effectively makes one input-output connection at a time, whereas the crossbar can handle parallel connections (see Figure 18.3 for an example of a crossbar switch). It follows that crossbar switching is preferable where high-speed switching is required. With regard to the method of switching, there are two approaches. In the store and forward approach, no decisions are made until the entire frame is captured. This introduces some latency, up to 1.2 ms for a maximum-sized frame,

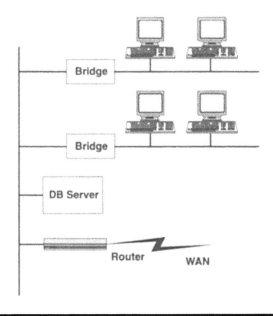

Figure 24.7   Use of Bridges

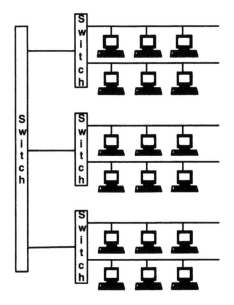

Figure 24.8   Use of LAN Switches

which may affect applications such as video streaming. Cut-through switching can commence as soon as the destination MAC address has been read, thus significantly reducing the latency. Finally, switches are cheaper and faster than routers but they lack a router's range of functionality.

Layer-3 switches support layer-2 switching and routerlike functionality, for example, IP datagrams on a per-port basis.

24.2.7 Inter-Data Center Communication

DWDM (Dense Wavelength Division Multiplexing) is a technique that maximizes the capacity of fiber links that are used to connect data centers. This is achieved by using different light wavelengths to transmit data. A useful analogy that I have seen equated a fiber link with a multilane highway where only one lane could be used; DWDM allows all the lanes to be used. DWDM devices strip off wavelengths and use each of them as a separate connection for potentially different purposes, for example, gigabit Ethernet, fiber channel, and so on. There are claims to support a total of 80 Gbps. DWDMs provide a popular means of connecting data centers, for example, for remote disk mirroring or remote backup purposes. They are expensive devices.

24.2.8 Scalable Networks

Before discussing scalability, the key watchword for a network design for any large or business critical system must be reliability. For example, there is little point in building expensive, high-availability server farms if the users cannot access them. It is critical to build resilience into a network design to provide a solid infrastructure for users and systems.

The principles of partitioning a workload that have been discussed in Chapter 7 apply equally to networks. The terminology that is used is different. At the bottom end segmentation is the term applied to splitting a LAN into discrete areas to contain purely local traffic so that it does not affect overall LAN performance. At the top end, terms such as hierarchical design and backbone are used. The main backbone will typically provide the fastest links and switches to support the required traffic with the minimum amount of latency. There may be several layers in the hierarchy, for example, core (corporate level), distribution (region), and access (office), as shown in Figure 24.9.

24.2.9 Citrix and Microsoft Terminal Servers

I mention Citrix and Microsoft terminal servers at this point, as the subject has significant network implications, and it is not addressed elsewhere.

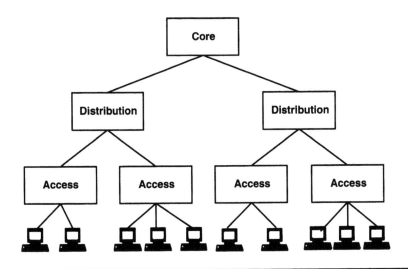

Figure 24.9   Scalable Network Hierarchy

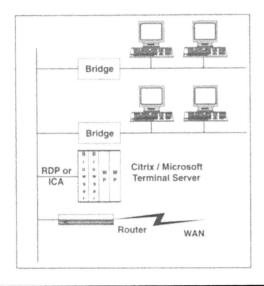

Figure 24.10   Citrix/Microsoft Terminal Server

In essence, they allow PC software (e.g., an Internet browser, word processing, and other office software packages) to be hosted on a server that is capable of supporting multiple concurrent users (see Figure 24.10). The user only requires a fairly simple, inexpensive terminal device (called a WID) to use the software rather than a fully functional PC. The reason for this is that the terminal is simply used as a means of input (key strokes and mouse movements) and output (screen display). ICA (Independent Computing Architecture) and RDP (Remote Desktop Protocol) are the protocols that supports WID-to-server communication. The inexpensive WIDs make the concept attractive, particularly to organizations in the public sector.

24.3 PERFORMANCE

A key network design objective is to minimize the number of hops that is necessary on both WANs and LANs for data to get from the source to the destination device. Each hop introduces a delay (a) to queue for the device, (b) to perform any necessary processing, and (c) in the transmission time between devices. Even blackbox products such as routers, firewalls, and switches will add overheads for a single packet — possibly submillisecond for a switch, a small number of milliseconds for a router — whereas the overhead can be greater for firewalls and load balancers, depending on the features that are used. Although the figures may sound modest, they can affect performance if there are a large number of hops and a reasonable number of packets to be moved. With respect to server LANs, Web, application, and DB servers can all generate significant network traffic, in addition to the delays imposed by their own processing loads, and therefore they can affect performance.

The use of utilization thresholds is a standard method of ensuring satisfactory performance. Any device, networking or otherwise, cannot be driven at high utilizations without the attendant danger that queues will form and ultimately degrade performance. Many devices (e.g., WAN links and Ethernet switches) can be driven at 60 to 70 percent with modest queueing. Other devices may benefit from running at lower utilizations. For example, Ethernet hubs have to handle collisions and they should be limited to 30 to 40 percent utilization for this reason. Ultimately, it depends upon what level of performance is required. If fast response times are justified by the business requirements lower utilization thresholds may be built into the design even for links or devices that could be driven at 60 to 70 percent; for example, it may be decided to limit WAN links to 40 percent utilization in an attempt to ensure good network performance.

The available WAN/LAN capacity should be used frugally by the applications. This comment appears in a number of places in this book. For example, the number of round-trips between requester and responder should be minimized, and only required data should be transferred, where possible.

Data compression is another method of reducing the use of network capacity. It has always been a prerequisite for the movement of images, and latterly other forms of multimedia, to allow anything like reasonable performance. With regard to the text, the usefulness of compression depends on the CPU overheads of compressing data at the sender's end and decompressing it at the receiver's end; there is little point in saving some network transmission time if more time is spent in compression/decompression. It helps if static files have previously been compressed; however, the move to greater use of dynamic content mostly nullifies the benefits of pre-compression in standard commercial systems. HTTP supports compression but there appears to be limited support for it among Web server products.

From a performance perspective, the overheads of establishing connections and sending/receiving packets assume greater importance than the volume of data that is involved. Where possible, keeping connections open and using larger messages can improve performance.

Traffic shaping is a set of methods for handling heavy bursts of network traffic. Approaches include prioritized queues to ensure that higher priority traffic gets preference when the network gets overloaded; and TCP rate control, where an application tells the client-side to reduce its packet rate.

Broadcast traffic and multicast traffic should be used sensibly, where possible. The heavy use of such facilities, particularly on IP systems, can adversely affect performance unless sensible LAN segmentation is used.

Where possible, security software other than firewalls or anti-virus checking should be nonintrusive, for example, passively sampling passing packets on a network rather than being part of the data flow and thereby introducing additional delays.

TCP is a "fat" protocol; that is, it contains much functionality relating to reliable delivery (its *raison d'être*) and network performance. On the latter subject there is a variety of tuning parameters that can be tweaked to improve overall performance/throughput, such as the window size (the number of packets that can be sent out before an acknowledgment is required). The main observation on TCP performance is that its focus is on overall network performance rather than the needs of individual applications or transactions. UDP will perform better but it does not provide reliable delivery; such a facility would have to be built into the application. Streaming video is a ready example where TCP is not fast enough to avoid "jitter." Protocols such as RTP (Real-Time Protocol) and RTSP (Real-Time Streaming Protocol) have been developed to support streaming, but they are typically built on top of UDP.

From a server perspective TCP is not particularly scalable over a single link. Vendors appear loath to mention the performance of their particular stack. It is noticeable that in benchmarks such as SPECWeb99 vendors will configure a one-gigabit link per CPU in an attempt to improve throughput. There are a number of possible reasons for poor performance:

the complex nature of the protocol, implementation in stack layers may produce a modular solution but hinder parallelization, parts of the stack that are serialized, the overheads of checksum processing, and context switching overheads (if the stack is not implemented in the kernel).

A frequently quoted mantra is that it requires 1 MHz of CPU power to support 1 Mbps. In theory, all things being equal, a 1-GHz CPU can therefore support a 1-Gigabit link (or so the inference goes). Even if the amount of processing is minimized, say by serving up the same cached HTML file over and over, there is usually little chance of getting anywhere near 1 Gbps on a single link; 200 to 300 Mbps is more likely for a full TCP implementation. TCP scalability was, and probably remains, an area of research. Refinements include increasing parallel processing (e.g., different CPUs handling different layers of the stack) and hardware-assisted solutions. The latter take the form of TCP accelerator cards, or "offload engines" as they are called. These cards may contain only a cut-down version of the full TCP/IP stack. They may be more appropriate for reliable interserver communication over a LAN (e.g., a NAS appliance), rather than for the vagaries of travel across an Internet to a Web server. The bottom line is to be wary of what throughput can be supported by a single server. In lieu of any better information I would assume no more than 200 to 250 Mbps per single 1-gigabit link.

Citrix and Microsoft terminal server systems must be carefully sized. In the first instance (and the reason why it is included here), there can be a great deal of communications traffic between the device and the server, significantly greater than was required to support dumb terminals on simple text-only systems before the arrival of Windows and the mouse. The network needs to be carefully designed to avoid poor performance. Apart from straightforward bandwidth considerations, I have seen examples where the WIDs were in one location and the server many hops away over the other side of a WAN. In these circumstances the simple echoing of a keystroke on the screen can be tortuous. In addition to the network concerns, the server itself requires careful sizing of CPU processing power, memory, and possibly disk. Vendor sizing guidelines that I have seen tend to be overly optimistic, and they should be viewed skeptically for systems with high transaction rates. In-house benchmarks are recommended, simulating the workload(s) that need to be supported, to aid the overall server and network sizing process.

24.4 GENERAL OBSERVATIONS

I make no apologies for repeating this message: Network resilience is hugely important. Working servers are of little use if nobody can get to them.

When procuring network services from a provider, ensure that you fully understand the resilience that is being offered. One project that I came across required a number of 4-Mbit connections. Each connection, for an area office, had to be resilient. The majority of vendors dutifully quoted 2 × 4-Mbit connections. However, one vendor quoted a resilient 4-Mbit connection, which in fact consisted of 2 × 2 Mbit. Needless to say, this was cheaper, and the client signed up for it, without realizing that he was not getting 4 Mbit when a failure occurred.

Procuring network bandwidth is often the point where the aggressive response time requirements of the client meet the cold light of cost reality. Fast response times will usually require that network links are run at low utilization levels, possibly as low as 20 to 30 percent, to minimize queueing, which means that more bandwidth must be configured. A frequent result is to decide that perhaps running at 50 to 70 percent utilization may be acceptable after all.

Be wary of vendor benchmark results on networks and network devices, including devices such as firewalls, server load balancers, and Web servers in the data center. Ensure that you understand how the benchmark applies to your situation. In particular, beware of the use of excessive network capacity and specialized, not fully functional, tests.

24.5 FURTHER READING

Stallings, W., *Data and Computer Communications*, 5th ed., Prentice-Hall, Englewood Cliffs, NJ, 1997.

Kumar, B., *Broadband Communications*, McGraw-Hill, New York, 1995.

Dooley, K., *Designing Large-Scale LANs*, O'Reilly, Sebastopol, CA, 2002. An excellent and practical book on LAN technologies.

Comer, D.E., *Internetworking with TCP/IP Volume 1; Principles, Protocols, and Architecture*, Prentice-Hall, Englewood Cliffs, NJ, 1991.

Yates, D.J., Nahum, E.M., Kurose, J.F., and Towsley, D., Networking Support for Large Scale Multiprocessor Servers, *SIGMETRICS*, 1996 can be found at www.citeseer.com.

Ravindran, K. and Singh, G., Architectural Concepts in Implementation of End-System Protocols for High Performance Communications, *ICNP 1996*. This paper can be found at www.citeseer.com.

Ya-Li Wong, A. and Seltzer, M., Evaluating Windows NT Terminal Server Performance, *Proceedings of the Third USENIX Windows NT Symposium*, 1999. This paper can be found at www.usenix.org. It provides a useful, dispassionate view of this technology.

25

FIREWALLS

Firewall technology is used to provide basic security protection against unauthorized access mainly into, but also out of, an organization. It forms part of an overall security solution. Firewalls are sold either as software only, or as blackbox solutions, usually termed appliances, consisting of both hardware and software.

25.1 BASIC TERMINOLOGY

- *Application* in this context refers to general-purpose communication software that provides useful facilities to developers. It does not typically refer to user applications. Examples include FTP (File Transfer Program), HTTP (HyperText Transfer Protocol), SMTP (Simple Mail Transfer Protocol), and TelNet (Terminal Emulation).
- *Latency* is the elapsed time taken for a packet of data to get through the firewall.
- *VRRP* (Virtual Router Redundancy Protocol) is used to provide resilience with multiple firewalls.

25.2 TECHNOLOGY OUTLINE

25.2.1 Functionality

The functionality can vary from product to product but the main categories are briefly described here.

- *Packet filtering*. This provides the most basic form of checking, including the protocol being used (e.g., TCP, UDF), the IP address of the sender, the packet destination, and port number of the

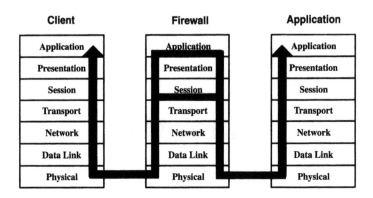

Figure 25.1   Proxy and Application Gateway Routes

application (e.g., HTTP, FTP, SMTP). This type of checking is also frequently deployed in routers. It is low in performance overheads; that is, it will perform well, but the level of security is modest.

■ *Proxy server.* See Figure 25.1. The objective is to prevent direct sessions between the client and the application and thus stop TCP- or IP-level attacks. After a client session is authenticated by the firewall it is terminated here and the firewall creates its own session with the internal application. There is obviously a performance overhead associated with the creation and tearing down of these additional connections.

■ *Cut-off proxy.* This term is arguably a misnomer. It provides the authentication of the client session, just as the proxy server does but then it allows subsequent direct connection between the client and the application, and uses packet filtering. This approach performs better than a proxy server but it is not as secure.

■ *Application-level gateway.* This is a refinement of the proxy server. Code is specifically developed for each application (e.g., FTP, HTTP, and Telnet), and is referred to as a gateway. An appropriate gateway is required to allow traffic through; for example, if only FTP and HTTP gateways are present only those types of traffic will be allowed through. Within a given gateway, further checks can be made by inspecting the contents of the packets. For example, FTP might be allowed from server to client but not from client to server. This provides better security but it is obviously more resource intensive.

■ *Stateful inspection.* This is a further refinement on the application-level gateway. It allows inspection of the packets using user-defined rules. This provides more control but once again there are potential performance implications, as more resources are required.

■ *Air gap.* In this approach inbound data is written to disk on the firewall and the recipient reads it from disk. This approach is relatively new and it is being hotly debated. Writing/reading to disk is a definite performance penalty.

The basic message from this overview is that better security requires more hardware resources.

25.2.2 High Availability (HA)

A firewall constitutes a single point of failure that can prevent users from accessing any services that reside on the servers that sit behind it. A simple method of providing resilience is to configure two firewalls and link them via VRRP, an industry standard protocol that supports HA for network devices, or a similar protocol. In essence, heartbeat-monitoring techniques are used to detect the failure of a firewall, the standby taking over when required. Changes to the rules on one firewall are replicated to the other firewall so that it is ready to take over when required. The target time for fail-over is typically within 30 seconds.

25.2.3 Scalability

See Chapter 26 for details of hardware and software approaches to scalability for stateless devices such as firewalls and server load balancers. Adding additional firewalls using either the hardware or software load-balancing approach can expand a firewall subsystem. Several vendors provide hardware solutions where a load-balancer (sometimes called a traffic switch) fronts a number of firewalls and load balances packets across them. There is at least one software solution available for load balancing across multiple firewalls. These solutions provide resilience as well as scalability.

25.3 PERFORMANCE

The functionality that is provided by a firewall, particularly the use of proxies, makes it important that firewall software be designed with care. As discussed in Chapter 14, the need to move between user mode and kernel mode, particularly when transferring packet data, results in frequent context switching, which can be a drain on performance. Any effort to minimize context switching, usually by performing the majority of processing in kernel mode, will be beneficial from a performance perspective.

Vendors frequently quote benchmark figures. Caution is required when assessing the figures provided. The first step is to check the network bandwidth that was configured in the tests and compare it with your likely available bandwidth. Beware of throughput figures that are based solely on the use of large packets unless that is your requirement; a smaller number of packets means less performance overhead and consequently more impressive figures. Throughput figures quoted over a range of packet sizes would be preferable. Figures are often quoted on the maximum number of connections that can be supported, for example, in relation to proxy server usage. However, what else is done during the test? If it is an artificial test that is simply creating/tearing down connections (and beware that it may not even be tearing them down) then that is not a particularly representative test. Latency (the time taken to pass through the firewall) is a key metric as it contributes to overall response times. However, it can be difficult to extract latency figures from vendors. When figures can be obtained it is important to understand how they were derived. *In extremis* it may be for a single simple rule with a low packet size, under no load, which is not terribly helpful. Ideally, latency figures should be provided for representative workloads and under varying load conditions.

Some firewalls will support SSL (Secure Socket Layer). Hardware accelerators are preferable to software, given the performance overheads of the latter.

25.4 GENERAL OBSERVATIONS

The performance of firewalls depends on the features used, the number of rules employed, the design of the firewall software, the power of the underlying hardware, and the network bandwidth. Vendor benchmarks will typically use large amounts of network bandwidth, a minimal rule set, and large packet sizes to get optimum results. It is important that these factors be taken into account when assessing what size firewall subsystem will be required to support your application.

Firewall latency is particularly important because it affects overall response times. Press vendors for figures or perform your own tests if you are reasonably worried. If you are concerned with response times do not be tempted to run firewalls at anywhere near the vendor-quoted figures as latency will undoubtedly be a factor, perhaps running at 30 to 50 percent of any vendor-quoted figures (or less depending on your concerns).

Firewall sandwiches are popular. By this I mean an outer firewall in a DMZ (Demilitarized Zone) in front of a Web server and an inner firewall that is sited somewhere between a Web server and either an application or DB server. Inner firewalls are a particular performance concern, as they can typically have to handle more traffic than the outer firewall. I have recently seen a system where significant NFS-based disk IO traffic went through a modest inner firewall. If inner firewalls must be used, it is important that they are sized correctly to avoid performance degradation.

When purchasing a firewall pair check to see if the two nodes run as active-passive (passive is essentially an idle standby) or if both are active.

If a firewall cluster is being considered, check out the overheads. For a software-based solution find out from the vendor what the LAN and CPU overheads are likely to be. For a hardware-based server load balancer, find out what additional latency the load balancer will add under varying load conditions.

Firewall appliances will typically provide better performance and scalability than server-based solutions, but typically at greater cost.

Finally, other security software (e.g., intrusion detection) should ideally be nonintrusive, for example, passively sampling passing packets on a network rather than being part of the data flow and thereby introducing additional delays. Anti-virus software (e.g., scanning of documents or e-mails) needs to be adequately sized to avoid undue latency.

25.5 FURTHER READING

RFC 2544 Benchmarking Methodology For Network Interconnect Devices. This document can be located on the IETF (Internet Engineering Task Force) Web site (www.ietf.org).

Vendors typically provide a range of white papers on their public-facing Web sites. Unfortunately, many are lacking in any reasonable level of technical detail and are really just marketing material. The exceptions that I have seen include the following.

Paul Henry. An Examination of Firewall Architectures (Cyberguard Web site).
Overview of Firewall Techniques (Chapter 1 of Tunix Firewall white paper).
Stateful Inspection (Check Point white paper).

26

SERVER LOAD BALANCING

This taster covers the use of facilities to split network traffic across multiple server devices, primarily firewalls, Web servers, and application servers, to provide a means of both resilience and scalability. There is a variety of options, ranging from software only to hardware-based blackbox solutions. This taster commences with the load balancing of devices such as firewalls and Web servers that typically do not need to store state information. Discussion continues with the implications of maintaining state on Web and application servers.

26.1 BASIC TERMINOLOGY

- *ASIC* (Application Specific Integrated Circuit) chips are purpose-built for a specified task.
- *DNS* (Domain Name Server) provides a mechanism to locate a required server.
- *HTTP* (HyperText Transfer Protocol) is the lingua franca of Web browsers and servers, allowing different programs to work together.
- *NLB* (Network Load Balancer) used to refer to a hardware load balancer.
- *Round-robin* is a technique where the first request is routed to server 1, the second to server 2, and so on to server n, and then back around to server 1.
- *SSL* (Secure Sockets Layer) is a protocol that provides encryption.
- *State* is any application- or system-level information that relates to a particular user session. A stateful server is one that retains state information in memory between requests for a given session. A stateless server is one that either does not need state information, or if it does it will retrieve the information from a shared source, for example, a database.

- *VRRP* (Virtual Router Redundancy Protocol) is used to provide resilience for hardware load balancers.

26.2 TECHNOLOGY OUTLINE

26.2.1 Load Balancing Approaches

Load balancing is performed at layers 3 to 7. Examples include: IP address (layer 3), TCP port (layer 4), and URL (layer 7). Greater throughput is achieved when it is possible to load balance at layers 3 and 4, as the processing overheads are usually modest. Parsing a URL at layer 7 is more processor intensive.

The methods of load balancing vary by product but the options include:

- Sticky sessions (specified session traffic always goes to the server that it is initially allocated).
- Round-robin (first message to server 1, second message to server 2, and so on).
- The best performing server means that the load balancer has to continually check the responsiveness of each server that can be an overhead.
- The server with the least number of connections.
- Weighted percentages. A bias can be given to specified servers so that they receive more or less traffic. This is mostly used where the target servers have different hardware specifications; for example, one server may be twice as fast as the others and it should therefore be weighted to receive twice the traffic.
- Using the contents of a cookie.
- Using the URL name or part of the name.
- SSL switch.

26.2.2 Software Load Balancing

Figure 26.1 shows a simple logical view of software load balancing. The actual approaches vary, as discussed below.

Domain Name Server (DNS) is the oldest, and arguably the simplest and cheapest approach. It provides a rudimentary round-robin facility but it tends not to handle failures of the target servers particularly well. It may be suitable for low-volume applications where there are a small number of devices to be load balanced.

Serious load balancing requires more sophisticated software than DNS. Techniques vary significantly. Some designs adopt a master and slaves approach, sometimes called a dispatcher-based approach. If the master has to distribute each item of work across the slaves then it may ultimately

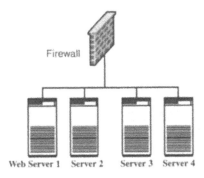

Figure 26.1   Simplified Software Load Balancing

become a bottleneck at high volumes, and affect response times. Performance may also be affected by the network overhead of having to redirect a large volume of traffic. A solution to this problem is to use "sticky sessions." Here the master only gets involved at the beginning of a session (e.g., user log-in) allocating a specified slave to a user. That slave is subsequently used for the life of the session and the master is bypassed. This approach can provide an effective solution although the load-balancing granularity may be somewhat coarse, a round-robin technique being frequently used. As the master is the cornerstone it is important that the software can cope with its loss; it should be possible for one of the slaves to assume the master role when required.

A recently popular approach is to remove the need for a master. In this technique packets are broadcast to each of the target servers, for example, by using IP multicast. An algorithm is run on each server to decide if it should process the packet or discard it. Obviously the idea is that only one node actually processes the packet. The servers communicate with each other and they can detect the failure of a server, or indeed the addition of new servers, and thereby feed that information into the algorithm to adjust the distribution of packets across the modified number of servers. The disadvantage of this approach is increased network traffic as the packet goes to every server, plus there is the CPU overhead in the server of handling packets that are discarded. Check with the vendor but there could be a ten to twenty percent CPU overhead on each target server.

26.2.3   Hardware Approach

A blackbox, sometimes called a server/network load balancer or a traffic switch, is placed in front of the farm of target servers; see Figure 26.2. It can be configured in a variety of ways to distribute the requests (see Section 26.2.1). There are two types of hardware load balancer, server-based and switch-based.

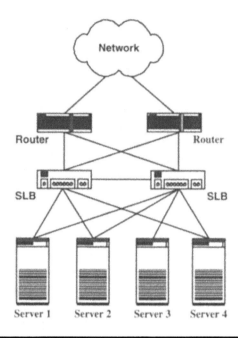

Figure 26.2   Hardware Load Balancing (High Availability)

Server-based systems typically employ a general PC-style design for the hardware. The use of faster CPUs is obviously preferred for performance reasons. Some implementations in fact employ dual CPUs. If SSL is required to support encryption for any significant volume of transactions, a system that is configured with hardware SSL acceleration is preferable to ensure reasonable performance, as software-based SSL is extremely onerous in performance terms. The operating system is usually OEMed or freeware although some vendors have their own purpose-built version.

Switch-based systems fully deserve the soubriquet "blackbox," as it can be extremely difficult to find information on their architectures. They use purpose-built, higher-performance ASIC chips to handle packets, sometimes in conjunction with a general-purpose CPU. They also have faster internal backbones. They tend not to have hardware support for SSL.

Any hardware load balancer should support Direct Return (sometimes called Out-of-Path return). This means that outgoing traffic from the target servers to the user community can bypass the load-balancing device as it is an unnecessary step.

26.2.4   Resilience

Hardware load balancers can be made resilient by configuring a pair of them. VRRP or an equivalent protocol is typically used to provide the necessary redundancy features. One load balancer is usually active while the other is passive. Any changes to the active load balancer are replicated to the passive SLB. This can be quite involved if there is a lot of state information that needs to be replicated in order to provide a truly hot standby capability. Check with the vendor that full hot standby is provided; that is, no state information is lost. It is also important that the passive load balancer communicate to connecting routers that it is passive, and hence that they know not to send packets to it.

Resilience for software-based load balancing is usually achieved by the individual nodes checking each other's heartbeat, and reconfiguring themselves to cope with fewer servers. In the case of the master–slave approach, if the master fails there must be a mechanism to allow one of the surviving nodes to take over as the master. Check with the software vendor as to precisely how they provide resilience.

26.2.5   The Implications of State

In essence, HTTP is a connectionless protocol that potentially allows many hundreds of concurrent users to browse a single Web site, as transactions are relatively lightweight in the sense that a request has no relationship with any other request from the Web site's perspective; that is, there is no need to maintain information, termed "state," on each user throughout his session. This stateless approach was (and is) suitable for Web sites that simply served up information in response to a browser request. As Web-based applications became more sophisticated, there was a requirement to maintain relevant information on a user and his session between individual user/server exchanges (transactions). An obvious example is a shopping basket in an online shopping system. This information is called state or session state. The basic premise in the following discussion is that the loss of state is unacceptable (although many nonmission-critical systems may accept such a situation).

To confuse matters, servers can be described as stateless or stateful. A stateful server is one that maintains state information in its memory. This usually means that all requests from a given user have to be processed by the server to which she is initially allocated. However, a stateless server is not necessarily one where state does not have to be maintained, merely that the state is not kept in the server's memory. Firewalls and Web servers can often be truly stateless, in the sense that state does not matter to them for the processing that they have to perform; they do not need to recognize user A from user B. However, some Web servers, but more typically application servers, will need to maintain state. Figure 26.3 shows a range of options: Web servers typically stateless, applications servers usually stateful, and a DB server that could be used to store state.

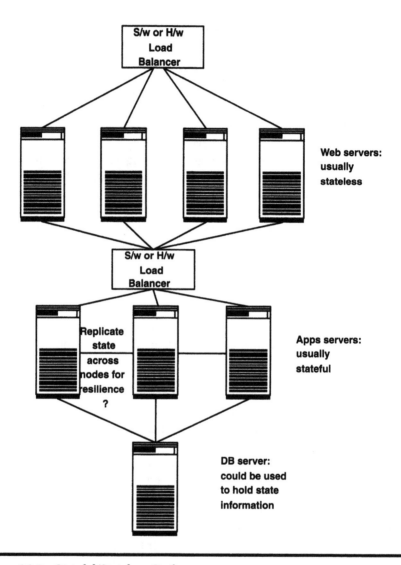

Figure 26.3 Stateful/Stateless Options

A stateless server that wishes to maintain state for a given user will have to store it somewhere other than its own memory so that it can be subsequently retrieved by the server that handles the next request from the same user.

The options for storing state in places other than the memory of a specified server include:

■ *Storing them in cookies.* This is only suitable for small amounts of data. The disadvantages for any significant amount of data are: the

network bandwidth overhead of sending and receiving the cookie, plus the processing overhead of packing and unpacking the data;
■ *Using hidden fields in the HTML*. More data can be stored in hidden fields but the network bandwidth considerations still apply; and
■ *Storing state on disk*. A database is usually the favored place, as it is easier to develop.

So, the downside of maintaining session state on a stateless server is the overhead of storing the state in one of these places and subsequently retrieving it. The upside is that full advantage can be taken of the available load-balancing techniques to spread the load dynamically across the available servers on a per-request basis, whereas on a stateful server the load balancing is on a per-session basis.

The problem with memory-based state is that it can be lost in the event of a software or hardware failure. As Web/application server software has a tendency to fail periodically, one solution is to use a separate or shared memory area that will not be affected if the Web server process fails-over. However, a preferable solution is to maintain a copy of the state on another hardware server. There is at least one application server product that offers state replication between server nodes. Taking my initial premises that simple stateful servers are not adequate for mission-critical, high-volume, highly available systems, state needs to be kept somewhere else for resilience, for example, on another server or on disk.

26.3 PERFORMANCE

Benchmark figures are often quoted by hardware load-balancing vendors, although usually not by the software load-balancing vendors. Published metrics should include:

■ Connections per second. This is important for HTTP with its large number of connections (one per object in HTTP 1.0) but not for UDP which is connectionless.
■ Concurrent connections supported. This is a memory issue but on the latest systems with large amounts of memory it is less of an issue than the other metrics.
■ Throughput. This is typically quoted in megabytes or megabits per second. Beware that large HTTP objects produce better performance figures because there are less connections per megabit. Throughput figures should also quote requests per second, which can help to provide a better handle on performance.
■ Figures for different functional tests. Layer 4 (protocol-level) switching provides much better performance than layer 7 (cookies and

URLs). I have seen four- and fivefold differences in performance. SSL support, if required, is extremely onerous without some form of hardware acceleration, for example, potentially a ten- to twelvefold reduction in performance in comparison to layer 4.

■ Latency figures are seldom provided, particularly under different load scenarios (more load equals more queueing equals greater latency). However, they are extremely important as they obviously have an impact on overall response times.

Storing session state in a database requires careful design consideration for high-transaction load systems. In one system, 70 percent of the total volume of SQL (for several thousand concurrent users) was related to handling state, and this was the area where the majority of the initial performance problems lay. It is particularly important that the state components not interfere with overall database performance; dedicated disks and possibly a separate database may need to be considered. The use of flat files would be preferable as they are less expensive in performance terms, although they are more expensive in development terms if the development product set does not support flat file-based state.

Custom replication of state across Web or application servers requires careful design to avoid performance overheads when there is likely to be significant internode traffic; lightweight sockets being infinitely preferable to (say) HTTP messages. Needless to say, the development of software to fail-over to the server that contains the replicated information is nontrivial.

26.4 GENERAL OBSERVATIONS

The choice of load balancer depends on the requirement. DNS can be adequate to load balance two or three Web servers. For more serious requirements software load balancing is cheaper than hardware load balancing but the facilities are not as comprehensive.

Where large numbers of servers have to be load balanced it pays to check that the balancing is satisfactory. Beware any favoring of servers that are near the top of the list as opposed to those that are farther down.

Be wary of the overheads of load balancing, and hence its possible impact on performance. This is particularly the case when using the more sophisticated features on hardware load balancers, for example, level 7 URL or cookie parsing. Press vendors for throughput figures when load balancing at level 4, level 7, and where appropriate, on SSL. Also, check out the overheads of using the best-performing server option, in particular, whether there are any practical limits to the number of servers that the load balancer can handle when it is checking on performance.

When used in combination, the individual prerequisites of Web-based middleware and of software/hardware load balancers may restrict the choice of load-balancing techniques that can be used, and precisely how state can be handled.

26.5 FURTHER READING

Bourke, T., *Server Load Balancing*, O'Reilly, Sebastopol, CA, 2001 is a useful guide.

27

WEB SERVER AND CACHE SERVER

This taster starts with the basic principles of Web server software to support the serving up of static content. It outlines the main performance problems and summarizes refinements that can improve performance. It continues with an overview of how dynamic content is supported. The use of scripting languages to drive the creation of dynamic content is not covered in this topic; see Chapter 29. Finally, the principles of cache servers (otherwise called caching proxy servers) are covered, including hierarchies and clusters of cache servers.

27.1 BASIC TERMINOLOGY

- *HTTP* (HyperText Transfer Protocol) is the lingua franca of Web browsers and servers, allowing different programs to work together.
- *CARP* (Cache Array Routing Protocol) provides a mechanism to load balance requests across a number of cache servers.
- *Harvest* is the name of the project that investigated cache servers in the mid-1990s. SQUID, a cache server whose source code is freely available, resulted from this project.
- *ICP* (Internet Cache Protocol) also resulted from the Harvest project. It supports cache server clusters.
- *UDP* (User Datagram Protocol) also sits on top of IP. It is thinner and faster than TCP but it lacks TCP's inbuilt reliability of transmission.

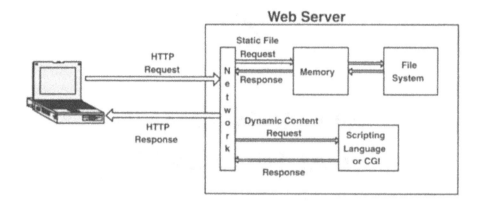

Figure 27.1 Web Request Overview

27.2 TECHNOLOGY OUTLINE

27.2.1 Web Server

As shown in Figure 27.1, the fundamental principles of Web server software are straightforward: to accept HTTP requests, and to either serve up static content or to pass the request to other software to generate dynamic content. In theory, this should lead to a simple design and implementation.

27.2.1.1 Static Content

Processing static content requests consists of accepting a request from the network, locating the file that contains the content, and sending it back to the requester over the network. Although accepting that it is slightly more complicated than this (e.g., handling connections and redirecting requests), the core requirement is relatively simple on the surface. There is little processing involved and, somewhat perversely, this can be a problem from a performance perspective; a Web server handling static content is heavily IO intensive (both network and disk IO). To provide good response times and optimum throughput it is necessary to make better use of the available CPU and memory resources. A basic Web server is an archetypal example of software that needs to be carefully designed (a) to handle multiple concurrent requests and (b) to minimize the overheads of handling large amounts of IO traffic. Many of the techniques that are required have been covered elsewhere, particularly in Chapter 14. They include the following.

- *Process or Thread-Based Design.* This is the same old argument of processes versus threads. Simple process-based solutions create a process for handling each request. The overheads of creating and killing processes are expensive in a high-volume system and they can limit performance. A refinement is to create a pool of processes at initialization and to reuse them. Although threads are more lightweight than processes (e.g., a thread context switch uses fewer resources than a process context switch), achievable performance depends on the design. Thread-based software can suffer from synchronization problems (e.g., parts of the system that have to be single-threaded to maintain integrity) that can easily nullify the advantages of threads. There are examples of reasonable performers in both camps.
- *Kernel-Based Software.* Standard software will usually run in user mode, making calls to low-level routines that reside in the kernel. Changing from user to kernel mode, or vice versa, requires a context switch. Software such as a Web server or a firewall that handles large volumes of inbound and outbound network traffic needs to pass data between system components. Usually this will be done via the kernel. It follows that there can be much copying of data, for example, from user buffer in process A to kernel buffer to user buffer in process C, and consequently much context switching. This can amount to a significant overhead. Moving the software to the kernel eliminates the need for copying and the resultant context switching.
- *Nonblocking IO.* Performance can be improved if a process or thread is not suspended while the IO that it has issued is in progress, which is what normally happens.
- *Memory Cache.* This cache is separate from any file system cache. It contains static content and it can be closely integrated with the network component to shorten the overall path length of a request by checking to see if the requested data is in this cache and serving it up immediately if it is. Some products offer this facility as an optional extra.
- *File System Cache.* In addition, a standard file system cache can obviously minimize the amount of physical disk IO that is necessary. The ability to transmit data directly from these buffers will assist performance.
- *Scatter/Gather IO.* Some operating systems support a feature whereby a single IO can be issued for noncontiguous data; for example, a network packet can be written using a single system call even though the various elements of the packet, such as HTML

headers and data, may be stored in noncontiguous locations. This saves on copying.

■ *Deferred Interrupts*. If the overall path length has been minimized, possibly by using some of the above techniques, it may be appropriate to aim to process a request as quickly as possible by limiting when it can be interrupted by tasks related to other requests. Deferred interrupts is a mechanism that can assist in this process.

■ *Log Writing*. It is important that writing Web logs does not impede performance. Write-behind can help to minimize the impact of log writing.

27.2.1.2 Dynamic Content

Much useful research work has gone into improving the performance of static content, but the world has moved on and many Internet-based systems are now using ever-increasing amounts of dynamic content. The initial method of invoking software that will generate dynamic content was CGI (Common Gateway Interface). In essence, a separate process was created to handle each request, loading and running the required script or software, generating the HTML response, and finally destroying itself. The natural subsequent refinement to this approach was to create a pool of reusable processes at initialization. This is FastCGI. Other interfaces have appeared with the advent of Web-based development toolsets that include the provision of scripting languages. Throughput and performance of software that generates dynamic content will in part depend on the effectiveness of the communication between the Web server and the application software. The main mechanisms are:

■ *Interthread*. Here the Web server and the scripting language reside in a single multithreaded process. Although this may be satisfactory for communication between the two components it can exacerbate any low-level thread synchronization problems in the Web server and it may throttle performance.

■ *Interprocess*. This may overcome the interthread synchronization problems but it still requires effective interprocess communication. Kernel-based sockets or shared memory are among the possible approaches. Whatever the approach, it requires careful design.

■ *HTTP request from Web server to software*. This is relatively simple to implement and it provides the potential for greater scalability as the target does not necessarily have to be on the same hardware server. The downside is that it is likely to be the worst performer, relatively speaking.

Generally, dynamic content is an area that needs further research to improve performance.

27.2.2 Cache Server

The concept of a caching forward proxy server for HTTP traffic was originally introduced to improve response times and to reduce network bandwidth requirements. As shown in Figure 27.2, a cache server (as I call it from this point forward) is sited somewhere between the users and the Web server. It receives browser requests; checks to see if it has a copy of the requested static content; if it has it sends the file back to the user; if not it sends the request on to the Web server, receives the response, stores the file on its disk for possible future use, and sends it to the user.

In theory, it protects the Web server from some requests when a hit occurs, saves network bandwidth (depending where it is sited, of course), and improves response times. In reality, these advantages depend on a reasonable hit rate; otherwise the cache server will actually degrade performance through its additional processing.

A cache server is heavily IO intensive, even more so than a Web server, as when a miss occurs it has the additional steps of sending the request to the Web server and storing the new content on its disks. It follows that many of the above-mentioned Web server refinements are equally applicable to a cache server. Any reduction of disk traffic is particularly useful.

Cache servers were extended to handle other traffic, for example, FTP and, more recently, streaming media.

Cache servers can be deployed as hierarchies or clusters. Figure 27.3 shows a simple hierarchy where each local area has its own cache server. Any misses lead to a request being forwarded to a regional cache before it has to go to the Web server.

A cluster is a group of cache servers that can jointly handle requests from users. Figure 27.4 shows the basic use of ICP (Internet Cache Protocol). Requests go to server B. If it does not have the requested file it asks servers A and C if they have it (note that a UDP packet is used for this question/answer, not HTTP). If Server A responds in the affirmative, Server B then issues an HTTP request to it for the file.

ICP is arguably the most-used protocol for clustering. An alternative is CARP (Cache Array Routing Protocol), which is an algorithm more than a protocol. It is effectively a load-balancing technique for spreading requests across the available servers.

Caching media (video and audio) presents a different set of problems. HTML and related files such as GIF and JPEG are typically modest in size, say 100 KB or less (usually much less). Media files, particularly video, are much larger. A one-hour compressed video may take up over 1 GB of storage. Whether a cache server is involved or not, the data has to be streamed to achieve acceptable performance at the browser, rather than a typical request/response mechanism. UDP tends to be used rather than TCP for this reason. On the cache server, more sophisticated memory-

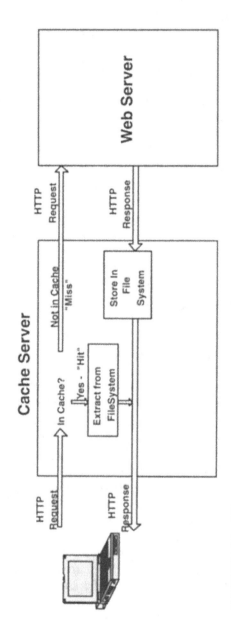

Figure 27.2 Request via Cache Server

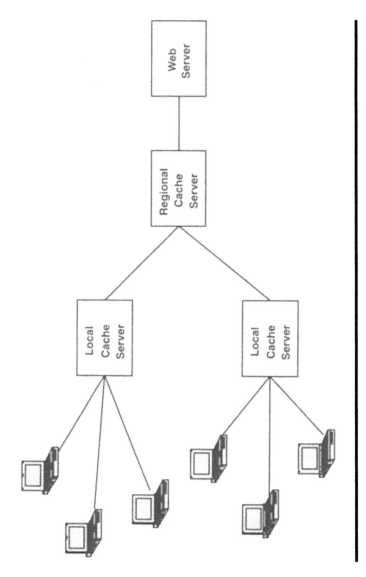

Figure 27.3 Cache Server Hierarchy

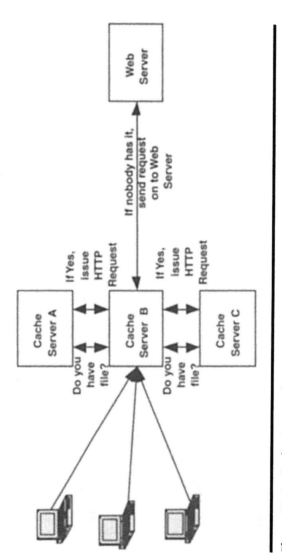

Figure 27.4 Cache Server Cluster

caching techniques are required than would be necessary for small files. It should be fairly obvious that any large volume media that are seldom requested should not be cached, particularly not on systems where disk space is at a relative premium, unless the data is likely to have a long shelf life and, ideally, it can be populated off-peak. In general the system needs to be aware of who is currently requesting what data; that is, it must be more intelligent than a simple cache for small files that can afford to be totally oblivious of such matters. File placement on disk is important, as disk IO must be highly performant; seek times in particular must not degrade performance. Several approaches may be considered, such as one disk per video, but more likely some form of disk striping will be required.

27.3 PERFORMANCE

Most vendors use the SPECWeb99 benchmark; it consists of 70 percent static and 30 percent dynamic content. Beware that most vendors configure the system for the benchmark with one 1-Gb/sec link per CPU in an attempt to maximize network throughput, which is unlikely for the majority of production systems.

In general, I consider that static content serving Web servers, despite improvements, are ultimately IO bound; that is, they are unlikely to drive the CPU(s) at high utilizations. This is due in part to design, and in part to single-threaded elements of the TCP protocol. The use of memory caches provides significant improvements for the performance of static content.

As mentioned elsewhere, SSL- (Secure Socket Layer) based encryption is processor intensive. Where it is used significantly (e.g., online payment), consider the use of SSL accelerator cards to improve throughput and performance.

It is difficult to discuss the performance of dynamic content, as it depends so much on what the application software has to do to produce the content. From a purely performance perspective I prefer the application code (whether script or program) to run in separate process(es) away from the Web server, although the communication between the two needs careful design.

Disk performance is important, even though every effort is made to minimize physical disk accesses. Web logs should be kept separate from the content, ideally on a separate disk. The content should ideally be spread over multiple disks, for example, via RAID striping.

Disk performance is doubly important on cache servers where the effective use of memory and file system caches is crucial.

Sensible caching strategies and effective file placement are necessary for handling large media files on cache servers.

The hit rate determines the success of cache server hierarchies. Low hit rates (less than 40 percent) may well degrade performance rather than improve it.

The success of cache server clusters using ICP can depend on the latency that is attributable to the traffic between the members of the cluster. This may be an issue if the servers are geographically separated and the resultant network latency is not negligible.

27.4 GENERAL OBSERVATIONS

In general, I do not recommend large SMP Web servers, as I am not convinced that they scale effectively. At this time I would not use anything larger than a dual-processor system, relying on some form of load balancing to scale out over multiple servers.

Some "high-performance" Web servers may not be fully featured. As a general comment, it is important to pay careful attention to the features that are supported by any product that comes with a "high-performance" label; there may be a trade-off between performance and features.

The move to the greater use of dynamic content appears to have affected the popularity of cache servers in the commercial world, although they are still attractive to ISPs and in areas of specialized usage such as streaming media. Cache appliances (blackboxes) are becoming popular, as opposed to general-purpose servers.

27.5 FURTHER READING

Yeager, N.J. and McGrath, R.E., *Web Server Technology*, Morgan Kaufmann, San Francisco, 1996. This is an exemplary work; it is a clear, concise, balanced description of Web architectures and potential problems.

Wessels, D., *Web Caching*, O'Reilly, Sebastopol, CA, 2001. This is an extremely useful book that includes chapters on cache hierarchies and clusters.

Hu, E.C., Joubert, P.A., King, R.B., LaVoie, J.D., and Tracey, J.M., Adaptive Fast Path Architecture, *IBM System Journal*, 45, 2 (March), 2001. This is a well-written article that provides useful insight into some of the problems that are encountered on Web servers.

Maltzahn, C., Richardson, K.J., and Grunwald, D., Reducing The Disk IO of Web Proxy Server Caches, *Proceedings of the USENIX Annual Technical Conference* 1999. This is an interesting paper on quite a technical topic.

Danzig, P., *NetCache Architecture and Deployment* can be found at www.netapp.com. It is a very useful paper.

28

LDAP SERVER

DAP (Directory Access Protocol) was introduced circa 1988 to provide open network support for directory services according to the X.500 standard. A directory typically, although not exclusively, holds information on individuals, for example, name, address, phone number, e-mail address, and so on. DAP's complexity made it unappealing to developers who were faced with implementing the client side of the protocol on limited resource devices such as PCs (they were limited in the early to mid-1990s). Hence the idea of a cut-down, lightweight version (LDAP) gained credence. Netscape, the University of Michigan, and 40 other companies initially promoted it in 1996.

LDAP has been used in mail and messaging systems for some time but it is now gradually being used as part of the security elements of application systems to control access to functions and data.

28.1 BASIC TERMINOLOGY

- *X.500* is an international standard that defines how global directories should be structured. X.500 directories are hierarchical.

28.2 TECHNOLOGY OUTLINE

LDAP allows a corporation to arrange its directory in a hierarchical form that reflects its geographical and organizational structures, as shown in Figure 28.1.

The LDAP protocol supports a lean set of functions to support this hierarchy, such as search, add, delete, and update.

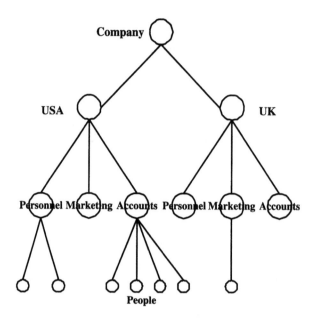

Figure 28.1 Corporate Hierarchy

28.2.1 Client/Server Communication

LDAP runs on top of TCP, as opposed to DAP which uses the OSI stack.

The individual stages that occur in the processing of a search, typically the most frequently used functions, are:

- *Open* establishes a connection between the client and the server.
- *Bind* operation is responsible for the authentication of the client.
- *Search*.
- *Unbind* terminates the session.

Multiple searches can be invoked before unbind is performed.

28.2.2 Replication

It is quite common to have multiple LDAP servers, either for resilience purposes, or to cater for distributed systems; for example, in Figure 28.1 there may be a server in each country. Multiple servers bring much additional complexity, as data has to be replicated across servers. There are a number of replication techniques but the major types, as shown in Figure 28.2, are multimaster and master–slave.

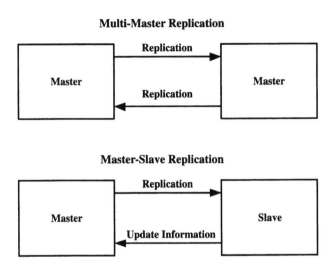

Figure 28.2   LDAP Replication Approaches

Multimaster is a peer-to-peer approach where changes can be made to either master that are eventually propagated across to the other master. In the master–slave approach the slave cannot do its own updates. Instead, it has to send details of the changes to the master who will update its database and then replicate the change back to this and other slaves.

There are advantages and disadvantages to the two approaches. In a system with a large number of LDAP servers the multimaster approach will typically perform better at the possible cost of more complex management. Conversely, the master–slave approach will typically have easier management at the cost of a possible performance penalty.

28.2.3   Deployment

LDAP server software typically employs a low-function, high-performance database, sometimes called a "small footprint DBMS."

LDAP server software can be purchased and deployed on a range of hardware running under UNIX, Linux, or NT/W2K.

LDAP functionality may be part of a product that provides a wider range of security and authentication features.

28.3   PERFORMANCE

LDAP currently appears to be a popular area for benchmarking by vendors and third-party organizations. The benchmarks that I have seen are limited to a single server. The items that you should be wary of when assessing a benchmark are as follows.

- The size of the directory — is it representative?
- Is it all cached in memory? If so, it will perform better. Is a totally memory-resident directory valid for your system?
- Is the workload mix representative? Simple searches are very light transactions and therefore they tend to perform very well. However, does the test include more complex searches and a representative volume of adds/updates/deletes?
- Are all transactions performed within the scope of a single bind operation? This improves performance. If so, this may not reflect actual usage, particularly in a custom application.
- Ideally, tests should be run with a representative amount of replication being performed although as stated earlier it is difficult to find such benchmarks.

28.4 GENERAL OBSERVATIONS

In general, LDAP is lightweight and therefore reasonable performance should be expected. With a satisfactory design, LDAP server software should scale well up to four CPUs on a single multiprocessor server, possibly more depending on the implementation. The area of most concern is the overhead of replication on multiple server implementations as this can be quite onerous, although it will naturally depend on the rate of change. Unfortunately, I have yet to see an LDAP benchmark that incorporated replication.

If the LDAP server coresides with other system functions on a single hardware server, performance may be affected.

Any set-up that contains a large number of reasonably volatile, disparate LDAP servers may suffer performance problems due to the overheads of replication.

Care is necessary where LDAP is used in applications as part of any comprehensive security mechanisms for authorization and authentication, as the frequency and complexity of LDAP calls may have sizing and performance implications.

28.5 FURTHER READING

Wang, X., Schulzrine, H., Kandlur, D., and Verma, D., Measurement and Analysis of LDAP Performance, *Proceedings of the 2000 ACM SIGMETRICS International Conference on Measurement and Modeling of Computer Systems*. This is well worth reading

Lightweight Directory Access Protocol — RFC 1777 on www.ietf.org contains details of the protocol.

Benett, G., *LDAP: A Next Generation Directory Protocol* on www.intranetjournal.com provides useful background material.

Sizing Up LDAP Servers on www.nwfusion.com contains a range of benchmark results.

29

MODERN SERVER-SIDE DEVELOPMENT TECHNOLOGIES

This taster discusses the concepts, design, and implementation issues that relate to the use of modern server-side technologies. Although there are other technologies in the field, the main players are arguably Microsoft with .NET and the Java community, and the observations apply predominantly to them. There is no attempt to compare the technologies, not least because there are too many products that come into the frame (e.g., MTS and COM+, as well as .NET in the Microsoft world), plus myriad application servers that support the J2EE specification.

29.1 BASIC TERMINOLOGY

- *COM* (Component Object Model).
- *DCOM* (Distributed Component Object Model) is a Microsoft term that provides a mechanism for objects to communicate across network boundaries; that is, it is a form of remote procedure call.
- *JDBC* (Java Database Connectivity) is the equivalent of ODBC in the Java world.
- *JVM* (Java Virtual Machine) is a platform-independent execution environment for Java code.
- *MTS* (Microsoft Transaction Server) is a form of TP Monitor.
- *ODBC* (Open Database Connectivity) provides a mechanism to access DBMSs from different vendors.
- *OLE* (Object Linking and Embedding) was Microsoft's initial facility for accessing objects from within another application. It pre-dated COM and DCOM.

29.2 TECHNOLOGY OUTLINE

29.2.1 Background

The current crop of server-side technologies has arguably evolved from three strands: transaction-processing monitors, object-oriented languages, and the Internet. For those who are old enough to remember, transaction-processing monitors date back to the mainframes of the 1970s, IBM's CICS being the most celebrated example. They provided a framework, including low-level services, within which developers could concentrate on building applications, typically in COBOL in those days.

The introduction of object-oriented design techniques, and programming languages such as Smalltalk and C++, led to the advent of object management architectures such as CORBA (Common Object Request Broker Architecture) from an industry consortium known as OMG (Object Management Group).

Web technologies were mainly used initially to deliver static content although CGI (Common Gateway Interface) was available to support the production of dynamic content. The introduction of ASP by Microsoft in 1996 saw a step change in the move towards the greater use of the Web for applications. An official release appeared in 1997 along with support for COM components; COM had evolved from Microsoft's OLE and DCOM technologies. MTS, Microsoft's transaction-processing monitor for COM components, appeared in 1998. The products went through several iterations over the next two years, including the merging of COM and MTS into COM+ when Windows 2000 appeared. In 2001, Microsoft introduced .NET, an evolution of these technologies, which introduced a simplified programming model.

In the Java camp, Sun initially announced JavaBeans and EJB (Enterprise Java Beans) in 1997. JSP (Java Server Pages), a direct competitor to Microsoft's ASP, and J2EE (Java 2 Enterprise Edition) appeared in 1999. J2EE is a specification, not a product. It has subsequently been implemented by a number of vendors, who have encapsulated it in products that typically come under the title of "application servers."

The rate of change in this area of the market has been unremitting. The applicability of comments on performance depends very much on the product, and indeed on the version of the product that is being used. The bottom line, particularly if these technologies are being evaluated, is to assess the deployment criteria with care. Any comprehensive evaluation of the technologies will cover many aspects other than performance, resilience, and scalability of deployed systems, but they are outside the scope of this taster.

Presentation	Thin Client Support	Fat Client Support	Web Services
Business Logic	Components		
Connectivity	ODBC / JDBC Drivers	Data Abstraction	SOAP
Execution	Runtime Environment		
Services	Threading	Garbage Collection	Security	Messaging

Figure 29.1   Typical Server-Side Architecture

29.2.2   Architecture

The architecture of deployed applications, shown in Figure 29.1, fits in with the popularity of multitiered solutions.

29.2.2.1   Presentation

The *presentation layer* is primarily based on the use of Web technologies (thin client). A scripting language is used to interface to a Web server, providing a means of producing dynamic content, and acting as the conduit to the business logic layer. Richer clients that support GUI interfaces are also available. As an aside, some software application vendors whose products pre-date the advent of the Web interface, typically supporting a GUI-style interface, have built a bridge to map the Web onto their existing user interface layer.

29.2.2.2   Business Logic

The *business logic layer* is developed using object-oriented techniques. Code can be written in a variety of languages, depending of course on the product.

29.2.2.3   Connectivity

Data is typically held in a proprietary database, usually, although not necessarily, on a separate hardware server. At the basic level, support is provided to access database(s) via an appropriate ODBC or JDBC software driver. However, the real push is to allow the developer to concentrate on the application logic rather than having to get involved with the intricacies of database/file handling. Hiding the technicalities of data access as much as possible, and simply allowing the developer to work with arrays or objects that contain the data achieve this. SOAP (Simple Object Access Protocol) provides a mechanism for issuing remote procedure calls using HTTP.

29.2.2.4 Execution

Components/beans are executed under the control of a run-time environment. This topic is discussed in later sections.

29.2.2.5 Services

One of the key selling points of these technologies is the concept of providing services that provide low-level management functionality that is expensive to develop, thus allowing the developers to concentrate on application functionality. The concept of support for threading, with the implication that scalable solutions can be readily deployed, is heavily promoted. Support for transactions is a key area, with heavy emphasis by the vendors on support for distributed transactions. Transactional support may be an inbuilt part of the product or it may be a general platform service that is available for use by other software. This applies to other services, in particular, messaging.

29.2.3 Programming Languages

A mixture of interpreted and compiled languages is supported, depending on the product. The terms "interpreted" and "compiled" have become somewhat muddied recently. The general tendency, whatever the language, is first to convert the code into a common intermediate form; Microsoft uses the term "Intermediate Language," and the Java world uses "bytecode." The second stage is to convert this common form into native code that can be executed. This may be done in batch mode, as per the archetypal compilation process, or on the fly using a JIT (Just in Time) compiler. The latter is particularly used for interpreted, or should I say dynamic, languages.

29.2.4 Memory

One of the other major pushes in the area of developer productivity is to ease the use of memory by removing the need to allocate and de-allocate it. In dynamic languages, memory management is largely performed by the system. The typical approach is that a heap (a common area of memory) is used for the majority of application memory requirements. Requests for memory are dynamically handled by the system without the need for the developer to define the requirements. Similarly, memory items that are no longer required are disposed of by the system; a garbage collector carries out this task.

29.2.5 Hardware Deployment Options

Although vendors will claim that their products can produce both scalable and resilient solutions, the actual flexibility of hardware deployment options will vary from product to product, and even from one version to another of the same product. Fully flexible solutions will allow:

- The presentation and business logic to be deployed on separate hardware servers;
- Multiple servers at both the presentation and business layers to cater for scalability of the solution;
- Multiple servers to provide resilience in case of server failure; and
- Ideally, seamless fail-over with no loss of user state in the case of server failure.

29.3 PERFORMANCE

This section contains generalized comments on performance. As stated previously, the ability of a given version of a given product to meet the requirements in a given area will vary. It pays to read the small print when evaluating products.

29.3.1 Threading

Although the products are marketed on the basis that threading is supported, with the implication that scalable solutions can be easily delivered, the actual implementation will vary. From a performance and throughput perspective there is little to be gained from fully supporting threading at the application level if it cannot be fully delivered at the execution level. The inability to support a comprehensively threaded system can be attributable to the programming language; some languages do not readily lend themselves to multithreading. It can also be attributable to the underlying platform; some operating systems have limited support for threads. See Chapter 14 for additional background. A typical indication that threading constraints exist is when a vendor talks about "different threading models."

Apart from the ability to provide a suitable threading execution environment it is important that thread synchronization issues do not cause significant problems. Synchronization is the term used to avoid multiple threads being concurrently executed where they need to access a common data structure. Synchronization issues can be minimized by good application design techniques. However, synchronization may also occur at the system level where the developer may have little or no control.

29.3.2 Run-Time Environment

Standard code interpretation can be a significant performance overhead on either scripting or programming languages. The recent move towards JIT compilation helps to minimize the problem. To be crude, this can be viewed as the batch interpretation of code components. Where feasible, it is imperative that once code is compiled it be retained for further use to avoid incurring the compilation overhead again. The compiled code will usually be cached in memory although some products allow it to be stored on disk if it is eventually crowded out of memory.

Locks that are generated by the controlling software can affect performance and throughput. They can be attributable to inbuilt features in the controlling software itself, or to the overheads of implementing synchronization on behalf of components to avoid memory corruption.

Network IO can be considerable in the world of distributed objects, even when they happen to be on the same machine! It is important that the controlling software can optimize communication between components, for example, by the use of multiplexing techniques.

Delays in the controlling software can affect scalability. For example, in the Java world the performance of individual JVMs can vary significantly. Observation of submitted results for some of SPEC's Java benchmarks can provide clues on the scalability of specific JVMs, for example, where multiple environments or instances are deployed to increase throughput. Similarly, there may be significant variation in the performance of individual servlet and EJB containers, plus JDBC (and indeed ODBC) drivers.

29.3.3 Garbage Collection

This is a crucial area from a performance perspective. The ability for developers to forget about memory allocation and de-allocation brings about the situation where they are more likely to abuse the feature by making ever more demands on memory, as discipline no longer appears to be required. This puts more pressure on the supplied garbage collection techniques to keep large heaps, which can run into gigabytes, in good working order. The danger for any high-volume system is that the system can be brought to a standstill periodically while the garbage collector does its work. Refinements have been made to collectors in attempts to minimize any noticeable delays. They include among others:

- Reference counts and traces (used to effectively identify objects that are no longer required)
- Separating small from large objects as they can benefit from different treatment
- Separating younger and older objects (younger object regions are more likely to produce candidates for collection)
- Pre-tenuring (allocating long-lived objects in regions that the garbage collector will seldom if ever access)
- Garbage collecting only part of the heap at a time (termed incremental or train collection)
- Parallel collectors (they naturally require multiple CPUs)

Although the list may indicate that garbage collection is no longer a significant problem, it still is, despite the improvements.

29.3.4 Intercomponent Communication

The observations in Chapter 7 apply fully in these technologies. Calls that cross process boundaries, and even more so, those that cross server boundaries, can impose significant overheads through the need to marshal parameters plus the levels of protocol that are used to effect the remote call. Beware that in some instances even local communication within the same process can result in similar overheads! Consider the requirement for any large-scale usage of "remote" communication and attempt to minimize it, where possible.

29.3.5 Mixing Technologies

It is often convenient (a.k.a cost effective) to mix technologies. At one extreme this can be the simple expedient of using previously developed components from an older version of the technology from within an application that is developed with the most recent version of the technology. At the other extreme it can be a bridge between totally different technologies, for example, .NET to J2EE or vice versa. The joy that is experienced by just being able to glue such disparate components together can just as easily disappear when performance is found to be unsatisfactory. This is often a case of even more significant intercommunication overheads. Think through the implications of any significant usage. This includes the use of other programming languages where the object is to improve performance of parts of the system. Excessive calls using, for example, JNI (Java Native Interface) may be counterproductive.

29.3.6 Reusing Objects

Objects are expensive to create and destroy. Where the technology allows it, recycle object containers; this type of feature is usually called object pooling. A further step, again where it is possible, is to retain the contents of any objects that are likely to be used by other components.

29.3.7 General Design Issues

There is a natural tendency to design a fully flexible application. This invariably results in large numbers of small objects with the concomitant overhead of large-scale object creation, destruction, and method calls. This is similar to the tendency to design fully normalized databases. A modicum of pragmatism is essential, weighing the cost of full flexibility against performance and hardware requirements.

Despite the architectural layers of presentation, business logic, and data access, there is still reasonable scope in deciding where a given piece of processing should reside. Where the performance capabilities of the product may be questionable, typically on high-volume systems, a standard solution is to move parts of the business logic into the database, as the latter products are much more mature, performant, and scalable.

29.3.8 Session State

This subject is generally addressed in Chapter 26. A range of mechanisms is available for supporting stateless and stateful solutions. Pinning a user to a specific server is a popular technique, as it tends to have the lowest performance overhead. The disadvantage is that a user's session state will be lost if the server fails. At least one product overcomes this problem by allowing session state to be replicated to another server, which can take over those sessions if the primary server fails. Storing session state in places other than memory between user transaction iterations incurs overhead, possibly considerable if there is a large amount of it, be it network overhead where cookies or hidden fields are used, or file handling overheads if a database or standard file system is used. The choice of how to handle session state requires careful consideration. Try to limit the amount of session state: one simple mechanism is to use defaults where specific options are stored, for example, the type of browser that is being used. If the session item corresponds to the default, say Internet Explorer V5.5, there is no need to store this information, as its absence when the session state is restored will indicate that the default is to be used.

29.3.9 Data Access

See Chapter 22 for information on ODBC and JDBC drivers. Use entity beans with care, as objects are persisted in the database, and where a relational DB is in use (the more normal case) there will be overheads of mapping between the object and relational forms.

29.3.10 Transactions

The technologies provide mechanisms to support transactions, usually termed a Transaction Manager (TM) that resides in a separate process, typically because it is a service that is available to other software. The implementation of a TM can be important in a high-volume system where it may be involved in a great deal of work. As vendors consider that the world is full of distributed transactions, the TM tends to implement a two-phase commit, even where only a single database is being updated. Two-phase commits impose an overhead. Try to avoid using them if they are not required.

29.3.11 XML and Web Services

These appear to be flavor of the month features. Full-blown XML can impose significant bandwidth and processing overheads. Although the overheads may well be justified in the open world of e-commerce and similar systems where information flows between organizations, they can be difficult to justify in closed systems. I have witnessed a design where it was proposed that more than 500 readings per second from outstation devices, circa 30 bytes of data each, be encompassed in XML that swelled the messages to over 500 bytes before communication protocol overheads were added. This was for a closed system where, to my untutored eye, the benefits were difficult to understand and the performance overheads were not justified. Apart from network bandwidth overheads, there is the overhead of parsing and validating XML messages.

In addition, there appears to be a desire to have XML databases. Current products in this area are suitable for modestly sized systems. Projects for larger systems may be attracted by the fact that relational databases claim to support XML. Issues here surround precisely how the document is stored by the RDBMS. The easy method is to simply store it as a BLOB. The disadvantages are that additional disk IO will be required for any reasonable-sized document; no detailed processing, such as a query, is possible by the RDBMS on individual elements within the document unless it can subsequently parse it, which brings additional overheads with it, particularly as it will have to parse it every time it is accessed; and there can be disk capacity issues, due to the verbose nature of the XML mark-up syntax, for example, the tags. The other approach is for the RDBMS to parse the document and store it in such a way that the individual elements can be subsequently accessed. The advantages are faster queries and updates plus reduced disk capacity requirements. The disadvantage is the initial hit on parsing and storing the document. Check out the facilities that are offered by your preferred RDBMS vendor.

If XML is used extensively in a large system, the sizing needs to cater explicitly for it; it cannot be lost in the noise as it might be on a small system.

Web services typically use SOAP, a lightweight XML-based protocol to provide a remote calling capability. There is a reasonable amount of baggage that comes with Web services, including: WSDL (Web Service Description Language), an XML-based language for documenting what messages a Web service will accept and generate; DISCO (Discovery of Web Services), advertising the location of Web services at a known URL; and UDDI (Universal Description, Discovery, and Integration), advertising the location of Web services when the URL is unknown, for example, through the use of a UDDI Business Registry). Once again, Web services are undoubtedly beneficial in interorganization systems, but careful consideration should be given to the possible effects before they are deployed on any large-scale closed system.

29.3.12 Programming Language

This subject has been left until last on the simple basis that only a modest amount of time, typically five to ten percent, is spent executing explicit application code. The majority of time is spent in the execution of management functions, for example, controlling intercomponent communication, data accessing, object and memory lifecycles, and transactional support. Every language ends up with useful sets of guidelines to optimize the code. A search of the Internet will usually uncover useful guidelines for an individual language. It is interesting that the same topics tend to appear almost irrespective of time and language, for example, string handling, buffered IO, method in-lining, and so on, put in perennial appearances.

29.4 GENERAL OBSERVATIONS

The pros and cons of these technologies keep zealots from both sides of the divide in employment. From the perspectives of deployment, performance, resilience, and scalability for large systems, the debate is not so much about the Java community versus Microsoft; it is product versus product. For example, it may be one application server versus another as much as it may be .NET versus Java application server; that is, this is about implementation rather than specification.

There are the usual competing claims about which technology is more mature. The blunt answer is that none of these technologies is mature. At the time of writing, they have been around for no more than five to six years and they are the subjects of rapid change, which does little to reinforce the idea of maturity. I was amused to read in one comparison of Microsoft and Java-based technologies that "the bottleneck is usually in the database." Well, it is only likely to be in the database when developers have gone out of their way to move processing over to the database because they have insufficient confidence in the technology. Otherwise, the problems will tend to reside in these technologies, which should be treated with great care where they are being considered for large systems.

They can be deployed successfully, but only when the key areas of risk have been addressed, and the sizing, design, and implementation take due cognizance of the problem areas. The fundamental architecture of a given product may well dictate the way in which the solution must be employed, which may not be the way that would be preferred; for example, large numbers of small servers may be required to circumvent scalability issues rather than a smaller number of larger servers. As mentioned above, a useful workaround can be to get the DBMS to do as much work as possible, that is, to execute some of the business logic, as DBMSs are mature products.

29.5 FURTHER READING

Hoffman, K. et al., *.NET Framework*, Wrox Press, Chicago, 2001, Ch. 1 to 12 provide a useful background to .NET.

Monson-Haefel, R., *Enterprise JavaBeans*, O'Reilly, Sebastopol, CA, 1999.

Ayers, D. et al. *Java Server Programming*, Wrox Press, Chicago, 1999. For information on Java Application servers look at the material that is available from the vendors, primarily on their Web sites. The quality of the information that is readily available is extremely variable. In this respect, WebLogic and WebSphere tend to provide more detailed information.

INDEX